THE ORACLE

The portrait of Gracián formerly exhibited
in the Jesuit College at Calatayud

BALTASAR GRACIÁN

THE ORACLE

A MANUAL OF THE ART OF DISCRETION

'ORÁCULO MANUAL Y ARTE DE PRUDENCIA'

The Spanish text and a new English translation,
with critical introduction and notes

by

L. B. WALTON M.A.; B.LITT.

*Head of the Department of Hispanic Studies
in the University of Edinburgh*

LONDON
J. M. DENT & SONS LTD

To the memory of my old master
JAMES FITZMAURICE-KELLY
this presentation and translation
of Gracián's *Oráculo*
is respectfully dedicated

L. B. W.

FOREWORD

THIS is not the first time that Baltasar Gracián's *Oráculo manual y arte de prudencia* has appeared in English dress. If the previous costumes had been at all adequate the present translator might well be charged with temerity. The already existing English renderings of this work are, however, very far from satisfactory. While Gracián is admitted by his own country-men to be an extremely difficult writer, the obscurity of the *Oráculo manual* has been exaggerated in England chiefly on account of the linguistic shortcomings of its readers and inter-preters.

In the case of the present rendering, I have made certain changes in punctuation where English usage seemed to demand them. When the interests of tolerable English have obliged me to depart very considerably from the original, I have called attention to the fact in the Notes at the end of this volume.

I should like to express my indebtedness to the Edinburgh University Carnegie Research Fund for a travelling grant which enabled me to visit the Biblioteca Nacional, Madrid, in con-nection with the preparation of this edition; to Professor Michael Grant of the Chair of Humanity at Edinburgh Uni-versity for some interesting comments on the Latin of the Epitaph which appears at the foot of the portrait of Gracián at one time exhibited in the Jesuit College at Calatayud and which is now the property of Señor D. Félix Sanz de Larrea; to Señor D. José María de Campoamor, Spanish Consul-General in London, for a transcription of the Epitaph and information as to the present ownership of the portrait; and to the *Mercure de France* for permission to reproduce the illustration of the portrait.

L. B. WALTON.

Edinburgh, 1953.

'Dabei ist es das Einzige seiner Art und nie ein anderes über denselben Gegenstand geschrieben worden; denn nur ein Individuum aus der feinsten aller Nationen, der spanischen, konnte es versuchen . . . . Dasselbe lehrt die Kunst derer Alle sich befleissigen und ist daher für Jedermann. Besonders aber ist es geeignet das Handbuch aller derer zu werden, die in der grossen Welt leben, ganz vorzüglich aber Junge Leute, die ihr Glück darin zu machen bemüht sind und denen es mit Einem Mal und zum Voraus die Belehrung giebt die sie sonst erst durch lange Erfahrung erhalten.' A. Schopenhauer, *Litterarische Notiz vor seine Übersetzung*.

'Taking the book as a guide, especially for those who intend to enter public life, I have never chanced to meet with anything which seemed to me even distantly to approach it. . . . It would possibly be rather difficult to disprove the thesis that the Spanish nation has produced the best maxims of practical wisdom, the best proverb, the best epitaph, and the best motto in the world. If I had to sustain it, I would point, with reference to the first head, to the *Oráculo manual*.' Sir M. E. Grant Duff on 'Baltasar Gracián' in the *Fortnightly Review*, March 1877.

CONTENTS

INTRODUCTION

I. Biographical Note

A HISTORY of literary reputations would make interesting, if
puzzling, reading. In such a work considerable space would
have to be devoted to the enigmatic figure of Baltasar Gracián,
several of whose books once enjoyed an extensive vogue
throughout Europe [1] and whose *Oráculo manual y arte de prudencia* was translated into German by Arthur Schopenhauer.
The closest parallel to the subsequent long neglect of Gracián,
both at home and abroad, can, perhaps, be found where our own
country is concerned, in the case of Hazlitt, whose *Characters*
were influenced by the *Maximes* of La Rochefoucauld,[2] and thus,
indirectly, may have points of contact with the thought of a Spanish writer who is, in some ways, so very un-Spanish; un-Spanish
because the genius of his country tends to be expansive, inclining
to rhetoric rather than concision. The native Iberian tendencies
are, indeed, already apparent in the work of Spanish-born
Romans such as Lucan and the elder Seneca. It is interesting to
note in this connection that Martial, a native, like Gracián, of
Bilbilis, the modern Calatayud, forms an exception to the general
rule. Does the environment of a writer affect his style? Is
there anything significant in the fact that Cordova produced
Lucan, Juan de Mena, and Góngora, all lovers of the purple
passage, while Bilbilis gave the world Martial and Gracián?
The geographer, the anthropologist, and the psychologist may,
some day, be able to provide an answer to a question which, in
such a context as this, one has time only to pose.

For full details of Baltasar Gracián's family history and career,
the reader of this brief Introduction should have recourse to
Adolphe Coster's masterly study of this writer in the *Revue*

---

[1] See Bibliography, p. 45, Section VIII. II. (iv), and Section IV of this
Introduction.

[2] For the possible influence of Gracián upon La Rochefoucauld, *vide*
Section IV of this Introduction.

Hispanique, vol. xxix, 1913, and to the other works mentioned in the bibliographical appendix. I should here like to express my especial indebtedness to M. Coster's study for much of the information recorded in the brief summary of Gracián's life given below.

Baltasar Gracián y Morales was born at Belmonte near Calatayud in 1601. In the baptismal register the name appears as 'galacián' and both forms, Gracián and Galacián, are found in the district to-day.

All Gracián's works, with two exceptions,[1] were published under the pseudonym of Lorenzo Gracián. His father Francisco Gracián, was a lawyer and may have been engaged in the administration of some great family estate in the neighbourhood, possibly that of the Luna family. The fact that he destined all his sons for the Church suggests that he was not overburdened with wealth.

Baltasar writes of his father with devotion and respect but says nothing of his mother, concerning whom we have no information other than the fact that her maiden name was Ángela Morales. We know that Francisco Gracián had a very poor opinion of women. 'The intelligence of the cleverest woman,' his son quotes him as saying, 'is no greater than that of any sensible youth of fourteen.'[2] Baltasar's experience, which, as a confessor, would not be inconsiderable, seems to have confirmed the views of his father who, like his uncle, Antonio Gracián, by whom Baltasar was educated at Toledo, was both a cynic and a wit.

Toledo, the ancient capital of the Visigoths, one of the most fascinating of Spanish cities, made a deep impression upon the youthful Gracián and he accords it high praise in his allegorical novel, the *Criticón*.[3] El Greco was living there at this time, also the eminent preacher Hortensio Paravicino,[4] one of the pioneers of the school of preachers and writers whose style was destined to have a profound influence upon the work of Gracián. It is a

---

[1] The first part of the *Criticón* (1651) and the *Comulgatorio* (1655).
[2] *Vide Agudeza y arte de ingenio,* Discurso xxiii.
[3] Part I, 1651; Part II, 1653; Part III, 1657.
[4] Hortensio Félix Paravicino y Arteaga (1580–1633).

curious fact that the latter, who prided himself upon his knowledge of the fine arts, never once mentions El Greco, although
he refers to Bosch, Velázquez, Michael Angelo, and Rubens.[1]

He is, however, eloquent in his praise of Paravicino, whom he
quotes freely in his *Agudeza y arte de ingenio*, although he may
not have been personally acquainted with him. He tells us that
he met in Toledo the eminent poets Antonio Hurtado de Men-
doza and Bartolomé Lupercio de Argensola.[2]

After his education at Toledo was concluded, Gracián probably returned to Aragon. He entered the Society of Jesus on
14th May 1619, taking the four vows on 25th July 1635. There
is little documentary evidence concerning this period of Gracián's
life, apart from the fact that he won a prize for Latin verse.[3]

It would be difficult to exaggerate the importance of the
influence which his upbringing as a Jesuit had upon the temperament and *Weltanschauung* of Gracián. To this matter we shall
return later. The significance of his Jesuit education seems to have
been overlooked even by so penetrating a critic as M. Coster.

We are not sure whether Gracián actually taught in the Jesuit
College at Calatayud, but we know that he was in that town in
1628.

It was not, however, in Calatayud, but in Huesca, that
Gracián met the personalities who were destined to exercise the
most profound influence upon his life and work. He was, we
know, in Huesca from 1646 to 1648. He had, however, made
friends there before that time.

Gracián's most important patron was Vincencio Juan de
Lastanosa, a cultivated nobleman with a flair for turning epigrams. Lastanosa had established an art gallery and scientific
museum at Huesca and was one of the leaders of a brilliant literary
salon in that town. He divided his time between his great
mansion at Figueruelas and his palace at Huesca, where his
brother also lived. Here were all the requirements for a truly
civilized life: art galleries, libraries, gardens; also unlimited
opportunity and leisure for conversation.

[1] Cf. Coster, op. cit., p. 360.
[2] *Vide Agudeza y arte de ingenio*, quoted by Coster, op. cit., p. 360.
[3] *Vide Agudeza y arte de ingenio*, quoted by Coster, op. cit., p. 364.

Those who still regard Spain as 'cut off from the light' during the Renaissance should dwell for a while upon the activities of the *salons* of Huesca in the age of Gracián.

Up to the time at which he took his vows Gracián had led an obscure life of intense intellectual activity. His ideas of men and things had yet to be tested in the crucible of experience, his knowledge of the world being still, in the main, theoretical. It was at this time that his *El Héroe*, dealing with the qualities of the ideal leader, appeared.[1] A copy of it was presented to Philip IV and it ran into six editions within seven years.

In April 1640 Gracián, already a marked man in the world of letters, was in Madrid. He visited the Buen Retiro, which had been erected only eight years before, and was introduced to a number of important personages. He also had his first and disagreeable taste of court manners. He comments, especially, upon the impudence of the servants and lackeys who hung about the palaces of the aristocracy and whose main amusement seemed to consist in being offensive to strangers.[2]

In December 1640 Gracián was again at Zaragoza in the household of the Duque de Nocera, whom he had chosen as his model for *El Héroe*. He also dedicated *El Político Don Fernando el Católico*,[3] his study of the ideal statesman, to Nocera.

He was not long in returning to Madrid, which he revisited in July 1641. He preached in that city with considerable success and there concluded one of his best-known works, the *Arte de ingenio, tratado de la Agudeza* licensed for publication in November 1641. The work probably appeared in February 1642[4] and was dedicated to the Infante Baltasar Carlos. By this time Gracián's pseudonym did not serve to conceal his identity from those acquainted with current literary developments.

We find him again in Zaragoza on 11th March 1642. The Catalans, in constant revolt and always a source of trouble to the centralized government in Castile, had just recognized Louis XIII as Count of Barcelona and the French Army was marching in

---

[1] 1637.
[2] *Vide* Gracián's correspondence published by Coster, op. cit., Appendix I, Letter 2.
[3] 1640.   [4] *Vide supra*, p. 9, footnote.

triumph through Aragon. This event coincided with the visit of Philip IV to Zaragoza for the purpose of encouraging his troops.

On 6th March 1643, Gracián was appointed Rector of the Jesuit College at Tarragona. He did not, however, continue in this appointment for the normal three years.

In December 1644 he was in Valencia on a mission of which we know nothing. He visited the site of ancient Saguntum and sent some medallions and coins to his friend and patron Lastanosa. These included a seal upon which was engraved the head of Ovid. In 1646 there appeared, at Lastanosa's expense, a study by Gracián of the ideal courtier and man of the world, *El Discreto*, dedicated to the Infante Baltasar Carlos.

We have no information concerning Gracián's activities in Valencia, apart from the amusing and characteristic incident of his 'letter from hell.' He announced that he had received such a missive and that he proposed to read it out from the pulpit. The episode was obviously intended as a joke which would give Gracián a chance to let off some verbal fireworks in the extravagant style of the pulpit oratory then in fashion.

He was annoyed with the Valencians for taking him seriously and he condemns them, not without justification on this occasion, as 'credulous.'

His little joke and his resentment at the lack of appreciation accorded to it mark an early stage in the growing hostility to a Jesuit who was coming to be regarded by his colleagues in the Order as 'too clever by half.'

Meanwhile, the French had occupied Lérida and the Marqués de Leganés appealed to the Valencian authorities for army chaplains. Gracián was sent out as an act of good riddance after the scandal excited by the 'letter from hell.' The regiment to which he was attached was commanded by Pablo de Parada.

He has left an account of one of the military expeditions of Parada.[1] He witnessed some frightful scenes of slaughter and a number of atrocities. Of these he writes in the objective manner one would expect of him. His chief interest was in the victory of the Spaniards and he was proud to have taken some part in it.

[1] *Vide* Coster, op. cit., Appendix I, Letter 14.

In December 1646 we find him again in Huesca with Lastanosa.   He was looking for poems for inclusion in a projected
new edition of his *Arte de ingenio, tratado de la Agudeza*,[1] which
he may have planned while in Valencia.   It was almost certainly
known in manuscript form before its official publication in 1648.
The second edition appeared at Huesca in 1649, after which date
we are uncertain of Gracián's whereabouts for a few years.

The decidedly unclerical and secular tone of his writings had
excited the wrath of more conventional ecclesiastics.   Fuel was
added to the flames by the publication of *El Oráculo manual y
arte de prudencia*, probably in 1647.[2]   Much malicious gossip
was abroad.   That personal jealousy of Gracián's social success
accounted to some extent for this attitude on the part of his
colleagues in the Order can scarcely be doubted.   He was moving
in circles closed to the majority of his fellow clerics, many of
whom, in any event, would have been incapable of appreciating
the cultural atmosphere of the Lastanosa *salon*.   From 1649 to
1651 he was probably engaged in preaching in various Aragonese
towns.   We find him at Pedrola in 1649 and at Zaragoza in 1651.
At this juncture, possibly to disarm scandal, he published the
Predicación fructuosa (1652) of Fr. Jerónimo Continente, a former
Rector of the College at Calatayud.   The work consists of
twenty-two sermons on religious topics such as death, confession,
and so forth.   Gracián wrote a short Preface to the work under
his own name, addressed to the Bishop of Huesca.

At this time there also appeared the first part of his allegorical
novel, *El Criticón*.[3]   He now adopted a new pseudonym, García
de Marlones, an anagram of the respective names of his parents.
The work was dedicated to his old commander, Pablo de Parada,
to whose regiment he had been chaplain.   Gracián now occupied
the post of Professor of Holy Scripture at Zaragoza and the
Criticón, worldly, cynical, and pessimistic in tone, seemed an odd
contribution to letters from the holder of a position obtained
through the influence of the Bishop of Huesca, or as a reward for
services in the army of Legañes.   Gracián made a little money

---

[1] *Vide* Coster, op. cit., p. 407.
[2] *Vide* Coster, op. cit., p. 410, for a full discussion of the date.
[3] 1651.

out of the work and used this for the purchase of books and coins, an action which was later to be condemned as a violation of his vow of holy poverty. It was at about this time that Gracián was denounced to the General of the Order in Rome. The publication of Part I of the *Criticón* gave his enemies the chance of a lifetime. For this work is, among many other things, a *roman à clef*, and definite personalities were soon recognized under their frequently thin disguises.

Gracián could cope with the Aragonese ecclesiastics because he had Lastanosa and other powerful friends behind him. The General of the Order, a German, Goswin Nickel, was, however, quite a different proposition. He informed the then Aragonese Provincial, Jacinto Piquer, that Gracián had published, without authority and pseudonymously, certain 'frivolous works' quite out of keeping with his profession. A pretext for getting him out of Zaragoza was being sought. We find him at Graus in November 1652. What was he doing there? A project had been formed for the establishment of a Jesuit college in this town and it may be that, in order to cloak Gracián's literary misdoings, the Bishop of Huesca had sent him to Graus in connection with the new scheme. However, he soon returned to Zaragoza. The new Provincial, Fr. Diego de Alastuey, was a mild man but a second letter from Nickel forced him to tackle the case of Gracián. He had been ordered to make an inquiry and, if the outcome was unfavourable, to deprive the author of the *Criticón* of his post.

Nevertheless, Gracián seems to have held on to his job for a time in spite of this trouble and, in collaboration with a friend, Andrés, produced a second edition of the *Oráculo manual*[1] and, at the same time, started work upon the second part of the *Criticón*, which appeared at Huesca in 1653. This second part was published under the old pseudonym of Lorenzo Gracián and was dedicated to Don Juan de Austria. At the same time, he submitted for the approval of the Provincial a religious work entitled *El Comulgatorio*, dedicated to Elvira Ponce de León, Marquesa de Valdueza, chief lady-in-waiting to the queen. He obtained a licence from Alastuey in February 1655, in which year

[1] 1653.

the book appeared under his own name. This may have been a deliberate move to regain favour with the ecclesiastical authorities. In 1655 he sent some chapters of the third part of the *Criticón* to Lastanosa for comment. He mentions the hostility of his colleagues and also writes to Lastanosa's brother, a canon, for some masses to say, as he is in need of money. On 30th July 1655 he sent some chapters of the third part of the *Criticón* to Lastanosa asking him to return them by the hand of some 'trustworthy person,' a request which indicates that he was being watched at the time. In 1656 we again lose track of him. The third part of the *Criticón* appeared in 1657 under the old pseudonym of Lorenzo Gracián. It was dedicated to the Dean of Sigüenza.

This third part was in the nature of a deliberate challenge, an act of open defiance. It was immediately denounced to the General of the Order and an inquiry was set afoot.

The mild Alastuey had been replaced by the aforementioned Jacinto Piquer, now reinstated as Provincial of the Order. Piquer gave Gracián a public reprimand, sentencing him to a fast on bread and water. He also exiled him from Zaragoza to Graus and deprived him of his Chair of Holy Scripture. Goswin Nickel devoted a great deal of his time to this affair. Gracián, he ordered, must be closely watched, his rooms must be searched, and he must be allowed to keep nothing under lock and key. If necessary, he must be deprived of ink, pen, and paper.

The appearance of Pascal's *Lettres provinciales* (1656-7) had excited a good deal of hostility to the Jesuit Order and such a work as Gracián's *Criticón* was an additional menace and another stick in the hands of the Jansenists. Gracián was humiliated and hurt by the public reprimand and wrote directly to the General, recalling the services which he, Gracián, had rendered to the Order and asking permission to abandon it for a mendicant one. Nickel replied reproaching Gracián with his violation of the vow of obedience. In the sequel, however, the rebel was sent on a mission to Alagón, near Zaragoza. This was an honourable appointment, and he met with considerable success. Nothing, however, could appease Nickel,

who maintained that Gracián must be inhibited from preaching in view of the fact that he had expressed a wish to leave the Order. Gracián was eventually silenced and sent to Tarazona.

Disgraced, embittered, and in poor health, he died at Tarazona on 6th December 1658. In later years, his Order made amends by displaying his portrait in the cloister of their college at Calatayud.

II. The Works of Gracián

In order to explain the significance of the *Oráculo manual* something must first be said concerning the works of which it is an epitome or anthology. Excluding *El Comulgatorio* (1655), which is no more than a guide to devotions, these works are five in number, *El Héroe* (1637), *El Político Fernando* (1640), *El Discreto* (1646), *Agudeza y arte de ingenio* (1648) (revised ed. of *El Arte de ingenio, tratado de la Agudeza*),[1] and *El Criticón* (1651-7).

In *El Héroe* Gracián gives us a kind of *catalogue raisonné* of the qualities, 'primores' he calls them, which should characterize the ideal leader and man of action.

The 'hero' of Gracián, be it noted, is no semi-mystical figure with the light of battle in his eyes, bearing a book and a sword. Nor is he a superman, nor a humanitarian philanthropist, nor yet an altruist. He is, first and foremost, an astute man of sound judgment, great-hearted, quick in action, and courageous. His most outstanding quality will be 'despejo,' a Spanish word which defies adequate English translation but which might be rendered, approximately, by 'ready wit combined with charm.' Some of the 'heroic' qualities enumerated by Gracián are of especial interest as revealing the author's own character and temperament. Moving, as he did, in a social circle superior to that in which he was born; dependent for success in his literary career upon the favours of the great, among whom, perhaps, he was never completely at his ease; an object of envy to his less cultured fellow priests, the quality most essential to him personally was discretion. He early came to realize that, as La Rochefoucauld

[1] 1642 (?). *Vide* Coster, op. cit., p. 394.

was to put it later, 'il n'y a rien d'aussi difficile que le commerce des hommes.' Seeing around him everywhere the disastrous consequences of human stupidity, he was almost fanatical in his detestation of fools. Warmth is not a characteristic of Gracián as a writer. It is, nevertheless, undoubtedly there when he is portraying an ass. We gather that he would have agreed up to a point with the proverbial division of mankind into 'knaves and fools' and there can also be little doubt that, in spite of his priestly office, he preferred the company of the former to that of the latter.

The hero, says Gracián, must be continually on his guard against fools and the shallow judgments of the mob. He should not reveal all his good qualities at once but should keep some distinction up his sleeve as a surprise.[1] The multitude never respects a man whom it thinks it has completely fathomed. The hero must, above all, know how to hold his tongue and if he has been guilty of some foolish blunder he must know how to cover it up.[2]

He should avoid the company of poor or unfortunate persons and should deliberately parade some weakness in order to appease the envious. Also, says Gracián,[3] we must not forget that sheer luck plays a large part in the careers of the great. The fault *is* sometimes in our stars that we are underlings and the tide in the affairs of men *is* frequently missed owing to sheer ill fortune.[4] *Pace* the moralists, our own experience surely bears out this view of Gracián's. Most men whom fortune has favoured will, if they are honest, admit that the secret of their success is about twenty per cent hard work, five per cent ability, and seventy-five per cent sheer luck.

One recalls La Rochefoucauld's later comment: 'Quelques grands avantages que la nature donne, ce n'est pas elle mais la fortune qui fait les héros.'

These awkward facts of experience, ignored by Samuel Smiles and the majority of Puritan moralists, did not escape the keen and observant eye of the Jesuit priest. We must, however, bear in mind that, as a priest, the Spanish writer would probably equate

[1] Cf. *Oráculo*, Maxim 94.   [2] Cf. *Oráculo*, Maxim 126.
[3] Cf. *Oráculo*, Maxim 36.
[4] Cf. *Oráculo*, Maxims 36, 38, 102, 139.

'fate' or 'luck' with the 'inscrutable designs' of Providence. Events have for the religious-minded an esoteric significance even when their outward aspect is purely fortuitous. The significant point is that, for Gracián, success in life is not necessarily the reward of piety and thrift. Also, from the Catholic point of view, wealth and power do not carry, as they do in our modern commercial civilizations, any necessary implication of superiority, or title to respect. In the age of Gracián, wealth was, in itself, no general social passport, even from the purely mundane angle.

El Héroe is the child of a mind well stocked from the classics and Italian writers on political philosophy. Gracián may also owe something to the *Honnête Homme* (1630) of Nicolas Faret.[1] It is interesting to note that he explicitly condemns Machiavelli in the *Criticón*, I. 7, as a 'falso político' although in the *Héroe* he may have intended to show that worldly success is not incompatible with Christian ethics. If so, he can scarcely be regarded as having attained his object.

El Político Don Fernando el Católico appeared at Zaragoza in 1640 and was dedicated to the Viceroy of Aragon, the Duque de Nocera. Its object was to depict a model ruler in the person of King Fernando I, 'the Catholic,' and to expound his political theories. Fernando, says Gracián, founded an empire, a task for which destiny alone can supply the necessary qualities. The two essential virtues in a monarch are courage and prudence. He must also be astute and able to conceal his true motives, especially when he is preparing for war. He must surround himself with trustworthy and able ministers. Gracián calls attention to the disunity of the Spain of his own day and contrasts it with the unity achieved by Fernando I (Queen Isabella is not mentioned, possibly because she was a woman!) and the comparative stability of France. There is nothing original in the *Político*, which is, indeed, inferior to the Italian political treatises of the time and to Quevedo's [2] political writings. Gracián's notion that

[1] *Vide* Coster, op. cit., pp. 461–5.
[2] Francisco Gómez de Quevedo (1580–1645), Spain's most famous satirist, author, among other works, of *La Política de Dios* and *Los Sueños*. The latter, a volume of satirical essays, was translated into English in 1667 by Roger L'Estrange.

distinctive ages of history produce distinctive types of ruler is interesting, if facile and unconvincing. In one era, he says, the monarch will be a statesman, in another a warrior, in another a voluptuary, and so on.

The *Político* simply sets down the facts concerning Fernando's policy, accompanied, invariably, by eulogistic comment. There is no attempt to evolve a philosophy of history, no attempt at character analysis. Gracián, was, however, like so many authors, an exceedingly poor judge of his own works. He thought very highly of *El Político* and in his *Criticón* ranks it with famous political treatises such as Machiavelli's *Il Principe*.

El Discreto (1646) is addressed to the ordinary man of the world. It is very difficult to find an appropriate English rendering of the title, which has also puzzled Gracián's French translators; Amelot de la Houssaie renders 'Discreto' by 'Discret,' while Fr. Courbeville paraphrases with 'L'Homme universel.' Gracián aimed at portraying what came to be regarded later as the distinguishing qualities of the eighteenth-century French 'honnête homme,' or of the English 'gentleman.'

As we have seen, prudence was a virtue much admired by Gracián and perhaps one need go no further than 'the man of discretion' in order to find his essential idea of the personality which he wishes to depict.

The qualities of the 'discreto' he calls 'realces' and each of the twenty-five chapters of the work deals with one of these. There is no fixed plan of composition. We find dialogues, letters, allegories, essays, all brought in to illustrate the virtues in question.

Some of the essays, which have as sub-title 'discurso académico,' may have been read at meetings of Lastanosa's *salon*.

The first chapter is important as throwing some light upon Gracián's use of the words 'genio' and 'ingenio.' One of the greatest difficulties which the translator has in dealing with Gracián is to be found in the variety of senses in which he uses certain quite common Spanish words. In *El Héroe*, 'ingenio' is used to indicate the intellectual faculties as opposed to 'agudeza,' 'finesse,' 'wit.' In *El Discreto* it also means 'aptitude for

acquiring knowledge,' while 'genio' is used in the sense of 'innate tastes' and 'character.' Vagueness in the use of words is characteristic of Gracián. Nevertheless, generally speaking, one may say that 'genio' and 'ingenio' were employed during his age as in the sense of the French 'génie' and 'esprit,' respectively.

A certain assurance of manner is a mark of the 'discreto,' an assurance which, in fools, takes the form of insolence and arrogance, common also, says Gracián, among the wealthy. He must be 'galante' (another troublesome word for the translator), and the Conde de Aranda is quoted as a model of 'gallantry.' He must be consistent and of equable disposition, urbane and tolerant. Lastanosa is given as a model of urbanity. He must be 'quick in the uptake' and must divine, up to a point, unspoken thoughts. The idea that a man of the world should be something of a mind-reader is characteristic of Gracián and he returns to it in the Criticón. He must have a sense of humour, but know when to stop joking.[1] He must have discrimination and must not be too easy-going.[2] He must know when he has gone far enough in a negotiation and be able to get out at the right moment; he must be able to display his merits without vulgar ostentation.[3] He must not give way to moods, nor be aggressive in conversation. 'He must,' says Gracián, employing a metaphor from the bullring, 'watch from behind the barrier of his wisdom the antics of the bulls of folly.'

Gracián's reputation as a cultivator of 'conceptismo' and 'culteranismo,' those often perverse forms of literary style so popular in Spain during the seventeenth century, is mainly due to his *Agudeza y arte de ingenio*[4] of which more will be said later. Here we need only comment on the curious fact that, while the *Oráculo manual,* so highly praised by Schopenhauer, has been neglected by the majority of Gracián's critics, the *Agudeza* was for long generally regarded as his only title to fame, or, perhaps we should say, infamy.

El Criticón[5] is Gracián's most ambitious work and embodies a lifetime of reading and experience. It might well be described

---

[1] Cf. *Oráculo,* Maxim 76.   [2] Cf. *Oráculo,* Maxims 70, 177.
[3] Cf. *Oráculo,* Maxim 277.   [4] *Vide supra,* p. 9.
[5] Part I, 1651; Part II, 1653; Part III, 1657.

as a secular *Pilgrim's Progress* and one episode, the visit to the
Fair of the World, recalls a similar incident in Bunyan's master-
piece.   It is, indeed, true that both books are allegorical romances.   There, however, the similarity ends.   The two works
differ from one another profoundly, as do the temperaments of
their respective authors.   Gracián is the aloof, objective observer
of human folly and wickedness, while Bunyan is the burning
enthusiast, proclaiming his 'message' on every page.   Gracián
approaches his theme in the spirit of a pagan philosopher
and develops it as a cultured man of the world.   It was less
dangerous for him to attack social evils through the mouths
of his characters than to indulge in direct criticism.   *El
Criticón*, nevertheless, was a major cause of his ultimate downfall
and disgrace.   It is, indeed, an extraordinarily courageous book
coming, as it did, from the pen of a Jesuit priest who did not
hesitate to criticize, although but implicitly, his own Order.   It
is also an indisputably great book which, if it had been written
in a less obscure and tortured style, might well have received as
much attention as the world's other great allegorical and satirical
romances.   More will be said later concerning the translations
of Gracián's works.   It is, however, interesting to note here that
Part I of the *Criticón* appeared in an English version by Paul
Rycaut as early as 1681 and it has been suggested that Defoe
may have derived the conception of Robinson Crusoe from this
rendering.[1]

The *Oráculo manual y arte de prudencia* (1647) is, as we have
observed, a kind of compendium or anthology of the apothegms,
maxims, epigrams, and general *obiter dicta* to be found scattered
throughout the other works of the author.

It is the book by which Gracián is best known outside Spain
and it has been translated into no less than eight modern European
languages.[2]   To what extent may one regard it as the product of
Gracián's unaided genius?   The three hundred Maxims of which
it consists are original in their mode of expression rather than in
their content.   As M. Coster rightly observes: 'On n'invente
pas en morale.'   Gracián has drawn upon the common stock of

---

[1] *Vide* Section IV of this Introduction.
[2] See Bibliography, p. 43, Section VIII. II.

Western European thought as exemplified, more especially, in the works of the Roman moralists, such as Seneca and the younger Pliny. There are indications that he was also acquainted with the works of Francis Bacon and he owes something to his own countrymen, Francisco Gómez de Quevedo and Antonio Pérez.[1] Borrowings of this kind were universal at the time, and if Gracián is to be charged with plagiarism he should, with justice, be accompanied in the dock by many figures greater than he. He is certainly as original as La Rochefoucauld who, directly or indirectly, probably laid him under contribution.[2] With this observation one may, perhaps, put aside a somewhat unprofitable topic and turn to matters of greater interest.

What kind of work is the *Oráculo?* It is, as the author describes it, a 'handbook' and its object is severely practical. The literature of the period abounded in guides to heaven above; the *Oráculo* is strictly concerned with man's fortunes on the earth beneath. It may seem strange that such a book as this, an odd compound of shrewdness, cynicism, and moralizing, should be the work of a minister of religion. Gracián, however, was a very special kind of minister, a Jesuit priest, with no inconsiderable experience of men and things both directly, in the palaces of the aristocracy and on the battlefield, and indirectly, in the confessional.

Whatever faults Roman Catholic priests may have, they are rarely, if ever, what the Americans describe, in picturesque simile, as 'yellow-mouthed.' The hearing of confessions over a long period must surely tend to eradicate any starry-eyed notions concerning human behaviour. It might be stretching the point rather far to say that the *Oráculo* could only have been written by a Catholic priest. It is, nevertheless, the kind of book which one might well expect from a cleric of Gracián's temperament, culture, and experience. As a priest, he was accustomed to advising penitents on spiritual matters. In the *Oráculo* he addresses his readers in his character of courtier and man of the world. He says to them, in effect: 'If you want to get on in life

---

[1] See, especially, Dr. Gregorio Marañón's study of Antonio Pérez (1952).

[2] *Vide* Section IV of this Introduction; also Coster, op. cit., pp. 682–3.

do what this book tells you, although I do not say that getting on in life should be your chief object, or even that it is a laudable object.' The approach of Samuel Smiles is very different. Gracián is nearer to Lord Chesterfield. His cynicism, however, goes deeper than that of the Englishman because the Spanish priest believed that 'getting on' in life was fundamentally unimportant. There is no cynicism more profound than that of the unworldly.

Apart from the deliberate opening gambit in which Gracián tells us that everything on earth has already been done as well as it possibly can be done, 'especially the job of being a great man,' the *Oráculo* is a book without a plan. The Maxims follow one another indiscriminately and there is no underlying conception to link them together. The same idea is frequently expressed in different forms. The quintessence of the advice which Gracián offers his readers might be summed up as follows: Know yourself, your weakness as well as your strength; [1] know also how to conceal shortcomings and make a discreet display of your merits.[2] Others, however, are at the same game, so *they* must be known as well. Penetrate behind their masks; be something of a clairvoyant, see through them and divine their thoughts.[3] Do not exaggerate, and remember, also, that truth itself can sometimes be used in order to deceive.[4] A wise man will have to deal, mainly, with fools because they are in the majority. He can, however, always get the better of them. Combine the subtlety of the serpent with the candour of the dove.[5] Think with the few and speak with the many.[6] Neither hate nor love on a permanent basis and remember that a friend turned enemy is the most dangerous of all foes, and that even the best friend may change.[7] One must, of course, have friends because they increase one's power, but do not trust them too far. One really good friend, and no more, is the ideal, but do not even venture to put all your eggs into that basket. Avoid poor and unlucky folk like the plague and cultivate those who can be of

[1] *Vide* Maxims 34, 89, 141, 161, 176.   [2] *Vide* Maxims 277, 289.
[3] *Vide* Maxims 26, 49.   [4] *Vide* Maxims 13, 41.
[5] *Vide* Maxim 243.   [6] *Vide* Maxim 43.
[7] *Vide* Maxim 217.

use to you.[1] Learn how to foster goodwill in others.[2] It is better that others should suffer than oneself.[3]

The *Oráculo* produces an impression of almost complete secularity. Its atmosphere is almost entirely of this world and its pessimism and cynicism were, later, to find an echo in the thought of La Rochefoucauld, Schopenhauer, and, possibly, Nietzsche. Was Gracián, then, a hypocrite and a double-dealer? Some of his critics have thought as much. Their judgment in this respect is almost certainly erroneous and arises either from lack of knowledge or from failure to appreciate the significance of Gracián's works. The Roman Catholic Church taught, and still teaches, that there are two orders of being, the natural and the supernatural; also that natural man, while not entirely corrupt, has but little to commend him. The Jesuits, while they believed in free will, regarded man's volition as enfeebled and perverted by original sin. While man is not altogether devoid of a certain natural benevolence, as distinct from supernatural charity, it would, from the Catholic point of view, be an occasion for surprise if people normally behaved well 'off their own bat,' so to speak. This, one feels, is the true explanation of Gracián's disarming observation at the end of the *Oráculo* to the effect that the best advice of all is: 'Be a saint.'

III. The Style of Gracián

Preciosity, Marinism, Gongorism, Euphuism, call it what you will, is not, as some critics would have us believe, a stylistic phenomenon which has its origins solely in the soil of Spain. It seems to flourish most luxuriantly at the point in its history when a civilization has reached its cultural zenith and is beginning to follow a downward spiral. When everything that can be said has been said upon a theme, for example, such as sexual love,

---

[1] *Vide* Maxim 31. [2] *Vide* Maxim 112.

[3] *Vide* Maxim 64.

the only task left to the erotic poet is to say the same things in a different way.   When all possible topics for moral exhortation have been exhausted, the preacher must keep the interest of his congregation alive by varying his technique, a fact of which ministers of religion in later days have been as conscious as were the Catholic clergy in the age of Gracián.

Rhetorical extravagance, striving after effect, abuse of metaphor, love of antithesis, all these are to be found in the Latin writers of the Silver Age, notably in the work of those Romans whose native land was Spain.   Medieval Latin writers, also, such as St. Augustine and St. Ambrose, delight in far-fetched parallelisms, antitheses, and, not infrequently, devastating puns. Gracián especially praises St. Augustine for his skill in the use of verbal fireworks and the Catholic clergy of his day did their best to live up to this tradition.   A glance at some of the sermons preached, in all seriousness, by the ablest pulpit orators of the time leaves one amazed and sometimes, if not often, amused. 'Preciosity' throve in the sermon for many years and the pulpit became its last stronghold.   The great preachers of the nineteenth century, both Protestant and Catholic, owed much of their success to sheer lung power but not a little, also, to the rhythmical structure of their periods which had an effect upon their congregations at once exciting and hypnotic.   Volumes could be written upon the oratory of the pulpit which, in Spain, reached the nadir of sonorous absurdity in the eighteenth century and was ridiculed, if not to death, into temporary coma, by Fr. Isla's entertaining satire *Fray Gerundio* (1758).

In Spain, 'preciosity' took two forms.   There was, on the one hand, 'culteranismo,' the art of playing with words, and, on the other, 'conceptismo,' the art of playing with ideas.   Marini [1] in Italy, and Luis de Góngora [2] in Spain, were outstanding exponents of the first technique, while Quevedo [3] distinguished himself in the second, and Gracián in both.   Quite apart from the influence of pulpit oratory and the general stylistic tendencies of his age, Gracián was temperamentally inclined towards highly

[1] 1569–1625.
[2] 1561–1627.
[3] *Vide supra*, p. 11, footnote.

sophisticated art forms. Anything which the mob, 'los necios,' the fools, could easily understand would naturally appear to him as of little, if any, value. Like Marini, he regarded obscurity as the essence of all great art. Where style is concerned, 'good' and 'difficult' were to him synonymous. Environmental influences in the form of Lastanosa's *salons* fostered cultural esotericism, and the wonder is not that Gracián became a 'cultista' and a 'conceptista' but that he was not more extreme in his practice of the stylistic techniques then so highly in favour. The maxims of the *Oráculo* are, it is true, difficult to interpret, and they are intentionally so. They are not meant to be swallowed at one gulp but to be rolled meditatively around the intellectual palate, as one might savour a fine old brandy with the physical organ. They presuppose a certain acquaintance with the classics and the contemporary literature of Italy and Spain. Some of them require a gloss for their proper elucidation. But surely similar things could also be affirmed of, say, the poetry of Mr. T. S. Eliot, who is now ungrudgingly awarded the approbation of the orthodox.

It is true that the *Criticón* abounds in obscure allusions to contemporary personalities and events, but so do the works of many non-Spanish writers who are hailed as geniuses. If Luis de Góngora, a far more obscure and difficult writer than Gracián, is accepted to-day as the genius which he undoubtedly was, why should some critics jib at the complexities of Gracián?

It is possible to find fault with the *Agudeza y arte de ingenio* on other and more serious grounds. While it is, professedly, a treatise on style, it has no clear plan and is replete with inconsistencies. With his head full of the writings of his greatly admired Alonso de Ledesma [1] and the sermons of Paravicino,[2] Gracián set out to produce a book of literary precepts for the guidance of would-be practitioners in the aforementioned styles. He does not even succeed in producing a satisfactory definition of either 'culteranismo' or 'conceptismo.' His theories concerning poetic diction, the use of neologisms and archaisms, are

---

[1] 1552–1633, author of *Conceptos espirituales y morales*, and one of the founders of the 'conceptista' school.

[2] *Vide supra*, p. 2, footnote.

ill presented and confused.   He praises the worst extravagancies
of Ledesma, and exalts the second-rate Luis Carillo y Sotomayor[1]
to the highest heaven of poesy.   For Gracián he is the prince of
Spanish 'cultistas.'   Luis de Góngora, the greatest poet of that
age, meets with slightly better treatment than his predecessor,
Herrera.   He is, says Gracián, a 'swan in his conceits' but the
most famous of all Góngora's 'cultista' poems, *Las Soledades*
and *El Polifemo,* are dismissed with the briefest of mention.
Quevedo is praised for his 'incessant puns' and Lope de Vega[2]
is somewhat unjustifiably ranked as an outstanding 'conceptista.'

It has been suggested that the *Agudeza* was a piece of plagiarism[3] and, whether this be the case or not, the work, which
has often been regarded as the sole criterion of Gracián's merits
as a writer, is not comparable in worth with either the *Oráculo*
or the *Criticón*.

Gracián's stylistic peculiarities may be summarized, very
briefly, as follows.[4]   The 'agudeza' is no new phenomenon in
literature.   The ancients knew it, although they had no theories
about it.   It is a 'beautiful concordance, an harmonious cor-
relation between intelligible extremes expressed by an act of the
intelligence.'   'What beauty is to the eyes and harmony to the
ears, the "concepto" is to the understanding.'   Another definition
of the 'concepto' is 'an act of the understanding which expresses
the correspondence which is to be found between objects.'
Gracián goes on to distinguish two species of 'agudeza,' the
second of which he subdivides into three varieties.   Much has
been written upon the precise nature of this treatise.   Croce
regards it as dealing with both 'conceptismo' and 'culteranismo'
while Menéndez y Pelayo says that it is exclusively 'conceptista.'
We shall not attempt to expound these arguments here but
merely call attention to the fact that Gracian makes a clear
distinction (one of the few such in the book) between 'natural'
and 'mannered' style ('estilo natural' and 'estilo artificioso')
and observes that the 'natural' variety is like bread, in that one
never wearies of it.   He also states quite clearly that two things

---

[1] 1583–1610.   [2] 1562–1635.
[3] *Vide* Coster, op. cit., Chap. XVI.
[4] Cf. Coster, op. cit., pp. 631–49, also Chap. XVIII.

are necessary to constitute a perfect style, the material element, which consists of the actual words employed, and the formal element, representing the ideas which the words express. Some, he says, are satisfied with the 'soul' of the 'agudeza' alone. This is not enough. It is difficult to interpret this observation as other than a statement of the author's belief that both 'conceptismo' and 'culteranismo' must be present to produce a perfect style. He emphasizes his point when he avers that if attention is paid merely to the words, their collocation and their material 'pulidez,'[1] the result will be a 'bastardo cultismo.' The older writers, he goes on to say, concentrated entirely on the 'concepto' while his contemporaries laid the main emphasis upon 'cultismo.' Of the two, Gracián maintains that the former were on more correct lines.

Gracián belongs, in fact, to both schools and his style is characterized by the following outstanding features: (1) careful avoidance of the simple and obvious idea or word; (2) forced antitheses of ideas and/or words; (3) comparisons and parallelisms; (4) plays on words; (5) inversion (subject placed after the verb); (6) constant use of metaphors, many of them forced and obscure; (7) use of words in a different sense from the normal one; (8) use of neologisms; (9) Latinisms (e.g. suppression of the article); (10) use of ellipsis; (11) use of odd epithets.

In spite of these mannerisms, most of his works have a superficial and deceptive appearance of simplicity, owing to the brevity of the sentences as compared with the long, meandering clauses so common in Spanish literature of the 'Golden Centuries.'[2] Everywhere, except in the *Criticón*, we sense an effort towards extreme concision. A maxim of the *Oráculo* is rather like one of those Chinese boxes which were fashionable playthings in the

[1] 'polish.'

[2] 1500–1700. Gracián represents, to some extent, one aspect of the European revolt against 'Ciceronianism.' Seneca and Tacitus became the new models and concision and brevity of expression tended to replace the 'purple passage.' Concision and concentration are not, however, characteristic of Spanish style. Gracián is, indeed, almost unique among Spanish writers in his succinctness of phrasing. For a recent comprehensive study of the anti-Ciceronian tendencies in European style, *vide The Senecan Amble*, by George Williamson (1951).

Edwardian era. It appears to be a complete object in itself but on opening it another box is revealed, and on opening that, another, and so on until one reaches the core, a miniature so small that it can scarcely be handled. The miniature box might be compared to the ultimate idea of a Maxim of the *Oráculo*. It has taken a great deal of time and much intellectual effort to discover it and when it is at last found it is sometimes a mere platitude dressed up to look like an epigram. But the process of discovering it in the original Spanish is entertaining and a valuable piece of intellectual gymnastics.

IV. GRACIÁN OUTSIDE SPAIN [1]

GRACIÁN is one of the most cosmopolitan of Spanish writers. As we have observed, a number of his works attracted the attention of distinguished foreigners, and the *Oráculo* is available in French, English, Italian, German, Dutch, Polish, Hungarian, and Latin versions.[2]

That he should have made a special appeal to the French is not surprising. His realism, cynical wit, and love, if not of clarity, of concision, soon found a discriminating public in the land of La Bruyère and La Rochefoucauld. The points of contact between Gracián and the latter are interesting. It is not yet clear, however, to what extent direct influence may have been at work. The *Maximes* of La Rochefoucauld appeared in 1665, eighteen years after the *Oráculo manual* of Gracián, which was translated into French by Nicolas Amelot de la Houssaie in 1684. La Rochefoucauld's friend, Madame de Sablé, certainly knew the *Oráculo*, and probably in the original, for she had some acquaintance with Spanish. Coster tells us that of the eighty-one Maxims, published later by l'Abbé d'Ailly as the work of Madame de Sablé, sixteen are translations or paraphrases of Gracián.[3] The *Caractères* of La Bruyère appeared in 1688, four years after

---

[1] *Vide* Bibliography, pp. 43–6.   [2] *Vide* Coster, op. cit., p. 682.
[3] *Vide* Coster, op. cit., p. 682.

Amelot's translation of the *Oráculo* was published, so there is no chronological objection to the view that La Bruyère may have been acquainted, indirectly, with the Spanish work.

It was not, however, the *Oráculo* which first attracted the interest of French men of letters. *El Héroe* was translated by Nicolas Gervaise and published in 1645. Gervaise's knowledge of Spanish was, however, inadequate for the performance of his task. In his *Le Héros français*, of the same date, Ceriziers is directly inspired by Gracián, whom he mentions in his Preface. Some passages are free translations of Gracián's *El Héroe*, others follow the original word by word. The only real difference between the two works is that Ceriziers substitutes Henri de Lorraine, Comte d'Harcourt, as his ideal hero, in place of the personalities mentioned by Gracián.[1] In 1671, a French Jesuit, Fr. Bohours, imitated Gracián, while attacking him in his *Entretiens d'Ariste et d'Eugène*. The main credit for introducing Gracián to France and to Europe must, however, go to Nicolas Amelot de la Houssaie (1634–1706), the translator of Machiavelli's *Il Principe*. Amelot produced a French version, *L'Homme de Cour*, of the *Oráculo*, and also translated considerable portions of *El Héroe* and *El Discreto*.[2] Bayle wrote a eulogistic article on Amelot's *L'Homme de Cour* for the *Nouvelles de la République des Lettres* in July 1684, the year in which the translation appeared at Paris and The Hague. It ran into fourteen editions between 1685 and 1716 and four editions between 1732 and 1808. Another translation of the *Oráculo* (*Maximes de Baltazar Gracián*) by Fr. Joseph de Courbeville, who had previously done *El Discreto* (*L'Homme universel*) (1723) and *El Héroe* (*Le Héros*) (1725) into French, appeared in 1730. Courbeville was also responsible for a French version of *El Político Fernando* in 1732. It is interesting to note that Voltaire came to know Gracián through Courbeville's rendering of *El Héroe*.[3]

We have, indeed, yet much to learn concerning the vogue and influence, direct and indirect, of Gracián in France. We have mentioned the case of La Rochefoucauld and that of La Bruyère. Coster suggests that Fénelon may owe something to Gracián in

[1] *Vide* Coster, op. cit., p. 465. [2] *Vide* Coster, op. cit., pp. 672–5.
[3] *Vide* Coster, op. cit., p. 680.

his conception of the character of Mentor in *Télémaque*. In his *Traité du vrai mérite de l'homme*, (1734) of which four editions appeared between 1734 and 1742, Le Maître de Claville quotes Gracián from Amelot's version.[1] The opening passages of Rousseau's *Émile* recall the first paragraph of the *Criticón* and Vauvenargues seems to have been acquainted with the *Oráculo manual*. The majority of translations of Gracián into languages other than French were made from French renderings. In 1652 there appeared 'The Hero of Lorenzo Gracian, or the way to eminence and perfection. A piece of serious Spanish wit, originally in that language written, and in English translated by Sir J. Skeffington.' This work is of special interest to English scholars for the Preface is by no less a person than Izaak Walton.[2]

Paul Rycaut's English rendering of Part I of the *Criticón* ('The Critick') was published in 1681. Rycaut tells us that he knew Spanish and that he had studied at Alcalá, where his attention had been called to Gracián's allegorical romance. In 1694 there appeared *The Courtier's Oracle*, a translation based on Amelot's French version of the *Oráculo*. This translation was the basis of Savage's *Art of Prudence* (1702). In 1726 an English version of *El Héroe* was published, based on Courbeville's rendering, and *El Discreto* appeared as *The Complete Gentleman* (1726) (2nd ed.) in an English version by T. W. Salkeld. More than a hundred years were to elapse before Gracián again attracted attention in England through a translation by Mariana Monteiro of *El Comulgatorio* (*Sanctuary Meditations*). This translation was republished in 1876 and 1900. In 1892 there appeared a new translation of the *Oráculo* by Joseph Jacobs, *The Art of Worldly Wisdom*.

In Germany, Gracián owes his fame mainly to Schopenhauer's rendering of the *Oráculo*.[3] As Coster observes, there can be no question as to the profound influence of Gracián upon Schopenhauer and, one might add, through Schopenhauer upon the European philosophy of pessimism in general. The opening passages of Nietzsche's *Also Sprach Zarathustra* recall a scene in

[1] *Vide* Coster, op. cit., p. 683. [2] *Vide* Coster, op. cit., p. 686.
[3] *Vide* Bibliography, p. 45.

El Criticón and it is possible that Nietzsche had some acquaintance with Gracián's work.[1]

Karl Borinski cites Christian Weise's *Die drei ärgsten Erznarren*
and its sequels *Die drei klugsten Leute* and *Der politischer Näscher*
as imitations of Gracián's *Criticón*. Goethe in his Journal, dated
26th June 1810, notes that he has read Gracián's *Homme de
Cour*.

El Político appeared in a German version by Gaspar von
Lohenstein as early as 1672, and the first German version of the
Oráculo by Johannes Leonhard Sauter goes back to 1687.

There is an anonymous Italian translation (1679) of the
Oráculo and an Italian translation of Amelot's French version by
Francesco de Tosques, *L'Uomo di Corte* (1698). This latter
rendering was reprinted five times. The *Criticón* was translated
into Italian by Pietro Cattaneo in 1695 and ran into three further
editions. There is an anonymous Italian translation (1675) of
El Comulgatorio and Courbeville's French version of *El Discreto*
was done into Italian in 1725.[2]

V. Gracián, the Moralist

The futility of attempting to interpret the work of a writer in
isolation from the cultural and intellectual background of his age
is now generally admitted. The hasty generalizations of many
nineteenth-century critics with regard, for instance, to Shakespeare and Cervantes have been exploded by the more scientific
approach of our own day. We now realize that geniuses are,
like other men, to a great extent creatures of their upbringing and
environment. The problem of Gracián's alleged 'insincerity'
or, as some critics would even hint, cynical agnosticism, takes on,
for example, a very different aspect if viewed in the light of the
age in which he lived.[3] Gracián's education by the Jesuits is a

---

[1] *Vide* Coster, op. cit., p. 692.

[2] *Vide* Coster, op. cit., p. 689.

[3] In this connection it should be noted that the Madrid (1653) edition
of the *Oráculo* bears the official approbation of the ecclesiastical censor,
Fr. Alonso Muñoz de Otalora, who praises the book, its style, and its
teaching—'enseñanza que no disuena a nuestra fe. . . .'

factor of paramount importance in his intellectual formation and in order to understand him properly one must know something of the aims and methods of the Order. Its founder, Ignatius Loyola,[1] a former army officer of distinction, was by natural inclination a man of action. He was also a born psychologist or, perhaps one should say, psychiatrist, and had an intuitive understanding of human nature, its weakness and its strength. His approach to the problem of training a corps of priests to defend and propagate what he regarded as the one true Faith was fundamentally practical. His methods were phenomenally successful and their influence has been far-reaching, passing the bounds of the merely ecclesiastical and impinging upon the whole field of human activity. Foreshadowing views which have acquired a wide vogue in our own day, Loyola attached great importance to the function of the imagination in the determination of human behaviour. While the Jesuits espoused the cause of Free Will in the theological arguments of the age concerning Predestination, they taught, nevertheless, that man's will was corrupted by the Fall and inclined towards evil rather than good.

They did not, like Calvin and, later, the Scottish Church,[2] declare that man 'is utterly indisposed, disabled, and made opposite to all good.' They did, however, take a dismal view of the unaided human will as a means to salvation. By 'corresponding' with the 'grace of God' the will might be strengthened for the performance of good works and, from a purely human angle, might be used as an instrument for the direction and control of a more powerful natural incentive to action or contemplation, the imagination. In no sense a formal philosopher, Loyola, nevertheless, anticipates Descartes and Kant in the importance which he attaches to what goes on within the cerebellum. He regarded the average man as tossed like a buoy without moorings upon the restless ocean of the confused and

---

[1] 1491–1556.

[2] *Vide The Westminster Confession of Faith*, Chap. VI. 4. 'From this original corruption [i.e. the sin of Adam and Eve], whereby we are utterly indisposed, disabled, and made opposite to all good, and wholly inclined to all evil, do proceed all actual transgressions.'

chaotic impressions received from an external world whose ultimate nature was, humanly speaking, unfathomable.

His will enfeebled and corrupted, his powers of concentration almost non-existent, his mind a mass of confused and contradictory ideas, his emotions unstable and uncontrolled, little. indeed, could be expected of man in his unregenerate state, Nevertheless, by intense discipline of both mind and body, an ordered world of meaningful images, religious in character, could be brought into being from the comparatively formless void of 'everyday reality' and the 'world of common sense.' The view that man constructs, to some extent, his own world and that the latter is a reflection of his inner state and will, were, of course, to find their classic modern expression, in the philosophies of Kant, Schopenhauer, and von Hartmann. Loyola, however, was no metaphysician, no ambitious theorizer. He accepted the teachings of the Catholic Church upon the nature of God and man as unquestionable. He was concerned, merely, with the devising of aids to the cultivation of the supernatural life, which was far more significant, to him, than the 'realities' of everyday experience. His *Spiritual Exercises* aim at the conscious substitution, by an effort of the will and the imagination, of certain religious images in place of the normal impressions of daily life.

The 'science' of Loyola is a science of body and spirit conceived as a unity in action, of their dissociation, and of their subsequent synthesis by means of the will working upon the imagination.[1]

The new images created by the intellect and the imagination under the direction of the will are conceived by Loyola as existing in their own right. They are no mere products of mystical ecstasy or special illumination. They are actual experiences. In this emphasis upon the concrete, Loyola is typically Spanish. The devotion of the faithful in Spain is stimulated, to a notable extent, by material representations, by images, crucifixes, and so forth. For the initiate, Loyola endeavours to supply a stimulus of a higher order; actual experience of the events figured in the material images. There is nothing vague or nebulous about Spanish Christianity. To

[1] Cf. Rouveyre, op. cit., p. 87.

Loyola and his followers these things are as real as rain or the sun.
One has to wait until Emanuel Swedenborg for an equally
'solid' conception of the world of the spirit, more real, more
solid, to both Swedenborg and Loyola, than the physical earth
beneath their feet.   This point is also emphasized by the late
Miguel de Unamuno, in his *Tragic Sense of Life in Men and
Peoples*,[1] where he says that an immortality which is not of
'carne y hueso,' of 'flesh and bone,' is a meaningless abstraction.

The interior and exterior worlds are, then, conceived, in some
sense, as one; but while Schopenhauer envisaged the former as
the will of the species and desired it to be directed towards
voluntary self-annihilation, Ignatius wished it to be dominated
by the conceptions of Catholic orthodoxy and the supernatural
life.   From Loyola, Gracián gets his sense of the concrete and
his idea of the training of the mind by the consideration of specific
examples.   The Maxims of the *Oráculo* are, so to say, secular, as
contrasted with spiritual, 'Exercises.'   That this indicates a revolt
on the part of Gracián against the teaching of Loyola and its background is, one feels, very much open to doubt.   He undoubtedly
defied his superiors in proceeding with the *Criticón* but he had
good reason to believe that the motives for the prohibition were
dubious.   True, he had taken the vow of obedience 'perinde ac
cadaver,' and blind obedience to the direction of a superior in the
Order is the king-pin of the Jesuit system.   But a system of
discipline is one thing and a system of belief quite another.
Many Catholic priests found their vow of chastity extremely
irksome and were not, in Gracián's age, over-scrupulous in its
observance.   Priestly celibacy is, however, not an article of
belief, and the Roman Catholic Church does not invariably insist
upon it.[2]   Gracián may have found his vow of obedience intolerable.   This is, however, no indication that he was an apostle of
revolt and a forerunner, in the moral sphere, of Nietzsche.
Much has been made of the secular and cynical atmosphere which
pervades his works and it has been taken as revealing positive

[1] *El Sentimiento trágico de la vida en los hombres y en los pueblos* (Madrid,
1913).   English translation by E. Crawford Flitch (London, 1921).
[2] The Uniats, in full communion with Rome, are allowed a married
clergy.

hypocrisy on the part of their author. A similar charge of disingenuousness was brought by Charles Kingsley against certain sermons preached by Cardinal Newman in which the latter appeared to extol the wisdom of the serpent as opposed to the harmlessness of the dove. Newman lived in the dawn of the scientific era and may have had less reason for lack of candour than had Gracián, who wrote at a time when any openly expressed disbelief in the tenets of the Church was fraught with the utmost danger to life and limb. To understand his mentality one must appreciate the fact that the existence of two 'orders of being' and two 'orders of value,' the super-natural on the one hand, the natural on the other, was almost universally accepted in the age of Gracián. 'Natural' man was wont to behave in such and such a way, in such and such circumstances. It was regarded as part of a priest's job, especially a Jesuit priest's, to study men's 'natural' behaviour and to know thoroughly the kind of creature with which he had to deal. The confessional gave him ample opportunity to probe to its innermost core the moral mechanism of the human animal. Gracián is not concerned with saints but with ordinary men and women, especially the educated men and women who moved in the fashionable society of his day. These he knew intimately, from the outside, as a courtier, *littérateur*, and man of the world and, from the inside, as a father confessor.

'If you want to get on in the world,' he says, in effect, 'follow the advice of my Oracle. This is how successful people, in the worldly sense, behave.' The sting, however, is in the tail, in the last Maxim of the *Oráculo*, in the somewhat disarming advice to 'be a saint.' It is difficult to believe from a study of his works as a whole that Gracián attached great importance to worldly success, although he undoubtedly enjoyed the good things of life, good food, good wine, and, above all, good books and good conversation. Incidentally, Jesus Himself has been accused of hypocrisy in respect of his famous utterance concerning the 'children of Mammon' and the advisability of acquiring wisdom from them.

It is, indeed, somewhat difficult to understand the positively

anti-Christian principles which Gracián appears at times to inculcate. To ignore Christian morality is one thing; to go out of one's way to attack it is another. The difficulty, however, is not insurmountable when one bears in mind the fact that Gracián's eyes are directed throughout the *Oráculo*, with the notable exception of the last Maxim, exclusively upon this world. There are, indeed, many who would regard the aforementioned counsels as pernicious even from a purely secular point of view. Nevertheless, the majority of successful people undoubtedly followed them in Gracián's day and continue to do so in our own, even though some of these would certainly 'profess and call themselves Christians.'

That truth has two facets, one material, one spiritual; that in order to combat 'the serpent' one must acquire some of his wisdom; that the 'children of Mammon are wiser in their generation than the children of light,' are all statements that have little meaning for, or relevance to, an increasingly secular and scientific age such as our own. They are, none the less, of significance in relation to the times of Gracián and do much to explain the inner content of his work and thought. While the beliefs of his Church and Order seem to mean less and less to the modern world, the techniques of obedience 'perinde ac cadaver,' physical austerity, and mental discipline, have been widely adopted by totalitarian states to-day. Loyola believed that human nature could be substantially changed or, rather, reorientated by rigid obedience to authority combined with severe mental and physical gymnastics. 'To serve humbly and without questioning' the purposes of the State is the ideal which has been substituted, in totalitarian countries, for Loyola's 'corpse-like' obedience to a religious Order and the humble service of an Almighty God. That both ideals should be repugnant to the scientific humanist is understandable. Nevertheless, their formidable dynamism must not, on that account, be underrated.

If the question of Gracián's sincerity is not so difficult of solution as might have been anticipated from the hostile comments of certain critics, the lack of recognition accorded to him by modern literary historians is indeed hard to understand. No less a person than Émile Faguet, for example, stresses the influence of

La Rochefoucauld upon Schopenhauer, without any mention of Gracián, avowedly the latter's favourite author![1]   This in spite of the fact that the German philosopher does not content himself with an odd passing reference to Gracián but goes out of his way to praise various aspects of his work, to call the *Criticón* the greatest allegorical romance ever written, and to make the translating of the *Oráculo* into German a major literary preoccupation.

We have already referred to the possible influence of Gracián upon La Rochefoucauld, especially through Madame de Sablé.[2] Its precise nature is open to doubt, but where Gracián and Schopenhauer are concerned there can be no room for any vestige of uncertainty.   For Schopenhauer, Gracián was a major formative influence and, as M. Rouveyre has pointed out, there is a striking similarity in conception between *Die Welt als Wille und Vorstellung* and the *Criticón*.[3]   Schopenhauer jettisons the metaphysico-religious ideas of Kant in favour of a return to the human creature as an organism, a whole rather than a perambulating cerebellum just as, in his *Oráculo* and the *Criticón*, Gracián subordinates the religious ideas of his Order to a study of the human mechanism for its own sake.   That the results of his investigations should be gloomy, as gloomy as those of Schopenhauer, is not in the least surprising.   There is, as we have seen, a strong vein of pessimism in Catholic Christianity which, in certain Spanish religious writers, seems to join hands with Buddhist thought.   'The greatest crime which man has committed is to have been born,' says Calderón in *Life's a Dream*[4] and we are not surprised to learn that Calderón was also one of Schopenhauer's favourite authors.   Catholic pessimism is, nevertheless, shot through with hope, and so is not a complete pessimism.   Even with regard to this 'vale of tears,' Catholic thinkers do not altogether abandon belief in the utility of human

[1] 'Mein Lieblingschriftsteller ist aber dieser philosophische Gracián.' A. Schopenhauer.   *Vide Schopenhauers Briefe*, ed. Schemann, Leipzig, 1893, p. 171, cited by Coster, op. cit., p. 691.

[2] *Vide* Section IV, *supra*.

[3] *Vide* A. Rouveyre: *Baltasar Gracián, Pages caractéristiques, Étude critique*, Chap. III.

[4] 'El delito mayor del hombre es haber nacido.'   *La Vida es Sueño*, Jornada I, Escena ii.

* B

effort.   As we have seen, man is not, for them, as for Calvin
and the Scottish Church, wholly evil.[1]   But what is one to make
of the following extract from the *Criticón* [2] concerning the nature
of human life?   'Nature has proceeded with cunning, if not with
deception, where man is concerned, at the moment in which he
comes into the world, by arranging that he should enter it without knowledge of any description so that he may not experience
any hesitation.   He arrives in darkness, and even still blind; he
begins to live without realizing that he is alive and without
knowing what life is.   Then he becomes a small child, so simple
that the merest trifle soothes him when he weeps and the smallest
plaything suffices to give him pleasure.   He imagines that he is
being introduced into a kingdom of felicities when he is really in
a fearful prison.   And when the eyes of his soul open and he
becomes aware of the deception, he finds himself committed
without any way of escape, he finds himself caught in a swamp
similar to the clay out of which he has come.   From that time
onwards, what is there for him to do but to walk in the morass,
trying to get himself out of it as best as he may?   I am convinced
that nobody would desire to come into so deceitful a world
without this universal lure, and that, once in it, few would agree
to continue living in the world if they had known in advance
what life really is.   For who would knowingly desire to set foot
in so false a kingdom, in reality a prison, to suffer there so many
and various pains?   In the physical realm, hunger, thirst, cold,
heat, fatigue, grief, illness; in the moral sphere, deceit, perse-
cution, envy, disdain, loss of reputation, sorrows, tribulations,
fears, anger, despair, to come in the end to a wretched death
losing everything that one has, home, wealth, dignities, friends,
parents, regretting the loss of even life itself, for this is the
moment in which one most loves it.   Nature has known very
well what she was doing and man has done very ill to accept the
position.   Let him who knows thee not esteem thee, O Life!
The disillusioned man would prefer to have passed from the
cradle to the grave, from the bed of childbirth to the tomb.   A
general presage of the miseries which await him is the fact that

---

[1] *Vide supra, The Westminster Confession of Faith.*
[2] *Criticón*, Part I, 5.   Rycaut's rendering.

man weeps on being born. Even the happiest of mortals has only a melancholy kind of bliss. The trumpet call which sounds the entrance of this Lord of Creation to the world is none other than his own groaning, a sign that his whole reign will be nothing but a series of sufferings. What can be expected of a life which begins with the groans of the mother who gives it and the tears of the infant who receives it? For, if he has not yet knowledge of the ills which await him, the new-born child has at least a presentiment of them. If he does not conceive them he divines them.'

Such a passage as this might well be taken from the works of a Buddhist mystic or from those of Schopenhauer and his disciples. There is nothing here of 'natural goodness or happiness,' no hint of consolations in a future existence. It were better not to have been born. Even when Gracián endeavours to portray a future state it is the 'isle of immortality' inhabited by the philosophers and sages, not the orthodox Christian heaven, with its angels and its saints.[1]

What is man to do in the dilemma in which he finds himself? Having realized that the only criterion of knowledge is within itself, and having gained control over its faculties in so far as it is able, to what should the disciplined ego devote itself? To the annihilation of the will to live, with Schopenhauer? To God, with Loyola? To the full and fearless development of the personality on the road to 'superhumanity,' with Nietzsche? If we look for answers to these questions in the works of Gracián we shall look in vain. He registers the facts and draws his limited conclusions from them. This is how things are, he says, and this is what you must do if you want to cope successfully with them. His analysis is cold, objective, calm. Only fools make him really angry. And after he has put 'economic man,' 'political man,' 'ecclesiastical man,' and 'civilized man,' on the dissecting table, after he has explored and revealed to his satis-faction the innermost nerve and sinew of their moral mechanism, he goes back quietly to his job as preacher and confessor, or writes a pious treatise to salve his conscience, or, more probably, to appease his superiors. 'Schizophrenia,' 'split personality,'

[1] *Criticón*, Part III, 12.

the psychologists may hiss.   Gracián remains, nevertheless, a complete man, a man in the round, a true Spaniard who is, at the same time, an outstanding example of the *homo europaeus* whose very existence is threatened by the ant-heap 'civilization' of our own day.

To see in his maxim 'Behave as though you were under continual observation' [1] a foreshadowing of the Kantian categorical imperative, or to hail him as a conscious forerunner of Nietzsche is, perhaps, unjustifiable.   Such a view propounded, *inter alios,* by so discriminating a critic as M. Rouveyre [2] marks a sharp reaction from the unwarrantable neglect of Gracián and is certainly nearer to the truth than the assessment which would dismiss him as a mere coiner of extravagant phrases and inventor of what Voltaire called a 'style d'Arlequin.' [3]   The concision of style which characterizes his *Oráculo*, quite apart from similarity of matter, makes him, as we have seen, unquestionably a forerunner of La Rochefoucauld and the latter's numerous imitators.

It is surely time that the key-position of Baltasar Gracián in the history of European thought and letters met with more general recognition than that which it has hitherto been accorded.

VI. THE UNIVERSALITY OF GRACIÁN

ANY work which claims to rank as a world classic should be, as the cliché has it, 'not of an age but for all time.'   There are, however, books which, while fulfilling this requirement as to universality of appeal, seem especially directed to the problems and needs of certain ages.   Cervantes's *Don Quixote* has found enthusiastic admirers ever since it was written and it appealed equally, although for different reasons, to the neo-classicists of the eighteenth, and the romantics of the nineteenth, century. To-day its main interest is, perhaps, psychological. [4]   The

---

[1] *Oráculo*, Maxim 297.

[2] *Vide* A. Rouveyre, op. cit., Étude critique, Chap. III.

[3] *Vide Dictionnaire Philosophique, art.* 'Figure.'

[4] *Vide* the writer's *Cervantes* in Cassell's Living Thoughts series; also his Introduction to the forthcoming new Everyman edition of *Don Quixote* (Motteux's translation).

universality of its appeal has, nevertheless, been affected to a comparatively small extent by evanescent literary fashions and 'climates of opinion.'

The works of Gracián have suffered, and more especially in this country, a different fate. We have already discussed the handicap under which he laboured in the matter of his translators. Nevertheless, the difficulty of his Spanish as compared, for example, with that of Cervantes, was probably less of a disadvantage to him in this country than his religious vocation and the idiosyncrasy of his thought. Mr. Joseph Jacobs's translation of the *Oráculo manual* [1] appeared at a time when prejudice against Roman Catholicism was rampant in this country and when the word 'Jesuit' automatically conjured up in the minds of the British Protestant pictures of activities as sinister as they were nefarious. Some years were to pass before these prejudices were crystallized, if not immortalized, in the novels of Mr. Joseph Hocking, but, outside a small group of aesthetes, many of whose members had leanings towards Rome, the mere fact that the *Oráculo* was the work of 'a Jesuit' was almost sufficient to condemn it out of hand. It may be replied that Cervantes, like the overwhelming majority of his countrymen, was also a Roman Catholic and that this did not interfere with the popularity of *Don Quixote*.

This is not the place to enter into a discussion concerning the precise nature of Cervantes's religious beliefs as revealed in his works. [2] He was, however, certainly not a Jesuit priest and it is almost impossible for this generation to realize the odium generally attached to the word 'Jesuit' by British citizens in the Victorian era.

Such prejudice was by no means confined to the uninstructed and unintelligent and it is a factor which any assessment of the vogue and value of Gracián must take into account. It is possible that, but for religious bigotry, Mr. Jacobs's rendering of the *Oráculo* would have been more widely known in this country and that the works of Gracián would have been as extensively read

---

[1] *Vide* Bibliography, p. 44.

[2] The most comprehensive study of the thought of Cervantes is Américo Castro's *El pensamiento de Cervantes* (Madrid, 1925).

and translated as those of the classical or French moralists.[1]
Possible, but not, one thinks, probable.   The general climate of
opinion, which favoured the idea of human perfectibility and
endless progress, was decidedly unpropitious.   If Gracián had
been widely studied by the exponents of perfectibility he would,
doubtless, have been condemned as a decadent pessimist and
cynic who did not even have the courage of his own erroneous
convictions in religious matters.   It must be borne in mind that
the doctrine of the 'double truth' and the 'two orders,' natural
and supernatural, was almost entirely unknown to Victorian
critics of Catholicism.   The whole sacramental conception of
human life was, to most of them, 'mummery and superstition'
and they did not even trouble to find out the facts about the
religion for which they had a traditional, instinctive antipathy.
Their hostility to Rome was ill-tempered and highly charged
with emotion.   They did not advance the many rational objec-
tions which can be maintained against the Catholic view of man
and the universe because they simply did not understand what
that view actually was.   The notion that man is essentially a dual
creature with a foot in two worlds, straddled, as it were, across
the bridge (the Church) between the natural and the supernatural,
was quite foreign to Victorian Protestants, at least in its Catholic
form.   In spite of Newman's ingenious verbal juggling, the
majority of Victorian members of the Church of England still
regarded the doctrine of Purgatory as a 'dangerous deceit' and
conceived it as peculiar to Rome.   British Protestantism had
also taken over from Calvinism the idea that material prosperity
was a sign of God's favour and the Catholic doctrine of 'holy
poverty' meant nothing to the respectable Protestant church-
goers of the nineteenth century.   They had, indeed, not the
slightest conception of Catholicism as a philosophy of life and
would, in consequence, have been quite incapable of understanding Gracián or, for that matter, Calderón, if the works of
these writers had been known to them.

   Catholicism was, indeed, to a large extent a tabooed subject,
except as a theme of abuse.   The Victorian Protestants

   [1] The deficiencies of his translation may have had something to do with
this lack of interest.

appeared, in the majority of cases, to have made no attempt to reconcile the general belief in progress and perfectibility which characterized their age with the Christian doctrine of the Fall of Man, a teaching which they, in common with Catholics and Calvinists, theoretically, at least, accepted. It may be argued that the belief in perfectibility was propagated by agnostics and rationalists rather than by Christians. There can be no doubt, however, that, in spite of the pessimistic view of human nature implied by the doctrine of the Fall, the Victorian Protestant tended to believe that this was the best of all possible worlds or, rather, that it was in rapid process of amelioration, mainly owing to the sound Protestantism and instinctive piety of the British race.

Apart from the few passing concessions to Christian teachings which we have already mentioned, the *Oráculo* of Gracián presents us, as we have seen, with a cynical and pessimistic conception of human nature. It would, indeed, be difficult to imagine any view less likely to flatter the illusions of Victorian perfectionists. It seems, therefore, probable that, quite apart from the almost universal antipathy towards the Jesuits, Gracián's secular philosophy would have met with but a poor response on the part of the Victorians if it had been more widely known to them.

The situation in our own day is quite different. Perfectionism of the nineteenth-century type is almost entirely discredited and a psychological approach to human problems which confines itself to registering modes of behaviour without passing moral judgments upon them renders us far more capable of understanding and appreciating the ideology of Gracián in its secular aspect than were our grandfathers. 'This,' says Gracián, in effect, 'is how men behave, whether you like their behaviour or not.' And upon this purely psychological basis (for, as we have seen, the religious element in his works, apart from *El Comulgatorio*, takes the form only of sporadic and somewhat inconsequential *obiter dicta*) Gracián proceeds to study concrete situations and tells us how a man wise in the ways of the world should tackle them if he prefers to be, in the Goethean sense, a hammer rather than an anvil.

The cold objectivity of his method, which truly merits the frequently abused epithet 'scientific'; the extreme concision of his style; his avoidance of the opinionated and long-winded, all render him congenial to our contemporary climate of opinion and scientific cast of mind. The disingenuous opportunism which characterizes so much of his advice is also in keeping with the tastes of an age of 'realism' in politics, both foreign and domestic. The widespread feeling that the creative spirit, in the realm, at least, of the arts, has exhausted itself and that there is nothing new under sun, moon, and stars apart, possibly, from the atomic bomb, is in harmony with the first Maxim of the *Oráculo*, 'Everything has already reached its peak of perfection'; the third provides a succinct summing-up of contemporary diplomatic approaches; the fifth illustrates the methods invariably employed by rulers, be they 'hidalgos' or plutocrats; the seventh should be engraved upon the hearts of all young men who aim at the 'glittering prizes' of politics; the two hundred and sixty-fourth will be heartily endorsed in an age when liberty-loving nations are apt to neglect their defences; the ninety-fourth should find especial favour with the general public, which always distrusts any signs of unusual intelligence; and the two hundred and thirty-second should be appreciated by our 'nation of shop-keepers.'

'Platitudes' some may say, and not without justification. Surely, however, the distinguishing mark of genius is the ability to make commonplaces sound original and to cause wisdom 'ever ancient' to appear as 'ever new'? Shakespeare, Goethe, Molière, La Bruyère, Saint-Simon, La Rochefoucauld, did not they all embellish platitudes? Genius might well be defined as the ability to make a platitude sound as though it were an original remark. Gracián excels in the renovation of platitudes and nearly all the goods in his second-hand store can pass as new.

Perhaps the most important effect which the reading of the *Oráculo* can have upon a man of our age is to make him ask himself whether the schizophrenia of the human race is really a permanent malady. Gracián, the courtier, often cites and approves conduct which Gracián, the Christian, must surely condemn. In this he resembles many of our contemporary writers of

leading articles and contributors of letters to the press. Machia-vellianism, we are inclined to say, has provided no remedy for the ills of the world. Opportunism appears to be leading us precisely nowhere. Yet is orthodox Christianity in very much better case? Are its ideals impossible of realization in this workaday world and, if so, was Gracián right to seek human salvation in another sphere and to conclude his moralizings with the abrupt and somewhat disconcerting exhortation: 'Be a saint!' One must, however, bear in mind that his favourite counsel, one which he never tires of reiterating throughout his works, can be summed up both briefly and accurately, as: 'Don't be an ass!' Could there be any better advice?

VII. On Translating Gracián

THE difficulties which face the would-be translator of Gracián are formidable. As is the case with the baroque poet, Luis de Góngora, certain works of the author require a special gloss to make them comprehensible even to Spaniards. Gracián's *Criticón* is especially remarkable for its obscurity and Rycaut's English rendering of Part I of that extraordinary book is little more than a defective paraphrase. The *Oráculo manual*, although difficult, is not, however, overwhelmingly so.

It has been pointed out that Gracián wrote for an esoteric, cultured circle and never for the, to him, always detestable mob. His rigid training in Latin under the Jesuits, with its emphasis upon ingenious turns of phrase, undoubtedly affected his Spanish style.

The task of rendering him into English is, in some respects, similar to that which confronts a would-be translator of an ancient classical author. The idiom of Gracián is so entirely remote from that of modern English that a literal rendering of the original is frequently impossible; impossible, that is, if the result is to be anything approaching tolerable English. This is not the place to deal with the controversial topic of translation in general. A case can, undoubtedly, be made out for the Italian maxim: 'To

translate is to betray.' I would merely suggest here that a basic *sine qua non* which a reader has the right to expect of a translator into English is reasonably good English! A precise word-for-word translation of any foreign work into our language would, admittedly, be a rendering into, at best, bad English and, at worst, sheer gibberish. This fact has always been recognized in the case of translations from the ancient classics. Some of the finest renderings of, for example, Horace, have been anything but word-for-word construes.

A second basic requirement is, I would suggest, direct work by the translator upon his original. Many of the world's classics have been made known outside the country of their origin in translations done at second hand. *Don Quixote* has suffered in this way, as did the novels of Scott in Spain. The same lot has, on occasions, befallen Gracián. In the case of the English versions of the *Oráculo manual*, the 1694 and 1702 renderings were made from the French version of Amelot de la Houssaie. Savage's rendering of 1702 is hardly more than a paraphrase and it differs very materially from the original Spanish in many respects. The translator had, nevertheless, some happy inspirations. Joseph Jacobs, who produced an English version in 1892, was a corresponding member of the Royal Spanish Academy of History and worked, so he tells us, mainly on two Spanish editions.

The result is a combination of good, bad, indifferent, and nonsensical. I have adopted one or two of Jacobs's happiest turns of phrase and acknowledgment of these will be found in the Notes at the end of this volume. One would hesitate to say, however, that, taking his work as a whole, it is anything more than a paraphrase in, at times, badly tortured English. I am especially indebted to Jacobs for the quotations from Schopenhauer and Sir M. E. Grant Duff which appear on p. viii of this book.

For the benefit of those readers who have some knowledge of Spanish, I will mention here a few cases in which I have departed from the precise sense of the original. It is frequently preferable to render an abstract noun in the original Spanish by a common noun in English. For example, 'sagacidad,' 'sagacity,'

may sometimes best be rendered by 'a sagacious person.' Gracián continually uses the perfect, and sometimes the future tense, where English demands the present. It is often necessary to supply words which, in the original Spanish, must be provided by the imagination of the reader. Gracián employs, indeed, a kind of mental shorthand which is, at first, somewhat confusing. The reader with a sound knowledge of Spanish will quickly become accustomed to it. In view, however, of the fact that this book will be read by some who know little Spanish, or none, the English rendering has been made as explicit as is consistent with the meaning of the original.

In many instances, it is quite impossible to supply a literal rendering of Gracián's rather devastating puns. To give only one example, in the same sentence the word 'pecho' is used in the sense of 'breast,' and in its other meaning of 'tribute.' It is impossible to carry over this play upon words into an English rendering.

Gracián is extremely fond of words and phrases with a double meaning and indulges extensively in antitheses, antinomies, and neologisms. The binary rhythm of his phrasing will already be familiar to many English readers in the works of John Lyly and other English euphuists.

In conclusion, I would like to say here how conscious I am of the imperfections of this English rendering of the *Oráculo manual*. It is, I think, closer to the original than any of the other English versions and, I hope, not entirely formless, as so many translations are apt to be. If my rashness in making this attempt has not qualified me for inclusion in Gracián's hated category of 'necios,' I shall be content.

Those who may make use of this book in order to revive or improve their knowledge of the Spanish language are reminded that they should refer to the Notes at the end of the volume. In these a literal rendering is given where considerable departure from the original has been deemed necessary.

No reference to translations of the *Oráculo manual* would be complete without allusion to the late A. Morel-Fatio's analysis of a number of passages from Schopenhauer's rendering. These he discusses in an article published in the *Bulletin Hispanique*,

vols. 11, 12, 1909–10.[1] He queries the verdict of Karl Borinski, who refers, in his *Balthasar Gracián und die Hofliteratur in Deutschland* (Halle, 1894) to 'Schopenhauers treue und sorgfältige Verdeutschung des spanischen Originals des Oráculo.'   While he agrees that Schopenhauer has, of all the translators, provided 'l'image la plus fidèle,' he points out that the German philosopher frequently missed the mark and that he treats Amelot de la Houssaie 'avec un dédain tout-à-fait injuste.'   Morel-Fatio also surmises that the obscurity of some of the cruxes in the text is due to typographical errors in the 1653 edition carried over into the 1659 edition, upon which latter edition Schopenhauer worked.   He points out that the Madrid edition of 1653 had never been properly collated with the Amsterdam edition of 1659 and suggests that the main differences between the two editions may be of a purely typographical nature.   I have been able to collate these editions, both of which are to be found in the Library of the British Museum, and have found that Morel-Fatio's conjecture is correct.   The faulty punctuation and mutilation of words which characterize the 1653 edition are frequently repeated in the edition of 1659, although the latter is less defective in these respects.   I have, in the main, followed the text of the 1659 edition, but have made a number of changes in the punctuation, which is chaotic in both editions.   I have also corrected the typographical errors, modernized the spelling, and italicized the opening sentence of each Maxim, following, in this last respect, the edition of the 1659 text by Dr. Alfonso Reyes (*vide* Bibliographical Note).   Morel-Fatio's more important comments upon the text of the *Oráculo* and upon Schopenhauer's rendering of certain passages have been included in a brief Appendix following the Notes at the end of this volume. The latter contain a number of my own observations upon the translations made, respectively, by Amelot, Schopenhauer, and Jacobs.   Morel-Fatio rightly observes that there is room for a good deal of further investigation into these renderings.

---

[1] 'Gracián interprété par Schopenhauer.

VIII. Bibliographical Note

I. SPANISH EDITIONS OF THE 'ORÁCULO MANUAL.'

ACCORDING to Latassa, the *Oráculo manual* was first published at Huesca in 1647 by Juan Nogués. So far as is known, no copy of the *editio princeps* survives. The earliest edition available is that published at Madrid in 1653:

Oracvlo| Manual y Arte| de Prvdencia| Sacada de los a| forismos que se discurren en| las obras de Lorenço| Gracián|. Publícala D. Vi| cencio Juan de Lastanosa.| Y la dedica| al Excelentísimo| Señor D. Luis Méndez| de Haro. Con licencia. En Madrid por Maria de Quiñones año de 1653. Véndese en casa de Francisco| Lamberto, en la Carrera| de San Gerónimo.

In the censor's licence there is a reference to a prior edition with which the Madrid edition is said to correspond ('corresponde con el antes impresso . . . que otras vezes ha sido impresso'). This is in accordance with the date given by Latassa for the *editio princeps* but, as Jacobs points out, it makes it difficult to understand Lastanosa's reference to the 'twelve Graciáns,' of which the *Oráculo* was the 'quintessence.' Four of these books only had appeared by that time and the two unpublished works would make up only half a dozen.[1] The date of the *editio princeps* must, then, be between 1647 and 1653.

The *Oráculo manual* was reprinted at Amsterdam in 1659 and from that time appeared in all the editions of the works of Gracián. Modern editions of the *Oráculo* are as follows: Rivadeneyra: *Biblioteca de Autores Españoles*, vol. lxv; *Biblioteca de Filosofía y Sociología*. Tom. XVIII (with *El Político*); ed. Alfonso Reyes in the Casa Editorial Calleja series. Madrid, 1918.

II. TRANSLATIONS OF THE 'ORÁCULO MANUAL.'

(i) *French*

L'Homme de Cour. Traduit de l'Espagnol de Baltasar Gracián. Par le sieur Amelot de la Houssaie. Avec des Notes.

---

[1] *Vide* Coster, op. cit., pp. 666–93, for much of the information contained in this Note.

A Paris chez la veuve Martin & Jean Boudot, rue de Saint Jacques, au Soleil d'or.   M.DC.LXXXIV.

Amelot's translation was reprinted fourteen times between 1685 and 1716 and, again, four times between 1732 and 1808. Coster writes of its 'exactitude et intelligence.' The former is, in fact, often dubious.   Schopenhauer is more precise.

Fr. Joseph de Courbeville criticized Amelot's rendering of the title of the *Oráculo manual* as '*L'Homme de Cour*' and undertook a new translation of the work in 1730: *Maximes de Baltasar Gracián, Traduites de l'Espagnol, avec les réponses aux Critiques de l'Homme universel et de l'Héros, traduits du même auteur.   A Paris, chez Rollin fils, quai des Augustins, à S. Athanase.   M.DCC.XXX.   Avec approbation & privilège du Roi.*

In his preface to this translation, Courbeville makes scathing and unjustifiable attacks on Amelot's general accuracy.   The new rendering did not meet with any great success and was not reprinted.   The majority of translations from Gracián's works into languages other than French were made from French versions.

(ii) *English*

An English translation of *El Oráculo manual* first appeared in 1694, based on the French version by Amelot de la Houssaie: *The Courtier's Oracle; or the Art of Prudence.   Written originally in Spanish And now done into English.   London*, 1694.

This version was revised by Savage in 1702 with the title: *The Art of Prudence; or a Companion for a Man of Sense.   Made English and illustrated with the Sieur Amelot de la Houssaie's notes, by Mr. Savage.   London*, 1702.   Savage's rendering was reprinted in 1705 and 1714.

An English rendering of the *Oráculo manual* by Joseph Jacobs appeared in 1892: *The Art of Worldly Wisdom by Balthasar Gracián.   Translated from the Spanish by Joseph Jacobs . . . London*, 1892.   This was reprinted in 1943, 1944, 1945, 1946, and 1950 (New York, The Macmillan Company).

(iii) *Italian*

An anonymous translation of the *Oráculo* appeared in Italy in 1679: *Oracolo manuale, e arte di Prudenza/Cavata dagli Aforismi,*

che si discorrono nell' Opre di Lorenzo Gratiano| Mandalo in Luce D. Vincencio Giovanni de Lastanosa. Diretto alla Nobilità Venetiana e dedicato all' Illustr. & Eccellentiss. Sig. Leonardo Pesaro ... In Venetia MDCLXXIX. This was reprinted in 1708, 1718, and 1790.

Amelot de la Houssaie's French rendering was done into Italian by Francesco Tosques in 1698 with the title *L'Uomo di Corte.* This version was reprinted in 1708, 1718, 1730, 1734, and 1761.

(iv) *German*

A German translation of the *Oráculo* by Leonhard Sauter appeared in 1687: *L'Homme de Cour Oder der heutige politische Welt- und Staats- Weise fürgestellt von Balthasar Gracián, Hispaniern, Und wegen seiner hohen Würde in unsre hochteutsche Sprache übersetzt, anitzo aus dem Original vermehret, und zum Andernmal hersausgegeben von Joh. Leonhard Sauter, J. U. D. Frankfurth und Leipzig,* 1687.

Another rendering, by C. Weissbach (under the pseudonym of Selintes) appeared in 1711. This was based on Amelot's French version. It was followed by A. F. Müller's version (1715–17).[1] Tosques's Italian rendering was done into German by Christoph Freiesleben in 1723. Another anonymous rendering appeared in 1786, and, in 1804, a version by P. H. Heydenreich. In 1826 yet another anonymous rendering was published, and, in 1838, a version by Fr. Kolle.

The most famous German rendering is that of Arthur Schopenhauer (1861): *Balthasar Graciáns Hand-Orakel und Kunst der Weltklugheit, aus dessen Werken gezogen von Don Vincencio Juan de Lastanosa| und aus dem spanischen Original treu und sorgfältig übersetzt von Arthur Schopenhauer.* This was republished in 1871, 1877, 1890, 1895, and 1910 (Kröner Verlag).

(v) *Dutch*

Amelot's rendering of the *Oráculo* was translated into Dutch in 1696 and republished in 1700.

---

[1] Reprinted in 1733.

(vi) *Other languages*

Amelot's version was done into Hungarian in 1750 (republished 1770–1, 1772, 1790, and 1837); into Polish in 1802; into Russian in 1742.   A Latin version appeared at Frankfurt in 1731, with the title, *Aulicus,* and this was reprinted in 1750.   Another Latin version appeared in 1734, by P. A. Ulrich.

III. MAJOR CRITICAL STUDIES OF GRACIÁN.

Coster, A.   'Baltasar Gracián.' *Revue Hispanique,*
                              vol. xxix, pp. 347–752. Paris, 1913.

(This is by far the most important and exhaustive study of Gracián which has yet appeared in any language.)

J. Liñán y Heredia   *Baltasar Gracián.*   1902.

Maldonado, F.   *Gracián como pesimista y político.* Salamanca, 1916.

Bell, A. F. G.   *Baltasar Gracián.*   Oxford, 1921.

Cossío, J. M. de   *Gracián, crítico literario.*   Madrid, 1923.

Marone, G.   *Moral y politica di B. Gracián.*   Naples, 1925.

Rouveyre, A.   Introduction to *Baltasar Gracián: Pages caractéristiques, traduites par V. Bouillier.*   Paris, 1925.

Farinelli, A.   *Estudio Crítico* (in his edition of *El Héroe and El Discreto,* Madrid, 1900).
                          'Gracián y la literatura de Corte en Alemania.'   (Univ. de Madrid. *Conferencias y trabajos,* 1924–5. Madrid, 1926.)

Bouillier, V.   'Gracián et Nietzsche.' *Revue de littérature comparée.* Paris, 1926.

Vossler, K.   'Introducción a Gracián.'   *Revista de Occidente,* 1935.

Correa Calderón, E.   *Introducción a las obras completas de Gracián,* 1945.

García López, J.   'Baltasar Gracián,' Editorial *Labor,* Madrid, 1947.

Epitaph

The following is a transcription of the Epitaph at the foot of the portrait of Gracián which was once displayed in the Jesuit College at Calatayud and is now the property of D. Felix Sanz de Larrea:

'P. Balthasar Gracian, ut iam ab ortu emineret, in Bellomonte natus est prope Bilbilim, confinis Martiali patria, proximus ingenio, ut profunderet adhuc xristianas argutias Bilbilis, quae poene exhaustae videbantur in aethnicis. Ergo augens natale ingenium innato acumine, scripsit ARTEM INGENII et arte fecit scibile quod scibile facit artes. Scripsit item ARTEM PRUDENTIAE et a se ipso artem didicit. Scripsit ORACULUM et voces suas protulit. Scripsit DISERTUM ut se ipsum describeret. Et ut scriberet HEROEM heroica patravit. Haec et alia eius scripta Mecenates [1] Reges habuerunt, Iudicem Admirationem Lectorem Mundum, Typographum Aeternitatem. Philippus 4^8 saepe illius argutias inter prandium versabat, ne deficerent sales regiis dapibus. Sed qui plausus excitaverat calamo, deditus Missionibus excitavit planctus verbo, excitaturus desiderium in morte qua raptus est 6 Decemb. 1658, sed aliquando extinctus aeternum lucebit.'

[1] *Sic.* For 'Maecenates.'

LASTANOSA'S PREFACE

AL LECTOR [1]

Ni AL justo leyes, ni al sabio consejos; pero ninguno supo bastantemente para sí. Una cosa me has de perdonar, y otra agradecer, el llamar Oráculo a este epítome de aciertos del vivir; pues lo es en lo sentencioso, y lo conciso. El ofrecerte de un rasgo todos los doce Gracianes, tan estimado cada uno, que el Discreto apenas se vió en España cuando se logró en Francia, traducido en su lengua, y impreso en su Corte: sirva éste de memorial en el banquete de sus sabios, en que registre los platos prudenciales, que le irán sirviendo en las demás obras para distribuir el gusto genialmente.

D. Vincencio Juan de Lastanosa.

TO THE READER

No LAWS for the just nor counsels for the wise: yet no one has known, on his own account, as much as he needed to know. You must forgive me for one thing and thank me for another: for calling this epitome of successful living an Oracle, since it is one in its sententiousness and concision; for introducing you all at once to all the twelve Graciáns, each one of his works being so highly thought of that his *Discreet Man* had scarcely appeared in Spain when it achieved success in France, being translated into the language of that country, and printed in its capital: let this be Wisdom's bill of fare at the banquet of her sages, the menu in which she sets down the dishes of discernment which she will serve to you in the other works, so that delight may be distributed in a pleasing fashion.

D. Vincencio Juan de Lastanosa.

[1] The spelling has been modernized throughout.

THE ORACLE

ORÁCULO MANUAL

The Madrid and Amsterdam editions, respectively, are cited in the footnotes to the text as 1653 and 1659. 'Reyes' refers to the edition of the 1659 text by Dr. Alfonso Reyes (Madrid, 1918). (J) refers to the English translation by Jacobs. Where a more or less literal rendering of the Spanish has been found possible, words which, although they do not have their counterpart in the Spanish text, are necessary in English to bring out the full sense of the original, appear in square brackets.

1

Todo está ya en su punto y el ser persona en el mayor; más se requiere hoy para un sabio que antiguamente para siete, y más es menester para tratar con un solo hombre en estos tiempos, que con todo un pueblo en los pasados.

2

Genio y ingenio. Los dos ejes del lucimiento de prendas; el uno sin el otro, felicidad a medias; no basta lo entendido, deséase lo genial; infelicidad de necio errar la vocación en el estado, empleo, región, familiaridad.

3

Llevar sus cosas con suspensión. La admiración de la novedad es estimación de los aciertos. El jugar a juego descubierto ni es de utilidad, ni de gusto. El no declararse luego suspende, y más donde la sublimidad del empleo da objeto a la universal expectación; amaga misterio en todo y con su misma arcanidad provoca la veneración; aun en el darse a entender se ha de huir la llaneza; así como ni en el trato se ha de permitir el interior a todos. Es el recatado silencio sagrado de la cordura. La resolución declarada nunca fué estimada; antes se permite a la censura; y si se saliere azar, será dos veces infeliz. Imítase, pues, el proceder divino para hacer estar a la mira y al desvelo.

THE ORACLE

1

Everything has already reached its peak of perfection and at the highest of these is [the art of] being a great man; more is required to make one sage to-day than was needed to produce seven in the past, and you need more wits in these times to handle one man than it took to manage a whole people in those gone by.

2

Genius and wit [are] the two poles around which the display of natural gifts revolves; [to possess] one without the other is to be happy by half; intelligence is not enough, genius is to be desired; it is the misfortune of fools to be mistaken in their choice of status, employment, place of abode, [or] circle of friends.

3

Keep your affairs in suspense. Admiration of their novelty causes achievements to be esteemed. There is neither profit nor pleasure in showing your cards. To refrain from showing your hand immediately keeps people in suspense, and more especially when the importance of your position gives rise to general anticipation; to do so hints at mystery in everything and your very secretiveness excites respect; you should avoid making yourself too clear even in your explanations; just as in social intercourse you should not wear your heart on your sleeve. A discreet silence is the sanctuary of wisdom. The declared purpose never inspires respect; rather does it invite adverse criticism; and should it meet with disaster you will be doubly unfortunate. Imitate, then, the methods adopted by Providence to keep men alert and vigilant.

4

El saber y el valor alternan grandeza; porque lo son, hacen inmortales: tanto es uno cuanto sabe, y el sabio todo lo puede. Hombre sin noticias, mundo a oscuras.   Consejo y fuerzas, ojos y manos; sin valor es estéril la sabiduría.

5

Hacer depender.   No hace el numen el que lo dora sino el que lo adora.   El sagaz más quiere necesitados de sí que agradecidos. Es robarle a la esperanza cortés fiar del agradecimiento villano, que lo que aquélla es memoriosa, es éste olvidadizo.   Más se saca de la dependencia que de la cortesía; vuelve luego las espaldas a la fuente el satisfecho, y la naranja exprimida cae del oro al lodo.   Acabada la dependencia acaba la correspondencia, y con ella la estimación.   Sea lición, y de prima en experiencia, entretenerla, no satisfacerla,[1] conservando siempre en necesidad de sí aun al coronado patrón; pero no se ha de llegar al exceso de callar para que yerre, ni hacer incurable el daño ajeno por el provecho propio.

6

Hombre en su punto.   No se nace hecho: vase de cada día perficionando en la persona, en el empleo, hasta llegar al punto del consumado ser, al complemento de prendas, de eminencias: conocerse ha en lo realzado del gusto, purificado del ingenio; en lo maduro del juicio, en lo defecado de la voluntad.   Algunos nunca llegan a ser cabales: fáltales siempre un algo; tardan otros en hacerse.   El varón consumado, sabio en dichos, cuerdo en hechos, es admitido y aun deseado del singular comercio de los discretos.

[1] *Vide* Appendix, p. 305.

4

Wisdom and courage make a mutual contribution to greatness; because they are themselves immortal they bestow immortality: knowledge is the measure of a man, and the wise man can do everything. A man without knowledge [lives in] a world of darkness. Prudence and strength [are] eyes and hands; knowledge without courage is sterile.

5

Make people depend upon you. It is not he who adorns but he who adores the idol that makes it divine. The wise man wants people who have need of him rather than grateful men around him. To have faith in the gratitude of boors is to do violence to gracious hope, for just as the latter has a good memory, so the former is quick to forget. More is to be had from dependence than from courtesy; he who has slaked his thirst immediately turns his back upon the spring, and the squeezed orange falls from its [plate of] gold into the gutter. When dependence disappears agreement departs with it, and esteem accompanies them both. The first lesson which experience should teach you is to foster hope in a dependant without satisfying him, keeping even a royal patron always in need of you; do not, however, carry reserve to such extremes as to fall into error, nor, for your own advantage, render another's ill incurable.

6

Man at his peak. We are not fully developed at birth: every day we advance towards perfection in our persons and in our callings, until we reach the peak of complete being, the full measure of [our] talents [and] of [our] high qualities: this stage can be recognized by the excellence of our taste, the clarity of our intelligence, the maturity of our judgment, the integrity of our purpose. Some men never attain completeness: there is always something lacking in them; others develop slowly. The complete man, wise in word, judicious in deed, is admitted to the special intimacy of the discreet and is even sought out by them.

7

Excusar victorias del patrón. Todo vencimiento es odioso, y del dueño, o necio o fatal. Siempre la superioridad fué aborrecida, cuanto más de la misma superioridad. Ventajas vulgares suele disimular la atención: como desmentir la belleza con el desaliño. Bien se hallará quien quiera ceder en la dicha y en el genio; pero en el ingenio, ninguno, cuanto menos una soberanía: es éste el atributo rey, y así, cualquier crimen contra él fué de lesa majestad. Son soberanos, y quieren serlo en lo que es más. Gustan de ser ayudados los príncipes, pero no excedidos, y que el aviso haga antes viso de recuerdo de lo que olvidaba, que de luz de lo que no alcanzó. Enséñannos esta sutileza los astros con dicha; que aunque hijos y brillantes, nunca se atreven a los lucimientos del sol.

8

Hombre inapasionable, prenda de la mayor alteza de ánimo; su misma superioridad le redime de la sujeción a peregrinas vulgares impresiones. No hay mayor señorío que el de sí mismo, de sus afectos; que llega a ser triunfo del albedrío; y cuando la pasión ocupare la personal, no se atreva al oficio, y menos cuanto fuere más: culto modo de ahorrar disgustos, y aun de atajar para la reputación.

9

Desmentir los achaques de su nación. Participa el agua las calidades buenas o malas de las venas por donde pasa; y el hombre las del clima donde nace. Deben más unos que otros a sus patrias, que cupo allí más favorable el cenit. No hay nación que se escape de algún original defecto, aun las más cultas, que luego censuran los confinantes o para cautela, o para consuelo.

7

Avoid victories over your superior. Every triumph is odious and if it is over your superior it is either foolish or disastrous. Superiority is invariably disliked, more especially by those who are themselves in high positions. Ordinary gifts can usually be concealed by the exercise of care: good looks, for example, can be belied by slovenliness. You may well find some people who may be willing to grant you pride of place in good fortune and character; but none in understanding, least of all a ruler: this attribute is kingly, and it follows that any offence against it ranks as *lèse-majesté*. Sovereigns are sovereigns, and like to be so in respect of the most regal of all qualities. Rulers like to be assisted but not to be outshone, and they prefer that advice should appear to be rather a reminder of something they have forgotten than a light upon something that is beyond their understanding. The stars set us a happy example of this tactfulness; for although they are children of the sun and shine brilliantly, they never venture to vie with him in splendour.

8

A man who is not passion's slave reveals the highest quality of soul; his superiority itself redeems him from subjection to passing, vulgar influences. There is no greater mastery than control over oneself and one's emotions; it comes to be a triumph for a man's free will; and if passion should dominate your personality do not let it threaten your position; and the less should it do so, the higher the latter may be: this is a polite way of avoiding troubles and even provides a short cut to fame.

9

Conceal your national failings. Water shares the good or bad qualities of the channels through which it flows, and a man the characteristics of the country in which he is born. Some owe more than others to their fatherland, for the stars have been more favourably inclined towards them there [than they would have been in another part of the world]. There is no nation, however civilized, that is free from some native failing which its neighbours are quick to censure, either from guile, or for their own

C

Victoriosa destreza corregir,[1] o por lo menos, desmentir estos nacionales desdoros; consíguese el plausible crédito de único entre los suyos: que lo que menos se esperaba, se estimó más. Hay también achaques de la prosapia, del estado, del empleo y de la edad, que si coinciden todos en un sujeto, y con la atención no se previenen, hacen un monstruo intolerable.

10

Fortuna y fama. Lo que tiene de inconstante la una, tiene de firme la otra. La primera para vivir, la segunda para después; aquélla contra la invidia, ésta contra el olvido: la fortuna se desea y tal vez se ayuda; la fama se diligencia; deseo de reputación nace de la virtud: fué, y es hermana de gigantes la fama; anda siempre por extremos: o monstruos o prodigios: de abominación, de aplauso.

11

Tratar con quien se pueda aprender. Sea el amigable trato escuela de erudición, y la conversación enseñanza culta; un hacer de los amigos maestros, penetrando el útil del aprender con el gusto de conversar. Altérnase la fruición con los entendidos, logrando lo que se dice, en el aplauso con que se recibe, y lo que se oye en el amaestramiento. Ordinariamente nos lleva a otro la propia conveniencia. Aquí, realzada, frecuenta el atento las casas de aquellos héroes cortesanos, que son más teatros de la heroicidad que palacios de la vanidad. Hay señores acreditados de discretos, que a más de ser ellos oráculos de toda grandeza con su ejemplo y en su trato, el cortejo de los que los asisten es una cortesana academia de toda buena y galante discreción.

12

Naturaleza y arte, materia, y obra. No hay belleza sin ayuda, ni perfección que no dé en bárbara sin el realce del artificio; a lo malo socorre, y lo bueno lo perficiona. Déjanos comúnmente a

---

[1] 1659 has 'corregir.'

amusement. It is a triumph of skill to correct or, at least, to conceal these national shortcomings; to do so will win you the praiseworthy reputation of being unique among your fellows: for what was least expected is the more highly esteemed. There are, also, defects of lineage, status, office, and age, which, if they are all united in one person and are not carefully forestalled, make an insufferable monster.

10

Fortune and fame. The one is as fickle as the other is steadfast. The first is for our lifetime, the second for hereafter; the former combats envy, the latter, oblivion. Fortune is courted, and sometimes assisted on her way; fame is won by dint of industry; a longing for good repute springs from virtue; fame [always] has been, and still is, the sister of giants; she invariably goes to extremes; [and creates] monsters or prodigies, [objects] of loathing, or [objects] of praise.

11

Associate with those from whom you may be able to learn something. Let friendly intercourse be a school of erudition, and company be a means of acquiring culture; make teachers of your friends and combine the advantages of learning with the delights of social intercourse. The intelligent enjoy a twofold satisfaction, pleasure from the applause which greets their words, profit from the instruction which they receive. We are usually attracted to another from motives of self-interest. In this case, the interest is of a higher type and the discreet man frequents those noble houses which are rather theatres of heroism than palaces of vanity. There are persons with a reputation for discretion who, in addition to being, themselves, oracles of every kind of nobility by their example and by their behaviour, also have as their retinue a courtly academy of all that is good, gallant, and discreet.

12

Nature and art, material and craftsmanship. There is no [such thing as] unaided beauty, and no excellence that does not degenerate into barbarism if it lacks the finishing touch of art; art redeems the bad and perfects the good. Nature usually lets us

lo mejor la naturaleza: acojámonos al arte. El mejor natural es inculto sin ella, y les falta la mitad a las perfecciones si les falta la cultura. Todo hombre sabe a tosco sin el artificio, y ha menester pulirse en todo orden de perfección.

13

Obrar de intención, ya segunda, y ya primera. Milicia es la vida del hombre contra la malicia del hombre; pelea la sagacidad con estratagemas de intención. Nunca obra lo que indica: apunta sí para deslumbrar: amaga al aire con destreza, y ejecuta en la impensada realidad, atenta siempre a desmentir. Echa una intención para asegurarse de la émula atención, y revuelve luego contra ella, venciendo por lo impensado. Pero la penetrante inteligencia la previene con atenciones, la acecha con reflejos; entiende siempre lo contrario de lo que quiere que entienda, y conoce luego cualquier intentar de falso: deja pasar toda primera intención, y está en espera a la segunda, y aun a la tercera. Auméntase la simulación al ver alcanzado su artificio, y pretende engañar con la misma verdad: muda de juego, por mudar de treta, y hace artificio del no artificio, fundando su astucia en la mayor candidez. Acude la observación, entendiendo su perspicacia, y descubre las tinieblas revestidas de la luz; descifra la intención, más solapada cuanto más sencilla. De esta suerte combate la calidez de Pitón, contra la candidez de los penetrantes rayos de Apolo.

14

La realidad, y el modo. No basta la substancia, requiérese también la circunstancia. Todo lo gasta un mal modo, hasta la justicia y razón. El bueno todo lo suple; dora el no, endulza la verdad, y afeita la misma vejez: tiene gran parte en las cosas el cómo, y es tahur de los gustos el modillo. Un bel portarse [1] es la gala del vivir: desempeña singularmente todo buen término.

---

[1] Both 1653 and 1659 have 'velportarse.'

down when we least expect it: let us, [then,] have recourse to art. Without art, the finest of natural endowments goes unembellished, and high qualities lack half their excellence if culture be to seek. Unrefined, artless knowledge is common to all men, and every kind of endowment needs polish.

13

Behave sometimes disingenuously, sometimes with candour. Man's life is a manœuvre against the malice of men; crafty schemes are the weapons of the shrewd. [Cunning] never behaves as appearances would suggest: it takes its aim, indeed, in order to provoke confusion: it skilfully contrives to keep its threats indefinite and carries them out in an unforeseen way, intent always upon dissimulation. It affords a glimpse of its purpose in order to ensure the attention of a rival, and then does the very opposite, triumphing by means of the unexpected. But keen intelligence shrewdly foresees this [and] lies in thoughtful ambush; it always comes to a conclusion contrary to the one it is intended to reach and at once recognizes any attempt at deception: it ignores every first and obvious aim and waits for the second, and even the third. Dissimulation is intensified when its trick has been detected and then endeavours to deceive by means of truth itself: it alters its play by some new feint, and turns simplicity into guile, basing its astuteness upon [a show of] extreme candour. Observation comes along and, its perspicacity seeing through the trick, unmasks the wolf in sheep's clothing; it detects the purpose [and sees it] as the craftier the more straightforward it appears. In this way, the cunning of the Python combats the candour of the searching beams of Apollo.

14

Substance and accidents. Substance alone is insufficient, accidents are also required. A bad manner ruins everything, even justice and reason. A good manner is a universal provider; it gilds a refusal, makes truth palatable, and even lends glamour to old age. The way in which things are done plays an important part in human life: and a good manner steals hearts away. A gracious deportment is the adornment of life: it provides the best way to the attainment of every worthy end.

15

Tener ingenios auxiliares. Felicidad de poderosos acompañarse de valientes[1] de entendimiento que le saquen de todo ignorante aprieto, que le riñan las pendencias de la dificultad. Singular grandeza servirse de sabios: y que exceden al bárbaro gusto de Tigranes, aquel que afectaba los rendidos reyes para criados. Nuevo género de señorío, en lo mejor del vivir, hacer siervos por arte de los que hizo la naturaleza superiores. Hay mucho que saber, y es poco el vivir, y no se vive si no se sabe. Es, pues, singular destreza el estudiar sin que cueste, y mucho por muchos, sabiendo por todos. Dice después en un consistorio por muchos, o por su boca hablan tantos sabios cuantos le previnieron: consiguiendo el crédito de oráculo a sudor ajeno. Hacen aquéllos primero elección de la lición, y sírvenle después en quintas esencias el saber. Pero el que no pudiere alcanzar a tener la sabiduría en servidumbre, lógrela en familiaridad.

16

Saber con recta intención. Aseguran fecundidad de aciertos. Monstruosa violencia fué siempre un buen entendimiento casado con una mala voluntad. La intención malévola es un veneno de las perfecciones, y ayudada del saber malea con mayor sutileza. ¡Infeliz eminencia la que se emplea en la ruindad! Ciencia sin seso, locura doble.

17

Variar de tenor en el obrar; no siempre de un modo, para deslumbrar la atención, y más si emula. No siempre de primera intención, que le cogerán la uniformidad, previniéndole y aun frustrándole las acciones. Fácil es de matar al vuelo el ave que le tiene seguido: no así la que le tuerce. Ni siempre de segunda

---

[1] *Vide* Appendix, p. 305.

15

Provide yourself with auxiliary wits. It is the good fortune of the powerful to be accompanied by clever bravoes who can get them out of any difficulty in which their ignorance has involved them, and can fight their hard battles for them. It is an outstanding [mark of] greatness to make use of wise men, and to do so is better than to follow the barbarous fashion of Tigranes, who delighted in making servants of the rulers he overcame. To enslave our natural superiors by the use of cunning is a novel kind of power, among the best that life can offer. There is much to be known, life is short, and life is not life without knowledge. It is, therefore, an excellent device to study without expense, and [to learn] much by means of many, acquiring knowledge from everybody. Later, you will speak in a council chamber as the mouthpiece of many, or as many sages speak with your lips as formerly gave you their advice. Thus, by the sweat of another's brow, you win the reputation of being an oracle. Those wise men first choose what lesson you are to learn, and afterwards serve up to you the quintessence of the wisdom they have acquired. Moreover, a man who cannot contrive to hold Wisdom in thrall should have her as a member of his household.

16

Knowledge and a right purpose. These ensure success in abundance. A sound understanding wedded to a perverse will always does violence to nature. A malevolent purpose envenoms all good qualities and, if backed by knowledge, works evil with the greater subtlety. Unhappy the talent devoted to evil ends! Knowledge without wisdom is doubly folly.

17

Vary your way of behaving; do not let it always be the same; so that you may puzzle anybody who is watching you, and more especially if he is competing with you. Do not always act openly, for your rivals will recognize this uniformity of behaviour and will forestall, and even frustrate, your actions. It is easy to shoot a bird on the wing if it flies straight: not so, one that twists

intención, que le entenderán a dos veces la treta. Está a la espera la malicia; gran sutileza es menester para desmentirla; nunca juega el tahur la pieza que el contrario presume, y menos la que desea.

18

Aplicación y Minerva. No hay eminencia sin entrambas, y si concurren, exceso. Más consigue una medianía con aplicación, que una superioridad sin ella. Cómprase la reputación a precio de trabajo; poco vale lo que poco cuesta. Aun para los primeros empleos se deseó en algunos la aplicación: raras veces desmienten al genio. No ser eminente en el empleo vulgar, por querer ser mediano en el sublime, excusa tiene de generosidad; pero contentarse con ser mediano en el último, pudiendo ser excelente en el primero, no la tiene. Requiérense, pues, naturaleza y arte; y sella la aplicación.

19

No entrar con sobrada expectación. Ordinario desaire de todo lo muy celebrado antes, no llegar después al exceso de lo concebido. Nunca lo verdadero pudo alcanzar a lo imaginado, porque el fingirse las perfecciones es fácil, y muy dificultoso el conseguirlas: cásase la imaginación con el deseo, y concibe siempre mucho más de lo que las cosas son. Por grandes que sean las excelencias, no bastan a satisfacer el concepto, y como le hallan engañado con la exorbitante expectación, más presto le desengañan que le admiran. La esperanza es gran falsificadora de la verdad; corríjala la cordura, procurando que sea superior la fruición al deseo. Unos principios de crédito sirven de despertar la curiosidad, no de empeñar el objeto. Mejor sale cuando la realidad excede al concepto, y es más de lo que se creyó. Faltará

and turns. Neither should you always behave disingenuously, for people will see through the trick the second time you try it on. Malice is on the watch; great skill is required to circumvent it: the sharper never plays the card his opponent is expecting, and still less the one which the latter wishes him to play.

18

Industry and intelligence. There is no distinction without both of these, and if they are conjoined, there is distinction in the highest degree. A mediocrity accomplishes more by means of diligence than a person of superior ability who lacks it. Fame is bought at the price of toil; what costs little is worth little. Even for [the attainment of] the highest positions, it is, in some cases, only application that is lacking; talent is rarely to seek. A noble mind may be excused for preferring a mediocre status in a high position to eminence in a humble one; but there is no excuse for being content with a mediocre status in the humblest position when it is possible to excel in the highest. Natural talent and skill are, therefore, both indispensable; and industry sets its seal upon them.

19

Do not arouse exaggerated expectations at the start. It is the common misfortune of everything which has been highly praised in advance never to come up, afterwards, to the exaggerated ideas which have been formed concerning it. Truth has never been able to rise to the heights of the imagined, because it is easy to conceive perfection and very difficult to attain it. Imagination is wedded to desire and always conceives things far beyond the bounds of what they are. However splendid high qualities may be, they are inadequate to satisfy the idea [you have formed of them], and as you have been deceived by extravagant hopes, you are readier to be disillusioned than to admire. Hope is a great falsifier of truth; wisdom should guard against this by seeing to it that achievement surpasses expectation. The beginnings of a reputation serve to excite curiosity but are no guarantee that you will gain your ends. Things turn out better when reality surpasses the idea formed concerning them and they are found to be more desirable than was expected. This rule will

*C

esta regla en lo malo, pues le ayuda la misma exageración; desmiéntela con aplauso, y aun llega a parecer tolerable, lo que se temió extremo de ruin.

20

Hombre en su siglo. Los sujetos eminentemente raros dependen de los tiempos. No todos tuvieron el que merecían; y muchos, aunque le tuvieron, no acertaron a lograrle. Fueron dignos algunos de mejor siglo, que no todo lo bueno triunfa siempre: tienen las cosas su vez, hasta las eminencias son al uso; pero lleva una ventaja lo sabio, que es eterno, y si éste no es su siglo, muchos otros lo serán.

21

Arte para ser dichoso. Reglas hay de ventura, que no toda es acasos para el sabio; puede ser ayudada de la industria. Conténtanse algunos con ponerse de buen aire a las puertas de la Fortuna, y esperan a que ella obre.[1] Mejor otros pasan adelante y válense de la cuerda audacia, que en alas de su virtud y valor puede dar alcance a la dicha y lisonjearla eficazmente. Pero bien filosofado, no hay otro arbitrio sino el de la virtud y atención; porque no hay más dicha ni más desdicha que prudencia, o imprudencia.

22

Hombre de plausibles noticias. Es munición de discretos la cortesana gustosa erudición: un plático saber de todo lo corriente; más a lo noticioso, menos a lo vulgar; tener una sazonada copia de sales en dichos, de galantería en hechos, y saberlos emplear en su ocasión, que salió a veces mejor el aviso en chiste que en el más grave magisterio. Sabiduría conversable valióles más a algunos que todas las siete, con ser tan liberales.

[1] *Vide* Appendix, p. 305.

not apply in the case of a bad reputation, for here exaggeration is itself helpful; it happily belies the general rule, and that which was dreaded as the extreme of villainy can even come to be regarded as tolerable.

20

A man and his times. Men of the very highest distinction are dependent upon their times. Not all of them have lived in the age which they deserved; and many, even though they did so, failed to take advantage of it. Some men have been worthy of a better age, for all good does not invariably triumph: [the] things [of this world] have their day, even the eminent have their vogue; but wisdom has one advantage, that of being eternal, and if this is not her age, many others will be.

21

The art of being lucky. There are rules for being lucky, because, for the wise man, all good luck does not come about by chance; it can be fostered by diligence. Some are content to stand confidently at Fortune's gates and wait for her to set to work. Others do better; they go ahead and profit by a wise audacity, for, on the wings of their virtue and their valour, they can overtake Fortune and flatter her to good effect. To philosophize truly, however, there are no means of winning success other than integrity and application; for there are no such things as good luck or bad luck, only prudence or imprudence.

22

The man with a well-stocked mind. The armoury of the discreet is polite, tasteful learning: a practical knowledge of all current affairs of an expert rather than a vulgar kind; the possession of a store of spicy witticisms and an abundance of gallant deeds upon which to know how to draw on the right occasion. For advice has often been better offered in jest than with most grave and magisterial solemnity. Colloquial wisdom has been of more use to some people than all the seven arts, be the latter ever so liberal.

23

No tener algún desdoro. El sino[1] de la perfección; pocos viven sin achaque, así en lo moral como en lo natural, y se apasionan por ellos, pudiendo curar con facilidad. Lastímase la ajena cordura de que tal vez a una sublime universalidad de prendas se le atreva un mínimo defecto, y basta una nube a eclipsar todo un sol. Son lunares de la reputación, donde pára luego y aun repara la malevolencia. Suma destreza sería convertirlos en realces. De esta suerte supo César laurear el natural desaire.

24

Templar la imaginación, unas veces corrigiéndola, otras ayudándola, que es el todo para la felicidad y aun ajusta la cordura. Da en tirana; ni se contenta con la especulación, sino que obra, y aun suele señorearse de la vida, haciéndola gustosa o pesada, según la necedad en que da; porque hace descontentos, o satisfechos de sí mismos. Representa a unos continuamente penas, hecha verdugo casero de necios; propone a otros felicidades y aventuras, con alegre desvanecimiento. Todo esto puede si no la enfrena la prudentísima sindéresis.

25

Buen entendedor. Arte era de artes saber discurrir; ya no basta: menester es adivinar, y más en desengaños. No puede ser entendido el que no fuere buen entendedor. Hay zahoríes del corazón y linces de las intenciones. Las verdades que más nos importan vienen siempre a medio decir; recíbanse del atento a todo entender; en lo favorable, tirante la rienda a la credulidad; en lo odioso, picarla.

[1] *Vide* Appendix, p. 305.

23

Have no blemish. There is no high quality without its 'yes' and 'no'; [1] few people are without some weaknesses, moral as well as physical, and they become obsessed by them, though they could easily be remedied. The virtue of others is offended if the slightest defect should happen to mar a host of high qualities, and one cloud is sufficient to eclipse a whole sun. Such failings are black spots on our good name and the malicious at once hit, and even dwell, upon them. It would be a master-stroke to turn such blemishes into adornments. In this way Caesar contrived to conceal his physical deficiency under his laurels.

24

Control your imagination. On some occasions curb it, on others give it free rein, for all our happiness depends upon it and it even puts common sense to rights. It can be a tyrant; and it is not content merely to speculate, but acts as well, and is even wont to control our lives, making them a pleasure or a burden to us according to its foolish whim; for imagination makes us either dissatisfied or contented with ourselves. To some it continually presents troubles, becoming the domestic executioner of fools; to others it holds out happiness and adventures, with cheerful irresponsibility. It is capable of all these things, if it is not controlled with the utmost discretion and sound judgment.

25

Be quick in the uptake. The ability to reason was once the art of all arts; it is no longer enough: you must be able to guess at things, and more especially in times of disillusionment. The man who is not quick to understand is unable to make himself understood. There are augurs of the heart and lynx-eyed fathomers of purposes. The truths which most concern us are always half-uttered; let the vigilant grasp their whole meaning; in auspicious matters, keep a tight rein upon your credulity; in those of ill omen, give it the spur.

[1] *Vide* Appendix, p. 305.

26

Hallarle su torcedor a cada uno. Es el arte de mover voluntades; más consiste en destreza que en resolución un saber por
dónde se le ha de entrar a cada uno: no hay voluntad sin
especial afición, y diferentes según la variedad de los gustos.
Todos son idólatras, unos de la estimación, otros del interés y los
más del deleite; la maña está en conocer estos ídolos para el
motivar, conociéndole a cada uno su eficaz impulso: es como
tener la llave del querer ajeno. Hase de ir al primer móvil, que
no siempre es el supremo; las más veces es el ínfimo, porque son
más en el mundo los desordenados que los subordinados.
Hásele de prevenir el genio primero, tocarle el verbo; después
cargarle con la afición, que infaliblemente dará mate[1] al albedrío.

27

Pagarse más de intensiones que de extensiones. No consiste la
perfección en la cantidad, sino en la calidad. Todo lo muy
bueno fué siempre poco y raro; es descrédito lo mucho. Aun
entre los hombres, los gigantes suelen ser los verdaderos enanos.
Estiman algunos los libros por la corpulencia, como si se es-
cribiesen para ejercitar antes los brazos que los ingenios. La
extensión sola nunca pudo exceder de medianía; y es plaga de
hombres universales, por querer estar en todo, estar en nada.
La intensión da eminencia, y heroica, si en materia sublime.

28

En nada vulgar. No en el gusto. ¡Oh, gran sabio el que se
descontentaba de que sus cosas agradasen a los muchos! Hartazgos de aplauso común no satisfacen a los discretos. Son
algunos tan camaleones de la popularidad que ponen su fruición,
no en las mareas suavísimas de Apolo, sino en el aliento vulgar.
Ni en el entendimiento, no se pague de los milagros del vulgo,

---

[1] 1653 has 'mate,' 1659 'mata.'

26

Find out everybody's weak spot. This is the art of setting wills in motion; to know how to get at every one is a matter of perspicacity rather than determination. There is no will without some special inclination, each differing from another according to the variety of tastes. All men are idolaters: some of reputation, others of self-interest, and the majority of pleasure; the skill consists in knowing how to make use of these idols as motives for action; to know each man's ruling passion is like having the key to the will of one's fellows. You must turn to the primary motive, which is not always the highest; in most cases, it is the lowest, for there are more licentious than self-disciplined people in the world. First you should ascertain a man's disposition, assaying his words; afterwards, get him carried away by his ruling passion, which will not fail to checkmate his free will.

27

Prize intensiveness more than extensiveness. Perfection does not reside in quantity, but rather, in quality. Everything superlatively good has always been quantitatively small, and scarce; abundance is discreditable. Even among men, giants are usually the real dwarfs. Some people judge books according to their bulk, as though they were written to exercise the arms rather than the wits. Mere extensiveness never rises above the mediocre; and it is the misfortune of men with wide general interests that, while they would like to have a finger in every pie, they have one in none. Intensiveness brings distinction, and heroic distinction, if the matter be a lofty one.

28

Be vulgar in nothing. [In the first place,] not in your taste. Ah, how profoundly wise the man who was unhappy because his achievements pleased the many! A glut of popular applause does not satisfy sensible men. Some are such chameleons of popularity that they delight, not in the gentle zephyrs of Apollo, but in the effluvia of the mob. [In the second place,] not in your understanding: take no delight in the marvels of the

que no pasan de espantaignorantes, admirando la necedad común, cuando desengañando la advertencia singular.

29

Hombre de entereza. Siempre de parte de la razón, con tal tesón de su propósito, que ni la pasión vulgar ni la violencia tirana le obliguen jamás a pisar la raya de la razón. Pero ¿quién será este fénix de la equidad? Que tiene pocos finos la entereza. Celebrándola muchos, mas no por su casa, síguenla otros hasta el peligro; en él, los falsos la niegan, los políticos la disimulan. No repara ella en encontrarse con la amistad, con el poder, y aun con la propia conveniencia, y aquí es el aprieto del desconocerla. Abstraen los astutos con metafísica plausible, por no agraviar, o la razón superior o la del estado: pero el constante varón juzga por especie de traición el disimulo; préciase más de la tenacidad que de la sagacidad: hállase donde la verdad se halla, y si deja los sujetos, no es por variedad suya, sino de ellos en dejarla primero.

30

No hacer profesión de empleos desautorizados: mucho menos de quimera, que sirve más de solicitar el desprecio que el crédito. Son muchas las sectas del capricho, y de todas ha de huir el varón cuerdo. Hay gustos exóticos que se casan siempre con todo aquello que los sabios repudian; viven muy pagados de toda singularidad: que aunque los hace muy conocidos, es más por motivos de la risa que de la reputación. Aun en profesión de sabio no se ha de señalar el atento: mucho menos en aquellas que hacen ridículos a sus afectantes: ni se especifican, porque las tiene individuadas el común descrédito.

31

Conocer los afortunados para la elección, y los desdichados para la fuga. La infelicidad es de ordinario crimen de necedad, y de

multitude, which are no more than baubles, for general folly admires where exceptional discernment is undeceived.

29

The upright man [is] always on the side of reason; with such tenacity of purpose that neither the passions of the mob nor the violence of the tyrant can force him to transgress its bounds. But who is this paragon of equity? For integrity has few intimates. While many praise her, they do not, however, admit her to their homes; others follow her even into danger; there, the false deny her and politicians affect not to know her. For she does not care whether she is at loggerheads with friendship, power, even self-interest, and here comes the rub of disowning her. The astute then indulge in plausible metaphysical abstractions, so as not to give offence to their superiors, or out of regard for public opinion. The honest man, however, regards dissimulation as a kind of treason; he sets more store by tenacity than shrewdness; he is to be found where truth is to be found and if he should desert people, it is not out of fickleness on his part but rather upon theirs, for having first abandoned truth.

30

Do not engage in unworthy occupations: still less in eccentric ones, for this serves to bring you into contempt rather than into good repute. There are many fancy sects and the wise man should avoid them all. There are exotic tastes which are always wedded to everything wise men repudiate; those who possess them delight in every kind of eccentricity; and, although this makes them notorious, it is rather as figures of fun than as men of good repute. A cautious man should not attract attention to himself even in a learned profession: still less in those which make such as engage in them ridiculous. And these are not specified because they have been singled out for general contempt.

31

Recognize the fortunate so that you may choose their company and the unfortunate so that you may avoid them. Misfortune is

participantes no hay contagión tan apegadiza: nunca se le ha de abrir la puerta al menor mal, que siempre vendrán tras él otros muchos, y mayores en celada. La mejor treta del juego es saberse descartar: más importa la menor carta del triunfo que corre, que la mayor del que pasó. En duda, acierto es llegarse a los sabios y prudentes, que tarde o temprano topan con la ventura.

32

Estar en opinión de dar gusto. Para los que gobiernan, gran crédito de agradar: realce de soberanos para conquistar la gracia universal. Esta sola es la ventaja del mandar: poder hacer más bien que todos; aquéllos son amigos que hacen amistades. Al contrario, están otros prestos en no dar gusto, no tanto por lo cargoso, cuanto por lo maligno, opuestos en todo a la divina comunicabilidad.

33

Saber abstraer: que si es gran lición del vivir el saber negar, mayor será saberse negar a sí mismo, a los negocios, a los personajes. Hay ocupaciones extrañas, polillas de precioso tiempo, y peor es ocuparse en lo impertinente que hacer nada: no basta para atento no ser entremetido, más es menester procurar que no le entremetan. No ha de ser tan de todos, que no sea de sí mismo; aun de los amigos no se ha de abusar, ni quiere más de ellos de lo que le concedieren. Todo lo demasiado es vicioso, y mucho más en el trato; con esta cuerda templanza se conserva mejor el agrado con todos y la estimación, porque no se roza la preciosísima decencia. Tenga, pues, libertad de genio, apasionado de lo selecto y nunca peque contra la fe de su buen gusto.

usually the crime of folly, and among those who suffer from it there is no malady more contagious: never open your door to the least of misfortunes, for, [if you do,] many others will follow in its train and greater ones will lie in ambush for you. In playing cards, the best device is to know how to discard: the lowest trump in the current round is worth the highest in the one already played. When in doubt, it is a good idea to stick to the company of the wise and the discreet who, late or soon, strike lucky.

32

Cultivate a reputation for being pleasant. It is a great credit to rulers if they give pleasure: a high quality in monarchs which enables them to win general goodwill. The only advantage of being a ruler is that you are able to do more good than every one else. Those who behave in a friendly way make friends. On the contrary, there are other people, averse in everything from divine sociability, who are quick to refrain from pleasing, not so much on account of the trouble involved as out of ill will.

33

Know how to keep yourself to yourself. For if one of life's major lessons teaches us how to refuse, a yet greater lesson teaches us how to control ourselves, our affairs, and [other] people. There are extraneous occupations which waste precious time, and it is worse to occupy yourself with things that do not concern you than to do nothing at all: for a careful man, it is not enough to refrain from being a busybody; it is more necessary for him to see that others do not pry into his affairs. You should not be so continually upon the doorstep of others that you have no time to be upon your own; you should not presume too much even upon your friends, nor demand more from them than they may [be prepared to] concede. All extremes are bad, and more especially so in personal dealings; by dint of a wise moderation the goodwill and esteem of every one is the better conserved, for thereby the most precious boon of propriety is not offended. Maintain, then, freedom of spirit, be zealous in the pursuit of what is choice, and never sin against the verdict of your good taste.

34

Conocer su realce rey. La prenda relevante, cultivando aquélla y ayudando a las demás. Cualquiera hubiera conseguido la eminencia en algo, si hubiera conocido su ventaja. Observe el atributo rey, y cargue la aplicación: en unos excede el juicio, en otros el valor. Violentan los más su minerva; y así, en nada consiguen superioridad: lo que lisonjea presto la pasión, desengaña tarde el tiempo.

35

Hacer concepto, y más de lo que importa más. No pensando, se pierden todos los necios: nunca conciben en las cosas la mitad, y como no perciben el daño o la conveniencia, tampoco aplican la diligencia. Hacen algunos mucho caso de lo que importa poco, y poco de lo que mucho, ponderando siempre al revés. Muchos, por faltos de sentido, no lo pierden. Cosas hay que se debrían observar con todo el conato, y conservar en la profundidad de la mente. Hace concepto el sabio de todo, aunque con distinción cava donde hay fondo y reparo; y piensa tal vez que hay más de lo que piensa; de suerte que llega la reflexión adonde llega la aprensión.

36

Tener tanteada su fortuna para el proceder, para el empeñarse. Importa más que la observación del temperamento; que si es necio el que a cuarenta años llama a Hipócrates para la salud, más el que a Séneca para la cordura. Gran arte saberla regir, ya esperándola, que también cabe la espera en ella, ya lográndola; que tiene vez y contingente, si bien no se la puede coger al tenor, tan anómalo es su proceder. El que la observó favorable, prosiga con despejo, que suele apasionarse por los osados, y aun

34

Know your strong point, your chief natural endowment; cultivate it and foster the others. Every one would have attained distinction in something if he had known his strong point. Take note of the quality in which you excel and apply yourself to cultivating it: some excel in judgment, others in courage. The majority do violence to their gifts and thus attain distinction in nothing: time disillusions us too late with that which is quick to flatter our passions.

35

Think things over, and more especially those which matter most. All fools come to grief through want of thought: they never see [even] the half of a matter, and just as they fail to perceive the loss or gain involved to themselves, neither do they apply themselves diligently [to their affairs]. Some make a lot of what matters little, and little of what matters a lot, always thinking things out in a topsy-turvy way. Many of them do not lose their senses because they have none to lose. There are things which ought to be observed with the closest attention and preserved in the innermost depths of the mind. The wise man thinks everything over but, unlike the fool, digs deeper and more carefully where there is ground for observation: and he considers that there may, perhaps, be more [at stake] than he imagines; so that reflection reaches the same goal as apprehension.

36

Weigh up your luck so that you may decide what action you should take and into what engagements you should enter. This is more important than studying your temperament; for if he is a fool who at forty applies to Hippocrates for health, he is a greater one who, at that age, goes to Seneca for wisdom. To know how to control your luck is a fine art, both while you are waiting for it, for waiting also plays its part, and also when it has come to you; it has its times and seasons; although its behaviour is so haphazard that you cannot tell what path it will follow. He who finds Fortune on his side should go briskly ahead, for she

como bizarra, por los jóvenes. No obre el que es infeliz,
retírese: ni le dé lugar de dos infelicidades. Adelante el que le
predomina.

37

Conocer: y saber usar de las varillas. Es el punto más sutil del
humano trato. Arrójanse para tentativa de los ánimos, y hácese
con ellas la más disimulada y penetrante tienta del corazón.
Otras hay maliciosas, arrojadizas, tocadas de la hierba de la
invidia, untadas del veneno de la pasión; rayos imperceptibles
para derribar de la gracia y de la estimación. Cayeron muchos
de la privanza superior y inferior, heridos de un leve dicho de
éstos, a quienes toda una conjuración de murmuración vulgar y
malevolencia singular no fueron bastantes a causar la más leve
trepidación. Obran otras, al contrario, por favorables, apo-
yando y confirmando en la reputación. Pero con la misma
destreza con que las arroja la intención las ha de recibir la cautela,
y esperarlas la atención: porque está librada la defensa en el conocer, y queda siempre frustrado el tiro prevenido.

38

Saberse dejar ganando con la fortuna: es de tahures de reputación. Tanto importa una bella retirada como una bizarra
acometida; un poner en cobro las hazañas, cuando fueren
bastantes, cuando muchas. Continuada felicidad fué siempre
sospechosa; más segura es la interpolada, y que tenga algo de
agridulce, aun para la fruición: cuanto más atropellándose las
dichas, corren mayor riesgo de deslizar, y dar al traste con todo.
Recompénsase, tal vez, la brevedad de la duración con la intensión
del favor. Cánsase la fortuna de llevar a uno a cuestas tan a la
larga.

is wont to favour the bold and even, gay lady that she is, the young. One who has had a stroke of bad luck should take no action and hold his hand: he should not open the door for a second stroke. If your star is in the ascendant, go ahead.

37

Know how to take and give hints. This is the most delicate aspect of human intercourse. Hints are thrown out in order to probe the mind and by their means the inmost recesses of the heart are sought out in the most secret way. There are others which are malicious, easily thrown out, verbal darts tipped with the poison of envy, anointed with the venom of passion; unseen thunderbolts destined to destroy favour and repute. Many men have forfeited the confidence of their superiors and subordinates because they have been injured by a passing remark of this kind, when a whole conspiracy of public slander and private malice would not have been enough to cause them the slightest perturbation. Other hints, on the contrary, work in your favour, upholding your reputation and making it secure. But caution must receive them with a skill equal to that with which malice delivers them and vigilance must foresee them, for defence depends upon knowledge and a shot which is anticipated is always futile.

38

To know how to abandon the game when their luck is in is characteristic of famous gamblers. A good retreat is as important as a spirited attack; it safeguards your achievements when they are adequate as well as when they are numerous. Continuous good luck is always open to suspicion; intermittent good fortune is safer, and let there be an element of the bittersweet about it even while you are enjoying it. The more your strokes of good luck crowd upon one another, the greater the risk you run of their slipping and bringing down the entire heap. The transience of a favour may sometimes be counterbalanced by its lavishness. Fortune soon tires of carrying one too long upon her shoulders.

39

Conocer las cosas en su punto, en su sazón, y saberlas lograr.
Las obras de la naturaleza todas llegan al complemento de su
perfección; hasta allí fueron ganando, desde allí perdiendo.
Las del arte, raras son las que llegan al no poderse mejorar.　Es
eminencia de un buen gusto gozar de cada cosa en su complemento: no todos pueden, ni los que pueden saben.　Hasta en
los frutos del entendimiento hay ese punto de madurez; importa
conocerla para la estimación y el ejercicio.

40

Gracia de las gentes.　Mucho es conseguir la admiración
común; pero más la afición; algo tiene de estrella, lo más de
industria; comienza por aquélla y prosigue por ésta.　No basta la
eminencia de prendas, aunque se supone que es fácil de ganar el
afecto, ganado el concepto.　Requiérese, pues, para la benevolencia, la beneficencia: hacer bien a todas manos; buenas palabras
y mejores obras, amar para ser amado.　La cortesía es el mayor
hechizo político de grandes personajes.　Hase de alargar la mano
primero a las hazañas y después a las plumas; de la hoja a las
hojas, que hay gracia de escritores, y es eterna.

41

Nunca exagerar.　Gran asunto de la atención no hablar por
superlativos, ya por no exponerse a ofender la verdad, ya por no
desdorar su cordura.　Son las exageraciones prodigalidades de la
estimación, y dan indicio de la cortedad del conocimiento y del
gusto.　Despierta vivamente a la curiosidad la alabanza, pica el
deseo, y después, si no corresponde el valor al precio, como de
ordinario acontece, revuelve la expectación contra el engaño y
despícase en el menosprecio de lo celebrado y del que celebró.
Anda, pues, el cuerdo muy detenido, y quiere más pecar de corto

39

Recognize the times and seasons in affairs and learn how to take advantage of them. The works of nature all attain to the full measure of their perfection; till then they have been on the up grade; from that point, they decline. Few works of art reach a stage beyond which they cannot be improved. It is a high privilege of good taste to enjoy everything in its perfect state: not every one is capable of doing this, and not all those who have the ability know how to do so. Even in the case of the fruits of the mind, there is that ripening point; it is important to recognize it so that you may set a right value upon it and make good use of it.

40

Popular favour. It is a great thing to win general admiration, but a greater one to win general regard; success in this depends, up to a point, upon luck, most of all upon diligence; luck provides an initial impulse and diligence develops it. Outstanding gifts are not enough, although one assumes that it is easy to win affection if one first wins esteem. For benevolence, then, beneficence is needed: do good abundantly; let your words be gracious and your actions even more so; love in order to be loved. Courtesy on the part of the great is the noblest of politic charms. You should first hold out your hand to great achievements and, afterwards, to the pen; turn from the blade to the book, for authors, too, grant favours, and they are undying.

41

Never exaggerate. Great care should be taken to avoid talking in superlatives, so as not to render yourself liable either to injure truth or damage your own [reputation for] wisdom. Exaggerations are excesses of the judgment and indicate limited knowledge and taste. Praise arouses lively curiosity, stimulates expectation and, if later, as usually happens, the value does not correspond with the price, anticipation turns upon deceit and avenges itself by despising both the praised and the praiser. So the wise man goes to work very cautiously and prefers to err by understatement rather than by overstatement. Great gifts are

que de largo. Son raras las eminencias: témplese la estimación. El encarecer es ramo de mentir, y piérdese en ello el crédito de buen gusto, que es grande, y el de entendido, que es mayor.

42

Del natural imperio. Es una secreta fuerza de superioridad. No ha de proceder del artificio enfadoso, sino de un imperioso natural. Sujétansele todos sin advertir el cómo, reconociendo el secreto vigor de la connatural autoridad. Son estos genios señoriles, reyes por mérito y leones por privilegio innato, que cogen el corazón y aun el discurso a los demás, en fe de su respeto; si las otras prendas favorecen, nacieron para primeros mobles políticos, porque ejecutan más con su amago, que otros con una prolijidad.

43

Sentir con los menos y hablar con los más. Querer ir contra el corriente es tan imposible al desengaño cuanto fácil al peligro. Sólo un Sócrates podría emprenderlo. Tiénese por agravio el disentir, porque es condenar el juicio ajeno; multiplícanse los disgustados, ya por el sujeto censurado, ya del que lo aplaudía: la verdad es de pocos, el engaño es tan común como vulgar. Ni por el hablar en la plaza se ha de sacar el sabio, pues no habla allí con su voz, sino con la de necedad común, por más que la esté desmintiendo su interior: tanto huye de ser contradicho el cuerdo, como de contradecir: lo que es pronto a la censura, es detenido a la publicidad de ella. El sentir es libre; no se puede ni debe violentar; retírase al sagrado de su silencio, y si tal vez se permite, es a sombra de pocos y cuerdos.

44

Simpatía con los grandes varones. Prenda es de héroe el combinar con héroes; prodigio de la naturaleza por lo oculto y

rare; so be moderate in your esteem. Exaggeration is an off-shoot of lying, and by it you sacrifice your reputation for good taste, which is a serious matter, and for good sense, which is more serious still.

42

Of natural leadership. This is a secret virtue of superiority. It should not proceed from vexatious artifice but from an inborn capacity to rule. All submit to it without knowing why, recognizing the secret power of innate authority. Natural leaders are masterful characters, kings by [personal] merit and lions by innate privilege, who capture the hearts and even the minds of others by virtue of the respect which they inspire; if their other qualities are favourable, such men are born to be the prime movers in affairs of state, for they achieve more by a hint than others are able to do by a lengthy harangue.

43

Think with the few and speak with the many. It is as impossible to root out error as it is easy to run into danger by trying to swim against the stream. Only a Socrates could attempt to do that. Disagreement is regarded as offensive because it is a condemnation of the views of others; the numbers of the disgruntled grow, either on account of some matter which has been the object of censure or of some person who has praised it: truth is for the few, error is as usual as it is vulgar. Nor is the wise man to be recognized by what he says in the market-place, for he speaks there not with his own voice, but with that of universal folly, however much his inmost thoughts may gainsay it: the wise man avoids being contradicted as sedulously as he avoids contradicting: the publicity of censure is withheld from that which readily provokes it. Thought is free; it cannot and should not be coerced; retire into the sanctuary of your silence and if you sometimes allow yourself to break it, do so under the aegis of a discreet few.

44

Fellow-feeling among the great. It is the mark of great men that they seek one another's company; it is a miracle of nature

por lo ventajoso. Hay parentesco de corazones y de genios, y son sus efectos los que la ignorancia vulgar achaca [a] bebedizos. No pára en sola estimación, que adelanta benevolencia y aun llega a propensión; persuade sin palabras, y consigue sin méritos. Hayla activa y la hay pasiva; una y otra felices, cuanto más sublimes. Gran destreza el conocerlas, distinguirlas y saberlas lograr, que no hay porfía que baste sin este favor secreto.

45

Usar, no abusar, de las reflexas. No se han de afectar, menos dar a entender; toda arte se ha de encubrir, que es sospechosa, y más la de cautela, que es odiosa. Úsase mucho el engaño: multiplíquese el recelo, sin darse a conocer, que ocasionaría la desconfianza; mucho desobliga y provoca a la venganza; despierta el mal que no se imaginó. La reflexión en el proceder, es gran ventaja en el obrar; no hay mayor argumento del discurso. La mayor perfección de las acciones está afianzada del señorío con que se ejecutan.

46

Corregir su antipatía. Solemos aborrecer de grado, y aun antes de las previstas prendas; y tal vez se atreve esta innata vulgarizante aversión a los varones eminentes. Corríjala la cordura, que no hay peor descrédito que aborrecer a los mejores; lo que es de ventaja la simpatía con héroes, es de desdoro la antipatía.

47

Huir los empeños. Es de los primeros asuntos de la prudencia. En las grandes capacidades siempre hay grandes distancias, hasta los últimos trances. Hay mucho que andar de un extremo a otro, y ellos siempre se están en el medio de su

by reason of its occult quality, and the advantages which it bestows. There is an affinity of hearts and minds and its effects are imputed by the ignorant to magic potions. This sympathy does not stop at [mutual] esteem, merely, but promotes goodwill and even affection; it persuades without words and obtains its ends without deserts. There is active sympathy and there is passive sympathy; and, the more sublime these are, the greater the happiness they bring. It is a fine art to recognize, distinguish, and know how to win these types of sympathy; for no amount of striving will suffice if this secret gift be lacking.

45

Use, but do not abuse, caution. You should not delight in it, much less brag about it; all artifice should be concealed for it is open to suspicion, and more especially that of cunning, which is odious. Deception is frequently employed: so misgiving should be intensified without its becoming obvious, for, [if obvious,] it would excite distrust; it is very irritating, incites to revenge and stirs up unimaginable mischief. Caution in our behaviour is of great advantage in execution; there is no more striking evidence of wisdom. The highest quality of deeds is confirmed by the mastery with which they are performed.

46

Overcome your antipathies. We usually enjoy hating, and [this] even before we have any experience of the qualities we presume to be detestable; and great men may sometimes become the object of this antipathy, innate in the vulgar. Good sense should overcome this feeling, for there is nothing more descreditable than to hate the best; just as sympathy with the great is a mark of superiority in a man, so antipathy towards them redounds to his discredit.

47

Avoid incurring obligations. This is one of the first concerns of prudence. In men of great abilities extremes are always poles apart. There is a long way to go between one extreme and another, and such men always take their stand midway: they are

cordura: llegan tarde al cumplimiento; que es más fácil hurtarle el cuerpo a la ocasión que salir bien de ella.   Son tentaciones del juicio; más segura el huirlas que el vencerlas.   Trae un empeño otro mayor, y está muy al canto del despeño.   Hay hombres ocasionados por genio, y aun por nación, fáciles de meterse en obligaciones; pero el que camina a la luz de la razón, siempre va muy sobre el caso.   Estima por más valor el no empeñarse que el vencer, y ya que haya[1] un necio ocasionado, excusa que con él no sean dos.

48

Hombre con fondos, tanto tiene de persona.   Siempre ha de ser otro tanto más lo interior que lo exterior en todo.   Hay sujetos de sola fachada, como casas por acabar, porque faltó el caudal; tienen la entrada de palacio y de choza la habitación.   No hay en éstos dónde parar, o todo pára[2] porque acabada la primera salutación, acabó la conversación.   Entran por las primeras cortesías como caballos sicilianos, y luego paran en silenciarios, que se agotan las palabras donde no hay perennidad de concepto. Engañan éstos fácilmente a otros que tienen también la vista superficial, pero no a la astucia, que, como mira por dentro, los halla vaciados, para ser fábula de los discretos.

49

Hombre juicioso y notante.   Señoréase él de los objetos, no los objetos de él.   Sonda luego el fondo de la mayor profundidad; sabe hacer anatomía de un caudal con perfección.   En viendo un personaje, le comprende y lo censura por esencia.   De raras observaciones, gran descifrador de la más recatada interioridad. Nota acre, concibe sutil, infiere juicioso: todo lo descubre, advierte, alcanza y comprende.

---

[1] Reyes has 'no hay.'   [2] *Vide* Appendix, p. 305.

slow to act, for it is easier to avoid occasions for committing yourself than to come well out of a commitment. Such occasions test your judgment; it is safer to avoid them than emerge victorious from them. One obligation leads to a greater one, and you come very near to the brink of disaster. There are meddlesome people so constituted by temperament, and even by nationality, that they readily allow themselves to be compromised; but he who walks by the light of reason always proceeds with great circumspection. Regard it as more courageous not to become involved in an engagement than to win the battle, and where there is already one interfering fool, take care that there shall not be two.

48

A man is a personality according to the measure of his capacities. The interior should always and in every respect be a little bit more impressive than the exterior. There are people who are nothing but façade, like houses which remain unfinished because funds have run out; they have the entrance hall of a palace and the living-rooms of a cottage. You cannot stop in these places or, rather, everything stops in them, because conversation comes to an end with the first exchange of greetings. These men prance through the opening compliments like Sicilian steeds, and finish up as silent ones, for words are lacking where there is no continuity of thought. Such people easily deceive others who also take a superficial view of things, but not the astute, who, because they look beneath the surface, discover these folk to be empty-headed, doomed to be a byword among the discreet.

49

The judicious and observant man. He masters things, not they him. He at once plumbs the profoundest depth; he knows perfectly well how to anatomize a man's capacities. He understands and sums up a person's essential nature as soon as he sees him. Through his rare powers of observation, he is a great unraveller of the innermost secrets of the heart. He observes keenly, understands subtly, and infers wisely: he discovers, notices, grasps, and understands everything.

50

Nunca perderse el respeto a sí mismo, ni se roce consigo a solas.[1] Sea su misma entereza norma propia de su rectitud, y deba más a la severidad de su dictamen que a todos los extrínsecos preceptos. Deje de hacer lo indecente, más por el temor de su cordura que por el rigor de la ajena autoridad. Llegue a temerse, y no necesitará del ayo imaginario de Séneca.

51

Hombre de buena elección. Lo más se vive de ella: supone el buen gusto y el rectísimo dictamen; que no bastan el estudio ni el ingenio. No hay perfección donde no hay delecto; dos ventajas incluye, poder escoger, y lo mejor. Muchos, de ingenio fecundo y sutil, de juicio acre, estudiosos y noticiosos también, en llegando al elegir se pierden; cásanse siempre con lo peor, que parece que afectan el errar, y así, éste es uno de los dotes máximos de arriba.

52

Nunca descomponerse. Gran asunto de la cordura nunca desbaratarse. Mucho hombre arguye de corazón coronado, porque toda magnanimidad es dificultosa de conmoverse. Son las pasiones los humores del ánimo, y cualquier exceso en ellas causa indisposición de cordura; y si el mal saliere a la boca, peligrará la reputación. Sea, pues, tan señor de sí y tan grande, que ni en lo más próspero ni en lo más adverso pueda alguno censurarle perturbado, sí admirarle superior.

53

Diligente e inteligente. La diligencia ejecuta presto lo que la inteligencia prolijamente piensa. Es pasión de necios la prisa,

[1] *Vide* Notes, and Appendix, p. 305.

50

Never lose your self-respect, nor be too familiar with yourself when you are alone. Let your integrity itself be your own standard of rectitude, and be more indebted to the severity of your own judgment of yourself than to all external precepts. Desist from unseemly conduct, rather out of respect for your own virtue than for the strictures of external authority. Come to hold yourself in awe, and you will have no need of Seneca's imaginary tutor.

51

The man who knows how to make the right choice. Most things in life depend upon right choice: it implies good taste and the most accurate judgment, for study and intelligence are not enough. There is no perfection where there is no discrimination; the latter includes two qualities, the ability to choose and the ability to choose the best. Many men of fertile and subtle wit, of keen judgment, studious and observant too, are lost when they come to the point of choosing; they invariably become wedded to the worst and it would seem that they enjoy going astray. Thus the ability to choose aright is one of the greatest gifts from on high.

52

Never be put out. Sensible people make a special point of never being put out. It is the mark of a true man and of great nobility of soul, for it is always difficult to upset the magnanimous. The passions are the humours of the soul and any excess on their part entails a disordered judgment: and if the malady should escape through the lips, your reputation will be in peril. Have, therefore, so much and such great control over yourself that in neither the most favourable nor in the most adverse circumstances can any one judge you to be put out. Rather, indeed, be admired as rising above circumstances.

53

Diligence and intelligence. Diligence performs speedily what intelligence slowly excogitates. Haste is the besetting sin of

D

que como no descubren el tope, obran sin reparo. Al contrario, los sabios suelen pecar de detenidos, que del advertir nace el reparar. Malogra tal vez la ineficacia de la remisión lo acertado del dictamen. La presteza es madre de la dicha. Obró mucho el que nada dejó para mañana. Augusta empresa correr a espacio.

54

Tener bríos a lo cuerdo. Al león muerto, hasta las liebres le repelan: no hay burlas con el valor; si cede al primero, también habrá de ceder al segundo, y de este modo hasta el último. La misma dificultad habrá de vencer tarde, que valiera más desde luego. El brío del ánimo excede al del cuerpo: es como la espada; ha de ir siempre envainado en su cordura, para la ocasión. Es el resguardo de la persona: más daña el decaimiento del ánimo que el del cuerpo. Tuvieron muchos prendas eminentes, que por faltarles este aliento del corazón parecieron muertos y acabaron sepultados en su dejamiento, que no sin providencia juntó la naturaleza acudida la dulzura de la miel con lo picante del aguijón en la abeja. Nervios y huesos hay en el cuerpo; no sea el ánimo todo blandura.

55

Hombre de espera, arguye gran corazón con ensanches de sufrimiento: nunca apresurarse ni apasionarse. Sea uno primero señor de sí, y lo será después de los otros. Hase de caminar por los espacios del tiempo al centro de la ocasión. La detención prudente sazona los aciertos y madura los secretos. La muleta del tiempo es más obradora que la acerada clava de Hércules. El mismo Dios no castiga con bastón, sino con sazón.[1] Gran decir: 'el tiempo y yo a otros dos.' La misma fortuna premia el esperar con la grandeza del galardón.

[1] Reyes has 'razón.'

fools who, failing to see the snag, set to work heedlessly. Wise men, on the other hand, usually err on the side of dilatoriness, for heed gives birth to deliberation. The ineffectiveness of procrastination may sometimes nullify sound judgment. Promptitude is the mother of good luck. He who has put off nothing till to-morrow has done a great deal. 'Make haste slowly' is a noble motto.

54

Be bold, but discreetly so. Even hares nibble at the mane of a dead lion: there is no playing about with courage; if you give way to the first comer you will have to yield to the second also, and so on, until the last. You will, in the end, have to overcome the selfsame difficulty which it would have been better to solve at the outset. The courage of the spirit is greater than that of the body: it is like the sword; it must always remain in the sheath of its wisdom ready for use when occasion arises. It is the shield of the personality: poor-spiritedness does more harm than physical weakness. Many people have possessed outstanding qualities but have seemed to be dead because they lacked a stout heart, and they have ended by being buried in the grave of their own pusillanimity. For it was not without foresight that our watchful mother Nature combined the sweetness of the bee's honey with the sharpness of its sting. There are muscles and bones in the body; the spirit should not be entirely soft.

55

The man who knows how to wait. To know how to wait is the sign of a great heart endowed with an all-embracing patience: never be in a hurry, nor lose your temper. First master yourself and, later, you will master others. You must traverse the domains of time in order to reach the goal of opportunity. A prudent dilatoriness ripens one's aims and brings secret schemes to maturity. The crutch of time does more than the nail-studded club of Hercules. God Himself punishes opportunely, not with the rod. 'Time and I against any two others,' is a fine saying. Fortune herself rewards those who wait with a magnificent prize.

56

Tener buenos repentes. Nacen de una prontitud feliz: no hay aprietos ni acasos para ella en fe de su vivacidad y despejo. Piensan mucho algunos para errarlo todo después, y otros lo aciertan todo sin pensarlo antes. Hay caudales de 'antiperístasi' que empeñados obran mejor; suelen ser monstruos que de pronto todo lo aciertan y todo lo yerran de pensado; lo que no se les ofrece luego, nunca, ni hay que apelar a después. Son plausibles los prestos, porque arguyen prodigiosa capacidad: en los conceptos, sutileza; en las obras, cordura.

57

Más seguros son los pensados, harto presto, si bien; lo que luego se hace, luego se deshace; mas lo que ha de durar una eternidad ha de tardar otra en hacerse. No se atiende sino a la perfección, y sólo el acierto permanece. Entendimiento con fondos logra eternidades: lo que mucho vale, mucho cuesta, que aun el más precioso de los metales es el más tardo y más grave.

58

Saberse atemperar. No se ha de mostrar igualmente entendido con todos; ni se han de emplear más fuerzas de las que son menester. No haya desperdicios ni de saber, ni de valer. No echa a la presa el buen cetrero más rapiña de la que ha menester para darle caza. No esté siempre de ostentación, que al otro día no admirará. Siempre ha de haber novedad con que lucir: que quien cada día descubre más, mantiene siempre la expectación y nunca llegan a descubrirle los términos de su gran caudal.

56

Cultivate a happy spontaneity.   It is the offspring of a ready wit: on account of its vivacity and charm, it knows no constraints and no mischances.   Many think deeply only to miss the mark completely later on, and others are completely successful without forethought.   There are paradoxical natures which function best under pressure; these are usually prodigies who, from the outset, succeed in everything they do without premeditation, and fail in everything they think out beforehand; what does not occur to them at once never occurs to them at all, nor, for them, is there any subsequent court of appeal.   The quick-witted win praise because their qualities imply outstanding ability; subtlety of judgment; wisdom in execution.

57

The safest men are those who think things out beforehand; quickly enough done, if well done.   What is soon done is soon undone; but that which is to last for an eternity will take another eternity to produce it.   Perfection is the only thing that counts and successful achievement alone endures.   A well-stocked mind attains immortality; what is worth much costs much, for even among metals the most precious is the densest and the heaviest.

58

Adapt yourself to your company.[1]   You should not display the same degree of intelligence to every one; nor should you use more effort than is necessary.   There should be no waste of either knowledge or worth.   The good falconer does not release more birds than are needed for the chase.   Do not always be showing off for, if you do, there will be nothing to excite admiration later on.   There must always be some new quality yet to be displayed: for the man who reveals something more each day always keeps hope alive and people never contrive to gauge the limits of his great capacity.

[1] (J).

59

Hombre de buen dejo. En casa de la fortuna, si se entra por la puerta del placer, se sale por la del pesar, y al contrario. Atención, pues, al acabar, poniendo más cuidado en la felicidad de la salida que en el aplauso de la entrada. Desaire común es de afortunados[1] tener muy favorables los principios y muy trágicos los fines. No está el punto en el vulgar aplauso de una entrada, que ésas todos las tienen plausibles, pero sí en el general sentimiento de una salida, que son raros los deseados; pocas veces acompaña la dicha a los que salen; la que se muestra de cumplida con los que vienen, de descortés con los que van.

60

Buenos dictámenes. Nácense algunos prudentes: entran con esta ventaja de la sindéresis connatural en la sabiduría, y así tiene la mitad andada para los aciertos. Con la edad y la experiencia viene a sazonarse del todo la razón, y llegan a un juicio muy templado; abominan de todo capricho, como de tentación de la cordura, y más en materias de estado, donde por la suma importancia se requiere la total seguridad. Merecen éstos la asistencia al gobernalle, o para ejercicio o para consejo.

61

Eminencia en lo mejor. Una gran singularidad entre la pluralidad de perfecciones. No puede haber héroe que no tenga algún extremo sublime. Las medianías no son asunto del aplauso. La eminencia en relevante empleo saca de un ordinario vulgar y levanta a categoría de raro. Ser eminente en profesión humilde, es ser algo en lo poco; lo que tiene más de lo deleitable, tiene menos de lo glorioso. El exceso en aventajadas materias es como un carácter de soberanía, solicita la admiración y concilia el afecto.

[1] *Vide* Appendix, p. 306.

59

A happy leave-taking. If you enter Fortune's house by the gate of pleasure, you leave it by the door of sorrow, and vice versa. Pay attention, therefore, to the final result, taking more care to have a happy exit than to receive applause upon entering. It is the general misfortune of the lucky to win great favour at the start and to come to an exceedingly tragic end. The applause of the mob when you come on the scene is not the point, for everybody's entrance is applauded, but what really matters is the general feeling on your exit, for few people are wanted; Fortune rarely shows any one to the door; her civility towards those arriving is matched by her rudeness towards those who are leaving.

60

Sound judgment. Some people are born prudent; they come into the world with that gift of good judgment which is innate in the wise, and so they are already half way along the road to success. With age and experience their reason comes to full maturity, and they come to acquire an exceedingly well-balanced judgment; they detest all caprice as a snare set for wisdom, especially with regard to affairs of state, in which, because of their high importance, complete reliability is essential. Such men deserve to be at the helm of government, either in an executive or in an advisory capacity.

61

Excellence in what is best. This is a great rarity among the multitude of high qualities. There can be no great man who does not possess some high, outstanding talent. Second-raters never provide a theme for eulogy. Eminence in an important position distinguishes you from the common herd and raises you to the ranks of the exceptional. To be eminent in a humble profession is to be a big frog in a little pond: the more delectable the job, the less glorious it is. Exceptional achievement in affairs of consequence is, as it were, a hall-mark of sovereignty; it courts admiration and wins goodwill.

62

Obrar con buenos instrumentos. Quieren algunos que campee el extremo de su sutileza en la ruindad de los instrumentos: peligrosa satisfacción, merecedora de un fatal castigo. Nunca la bondad del ministro disminuyó[1] la grandeza del patrón; antes toda la gloria de los aciertos recae después sobre la causa principal, así como, al contrario, el vituperio. La fama siempre va con los primeros. Nunca dice: aquél tuvo buenos o malos ministros, sino aquél fué buen o mal artífice. Haya, pues, elección; haya examen, que se les ha de fiar una inmortalidad de reputación.

63

Excelencia de primero y, si con eminencia, doblada. Gran ventaja jugar de mano, que gana en igualdad. Hubieran muchos sido fénix en los empleos a no irles otros delante. Álzanse los primeros con el mayorazgo de la fama, y quedan para los segundos pleiteados alimentos; por más que suden, no pueden purgar el vulgar achaque de imitación. Sutileza fué de prodigiosos inventar rumbo nuevo para las eminencias, con tal que asegure primero la cordura los empeños. Con la novedad de los asuntos se hicieron lugar los sabios en la matrícula de los heroicos. Quieren algunos más ser primeros en segunda categoría, que ser segundos en la primera.

64

Saberse excusar pesares. Es cordura provechosa ahorrar de disgustos. La prudencia evita muchos: es Lucina de la felicidad, y por eso, del contento. Las odiosas nuevas, no darlas, menos recebirlas: hánseles de vedar las entradas, si no es la del remedio. A unos se les gastan los oídos de oir mucho dulce en lisonjas; a otros de escuchar amargo en chismes; y hay quien no sabe vivir

---

[1] 1659 has 'desminuyó.'

62

Work with good tools. Some like the most striking evidence of their skill to reside in the wretchedness of the tools [which they employ]: a dangerous [source of] satisfaction, worthy of condign punishment. The excellence of an agent never diminishes the greatness of his principal; rather does all the glory of success afterwards revert to the first cause, just as, on the contrary, does blame in the case of failure. Fame always accrues to superiors. She never says: 'He had good or bad tools' but: 'He was a good or a bad workman.' So select your tools; try them out, for you will have to rely upon them to provide you with undying fame.

63

It is a good thing to be first in the field and, if [you acquit yourself] with distinction, doubly good. In a game where the players are equally matched it is a great advantage to have the first move. Many men would have been paragons in their jobs if others had not preceded them. Those who are first in the field get away with the entailed estate of Fame, and disputed portions go to second comers; however hard the latter may work, they are unable to clear themselves of the vulgar charge of plagiarism. It is the subtle skill of genius to open up new roads to distinction, provided that its undertakings are first backed by wisdom. Wise men have won a place for themselves on the roll of heroes owing to the novelty of their achievements. Some people would rather be first in the second rank than second in the first.

64

Learn how to avoid troubles. To save oneself vexations is a profitable kind of wisdom. Prudence avoids many of them: she is the midwife of good fortune, and, consequently, of happiness. Do not be the purveyor of bad news, much less listen to it: all entries should be barred to it, except that which opens the way to a remedy. Some men abuse their sense of hearing by listening to a host of agreeable flatteries; others by opening their ears to spiteful scandalmongering; there are some folk who cannot exist without their daily dose of annoyance, just as

* D

sin algún cotidiano sinsabor, como ni Mitridates sin veneno. Tampoco es regla de conservarse querer darse a sí un pesar de toda la vida por dar placer una vez a otro, aunque sea el más propio. Nunca se ha de pecar contra la dicha propia por complacer al que aconseja y se queda fuera; y en todo acontecimiento, siempre que se encontraren el hacer placer a otro con el hacerse a sí pesar, es lición de conveniencia que vale más que el otro se disguste ahora que no tú después y sin remedio.

65

Gusto relevante. Cabe cultura en él, así como en el ingenio; realza la excelencia del entender el apetito del desear, y después la fruición del poseer. Conócese la altura de un caudal por la elevación del afecto. Mucho objeto ha menester para satisfacerse una gran capacidad; así como los grandes bocados son para grandes paladares, las materias sublimes para los sublimes genios. Los más valientes objetos se temen y las más seguras perfecciones desconfían; son pocas las de primera magnitud : sea raro el aprecio. Péganse los gustos con el trato y se heredan con la continuidad : gran suerte comunicar con quien le tiene en su punto. Pero no se ha de hacer profesión de desagradarse de todo, que es uno de los necios extremos, y más odioso cuando por afectación que por destemplanza. Quisieran algunos que criara Dios otro mundo y otras perfecciones para satisfacción de su extravagante fantasía.

66

Atención a que le salgan bien las cosas. Algunos ponen más la mira en el rigor de la dirección que en la felicidad del conseguir intento; pero más prepondera siempre el descrédito de la infelicidad que el abono de la diligencia. El que vence no necesita de dar satisfacciones. No perciben los más la puntualidad de las circunstancias, sino los buenos o los ruines sucesos; y así, nunca se pierde reputación cuando se consigue el intento. Todo lo

Mithridates could not get on without his [draught of] poison. Nor is it a rule for self-preservation to take up a lifelong burden of trouble in order to give temporary pleasure to another, even though the latter be your nearest and dearest.   You must never spoil your own chances of happiness in order to please one who, while giving you advice, remains aloof; and in every case where giving pleasure to another may involve causing trouble for yourself, it is a convenient maxim that it is better for that person to be displeased now than that you should be so later on, and irremediably.

65

Good taste.   There is room for cultivation here, just as in the case of the mind; the excellence of the understanding enhances the appetite of desire, and, later on, the enjoyment of possession. The extent of a man's capacity is to be known by the loftiness of his taste.   Great ability requires many objects to satisfy it; just as large morsels are suited to big mouths, so are high matters to high minds.   The worthiest objects are mutually suspicious and the most stable qualities are mistrustful: there are few of the first magnitude, so be sparing with your appreciation.   Tastes are imparted by personal intercourse and are passed on by frequenting the society of one's fellows; it is a piece of great good luck to deal with someone who values you at your true worth. But do not profess to be displeased with everything, for that is one of the extremes of folly, and is more detestable when it arises from affectation than when it is caused by lack of balance.   Some people would like God to have created a different world and different beauties, in order to satisfy their wild whims.

66

Take care that your affairs reach a successful conclusion.   Some people are more concerned with the accuracy of their aim than with the satisfaction of attaining their object; but the disgrace of failure invariably counts for more than the recognition of diligence.   A victor need give no explanations.   The majority do not look closely into circumstantial detail but only at a successful, or unsuccessful, outcome; thus one's reputation never suffers if one's object is attained.   A satisfactory issue puts

dora un buen fin, aunque lo desmientan los desaciertos de los medios. Que es arte ir contra el arte, cuando no se puede de otro modo conseguir la dicha del salir bien.

67

Preferir los empleos plausibles. Las más de las cosas dependen de la satisfacción ajena: es la estimación para las perfecciones lo que el Favonio para las flores: aliento y vida. Hay empleos expuestos a la aclamación universal; y hay otros, aunque mayores, en nada espectables; aquéllos, por obrarse a vista de todos, captan la benevolencia común: éstos, aunque tienen más de lo raro y primoroso, se quedan en el secreto de su imperceptibilidad, venerados, pero no aplaudidos. Entre los príncipes, los victoriosos son los celebrados, y por eso los reyes de Aragón fueron tan plausibles por guerreros, conquistadores y magnánimos. Prefiera el varón grande los célebres empleos, que todos perciban y participen todos, y a sufragios comunes quede inmortalizado.

68

Dar entendimiento es de más primor que el dar memoria. Cuanto es más, unas veces se ha de acordar y otras advertir. Dejan algunos de hacer las cosas que estuvieran en su punto, porque no se les ofrecen; ayude entonces la advertencia amigable a concebir las conveniencias. Una de las mayores ventajas de la mente es el ofrecérsele lo que importa. Por falta de esto dejan de hacerse muchos aciertos; dé luz el que la alcanza,[1] y solicítela el que la mendiga; aquél con detención, éste con atención: no sea más que dar pie. Es urgente esta sutileza, cuando toca en utilidad del que despierta; conviene mostrar gusto, y pasar a más cuando no bastare. Ya se tiene el no, váyase en busca del sí, con destreza, que las más veces no se consigue porque no se intenta.

[1] 1659 has 'alança.'

everything to rights, although mistaken means may belie it. It is, therefore, an art in itself to transgress the rules of art, when there is no other way of winning the joy of success.

67

Prefer commendable occupations. We are dependent in most things upon the satisfaction we give to others: recognition is to great gifts what a gentle zephyr is to flowers, the very breath of life. There are some callings which are the object of universal esteem; and there are others which, although more important, are in no way commendable; the former, being pursued in full view of all, win general approval; the latter, although they are more refined and elegant, remain unnoticed in their obscurity, honoured but unsung. Among princes, the victors are those who attain fame, and it was for this that the kings of Aragon won so much praise as great-hearted warriors and conquerors. The great man should prefer a distinguished position which all may see and all may take note of, so that he may be immortalized by universal suffrage.

68

To inform is of more value than to remind. Nevertheless, on some occasions one has to remind and on others to inform. Some people fail to do the right thing at the right time because the opportunity to do so does not arise; on such occasions let friendly advice help them to recognize the times and seasons for action. One of the greatest gifts of the mind is its power to draw your attention to what is important. Many aims go unfulfilled because of its failure to carry out this function; let him who is enlightened provide enlightenment, and let him who lacks it ask for it; the former sparingly, the latter eagerly: it is enough for the former to clear the way for the latter. This device is indispensable when it affects the interests of the person whose attention you arouse. It is as well to give but a taste at first, and then pass on to more should that be insufficient. A negative attitude is already there; go skilfully in search of the positive, for, in the majority of cases, an object is not attained because no effort is made to attain it.

69

No rendirse a un vulgar humor. Hombre grande el que nunca se sujeta a peregrinas impresiones. Es lición de advertencia la reflexión sobre sí; un conocer su disposición actual y prevenirla; y aun decantarse al otro extremo, para hallar entre el natural y el arte el fiel de la sindéresis. Principio es de corregirse el conocerse; que hay monstruos de la impertinencia; siempre están de algún humor, y varían afectos con ellos, y arrastrados eternamente de esta destemplanza civil, contradictoriamente se empeñan; y no sólo gasta la voluntad este exceso, sino que se atreve al juicio, alterando el querer y el entender.

70

Saber negar. No todo se ha de conceder, ni a todos. Tanto importa como el saber conceder; y en los que mandan es atención urgente. Aquí entra el modo. Más se estima el no de algunos que el sí de otros, porque un no dorado satisface más que un sí a secas. Hay muchos que siempre tienen en la boca el no, con que todo lo desazonan. El no es siempre el primero en ellos, y aunque después todo lo vienen a conceder, no se les estima porque precedió aquella primera desazón. No se han de negar de rondón las cosas; vaya a tragos el desengaño; ni se ha de negar del todo, que sería desahuciar la dependencia. Queden siempre algunas reliquias de esperanza para que templen lo amargo del negar. Llene la cortesía el vacío del favor, y suplan las buenas palabras la falta de las obras. El no y el sí son breves de decir, y piden mucho pensar.

69

Do not give way to a vulgar impulse. He is a great man who is never swayed by outside influences. Introspection is the school of good counsel; [it teaches us] to know our present disposition and to forestall it; and even to go towards the other extreme in order to arrive at that just balance between nature and art which sound judgment demands. Self-knowledge is the beginning of self-improvement; for there are monsters of folly who are always at the mercy of some whim, and their inclinations vary according to its dictates. Perpetually a prey to this internal disharmony, they become involved in mutually irreconcilable obligations. This excess not only undermines their purpose but even attacks their power of judgment, perverting their will and understanding.

70

Know how to refuse. One should not give way in everything, nor to everybody. This is as important as knowing how to concede, and it is a pressing concern of those in authority. Here there comes in the way [in which you say a thing]. The 'No' of some men is more highly prized than the 'Yes' of others; for a gilded 'No' is more agreeable than a plain 'Yes.' Some people are always ready with a 'No,' and thereby make everything distasteful. 'No' always comes first with them, and even though they eventually grant everything, the concession is not appreciated because it was preceded by this unpleasantness at the start. Do not refuse things point-blank: let the disappointment be administered drop by drop; and do not let your refusal be complete, for that is to deprive a dependant of all hope. Let some dregs of hope always remain to temper the bitterness of denial. Let courtesy fill the vacuum left by the refusal of a favour, and fair words supply the deficiency of deeds. 'No' and 'Yes' are words quickly said, and they need a great deal of thought [before you utter them].

71

No ser desigual, de proceder anómalo, ni por natural, ni por afectación. El varón cuerdo siempre fué el mismo en todo lo perfecto, que es crédito de entendido; dependa en su mudanza de la de las causas y méritos: en materia de cordura, la variedad es fea. Hay algunos que cada día son otros de sí; hasta el entendimiento tienen desigual, cuanto más la voluntad y aun la ventura. El que ayer fué el blanco de su sí, hoy es el negro de su no, desmintiendo siempre su propio crédito y deslumbrando el ajeno concepto.

72

Hombre de resolución. Menos dañosa es la mala ejecución que la irresolución. No se gastan tanto las materias cuando corren como si estancan. Hay hombres indeterminables que necesitan de ajena premoción en todo; y a veces no nace tanto de la perplejidad del juicio, pues lo tienen perspicaz, cuanto de la ineficacia. Ingenioso suele ser el dificultar, pero más lo es el hallar salida a los inconvenientes. Hay otros que en nada se embarazan, de juicio grande y determinado; nacieron para sublimes empleos, porque su despejada comprensión facilita el acierto y el despacho; todo se lo hallan hecho, que después de haber dado razón a un mundo, le quedó tiempo a uno de éstos para otro, y cuando están afianzados de su dicha se empeñan con más seguridad.

73

Saber usar del desliz. Es el desempeño de los cuerdos. Con la galantería de un donaire suelen salir del más intrincado laberinto. Húrtasele el cuerpo airosamente con un sonriso a la más dificultosa contienda. En esto fundaba el mayor de los

71

Do not be inconsistent. Neither your natural inclination nor affectation should render your behaviour inconsistent. The wise man is always the same in all his good qualities, for this is the mark of a sound understanding; he must change his mind only on grounds of reason and on the merits of the case. Where wisdom is concerned, inconsistency is hateful. Some people are different persons from day to day; even their understanding vacillates; their wills are even more unstable, and even their luck is inconsistent. What was yesterday their obliging 'Yes' is to-day their displeasing 'No.' They always belie their own reputations and confound the opinion which others have formed of them.

72

The resolute man. Defective execution is less harmful than infirmity of purpose. Things do not deteriorate so much when they are on the move as when they are stagnant. There are irresolute men who have to rely upon the initiative of others in all their dealings; and this state of affairs is sometimes due not so much to perplexity, for their judgment is clear, as to ineffectiveness. It is usually clever to make difficulties, but it is far more so to find a way out of awkward situations. There are other men of sound and resolute judgment who are never perplexed by anything; they are born for the highest office because their clear grasp of things makes both aim and execution easy; everything that comes their way is as good as done already, for, after such a man has proved himself in one sphere there will still be time for him to do so in another; and when such a one has fortune behind him he enters upon an undertaking with all the greater assurance.

73

Know how to be evasive. That is how wise men get themselves out of difficulties. They can usually extricate themselves from the most intricate imbroglio with a gallant and witty remark. A cheerful smile will get them out of the most tiresome quarrel. The courage of the greatest of all great leaders had its

grandes capitanes su valor. Cortés treta del negar mudar el verbo: ni hay mayor atención que no darse por entendido.

74

No ser intratable. En lo más poblado están las fieras verdaderas. Es la inaccesibilidad vicio de desconocidos de sí, que mudan los humores con los honores; no es medio a propósito para la estimación comenzar enfadando. ¡Que es de ver uno de estos monstruos intratables siempre a punto de su fiereza impertinente! Entran a hablarle los dependientes de su desdicha, como a lidiar con tigres; tan armados de tiento, cuanto de recelo. Para subir al puesto agradaron a todos, y en estando en él se quieren desquitar con enfadar a todos. Habiendo de ser de muchos por el empleo, son de ninguno por su aspereza o entono. Cortesano castigo para éstos dejarlos estar, hurtándoles la cordura con el trato.

75

Elegir idea heroica, más para la emulación que para la imitación. Hay ejemplares de grandeza, textos animados de la reputación. Propóngase cada uno en su empleo los primeros, no tanto para seguir, cuanto para adelantarse. Lloró Alejandro, no a Aquiles sepultado, sino a sí mismo, aún no bien nacido al lucimiento. No hay cosa que así solicite ambiciones en el ánimo como el clarín de la fama ajena. El mismo que atierra la invidia alienta la generosidad.

76

No estar siempre de burlas. Conócese la prudencia en lo serio, que está más acreditado que lo ingenioso. El que siempre está

roots in this accomplishment. A courteous way of refusing is to change the subject; and there is no device more shrewd than to pretend you do not understand.

74

Do not be unapproachable. The real wild beasts are to be found in the most densely populated areas. Inaccessibility is the vice of those who are not sure of themselves, those whose disposition changes with the honours they receive; to start off by annoying people is not an appropriate way of gaining their regard. What a sight one of these unapproachable monsters is, always perched arrogantly upon his high horse! Those who depend upon his wretched temperament seek his ear as though they were about to wrestle with a tiger; they come armed with caution and fear in equal proportions. These unapproachable people have fawned upon all and sundry in order to rise to their present position, and, having attained it, wish to get their own back by irritating everybody. While their position demands that they should be accessible to many, they are, on account of their brusqueness or arrogance, approachable by none. A polite way of punishing such people is to leave them alone and thus deprive them of the opportunity to acquire wisdom through intercourse with their fellows.

75

Choose an heroic ideal, rather for emulation than imitation. There are models of greatness, living text-books of honour. Let every one keep in his mind's eye those who have excelled in his calling, not so much that he may follow in their footsteps but, rather, that he may outstrip them. Alexander did not weep for Achilles, dead and buried, but rather for himself, [because he was] not yet born to widespread fame. Nothing stirs ambition in the soul so deeply as the clarion call of another's glory. He who lays envy low fosters magnanimity.

76

Do not always be joking. Prudence is revealed by a serious mien, and is more highly prized than wit. The man who is

de burlas, nunca es hombre de veras. Igualámoslos a éstos con los mentirosos en no darles crédito; a los unos por recelo de mentira, a otros, de su fisga. Nunca se sabe cuándo hablan en juicio, que es tanto como no tenerle. No hay mayor desaire que el continuo donaire. Ganan otros fama de decidores y pierden el crédito de cuerdos. Su rato ha de tener lo jovial: todos los demás, lo serio.

77

Saber hacerse a todos. Discreto Proteo; con el docto, docto, y con el santo, santo. Gran arte de ganar a todos, porque la semejanza concilia la benevolencia. Observar los genios y templarse al de cada uno; al serio y al jovial seguirles la corriente, haciendo política transformación; urgente a los que dependen. Requiere esta gran sutileza del vivir un gran caudal; menos dificultosa al varón universal de ingenio en noticias y de genio en gustos.

78

Arte en el intentar. La necedad siempre entra de rondón; que todos los necios son audaces. Su misma simplicidad, que les impide primero la advertencia para los reparos, les quita después el sentimiento para los desaires. Pero la cordura entra con grande tiento: son sus batidores la advertencia y el recato: ellos van descubriendo para proceder sin peligro; todo arrojamiento está condenado por la discreción a despeño, aunque tal vez lo absuelva la ventura. Conviene ir detenido donde se teme mucho fondo. Vaya intentando la sagacidad y ganando tierra la prudencia. Hay grandes bajíos hoy en el trato humano; conviene ir siempre calando sonda.

79

Genio genial. Si con templanza, prenda es, que no defecto. Un grano de donosidad todo lo sazona. Los mayores hombres

always joking can never be taken seriously. We put these people on the same level as liars in giving no credit to what they say; for, in the case of the liars we suspect falsehood, and in the case of the jesters, their raillery. We never know when they are talking sense, which is as much as to say that they have none. There is nothing more contemptible than continual banter. Others win the reputation of being witty and lose that of being wise. Jesting should have its little day, seriousness all the rest.

77

Know how to be all things to all men. A discreet Proteus; a scholar among scholars, a saint among saints. That is the art, *par excellence*, of winning every one's regard, for similarity [of outlook] attracts goodwill. Take note of temperaments and adapt yourself to that of each person [you meet]; follow the lead of the serious and the jovial in turn, changing your mood discreetly; an indispensable device for dependants. This high skill in the art of living demands great ability; it is less difficult for the versatile, well-informed man of cultivated tastes.

78

Astuteness in undertakings. Folly always rushes in recklessly; for all fools are rash. Their very simplicity, which prevents them from first taking thought, renders them, later, impervious to rebuffs. Discretion, however, approaches very warily: her outriders are care and circumspection: they precede her in order to discover a safe road; although a happy issue may sometimes excuse a rash venture, discretion marks down all foolhardiness for destruction. It is well to proceed carefully where you suspect that the waters may be very deep. Let sagacity feel the way and prudence gain the ground. There are many shoals in the stream of human intercourse to-day; it is advisable to take continual soundings.

79

A genial disposition. If one has this to a moderate degree, it is a good quality, not a defect. A grain of wit gives spice to

juegan también la pieza del donaire que concilia la gracia universal, pero guardando siempre los aires a la cordura y haciendo la salva al decoro. Hacen otros de una gracia atajo al desempeño, que hay cosas que se han de tomar de burlas, y a veces las que el otro toma más de veras. Indica apacibilidad, garabato de corazones.

80

Atención al informarse. Vívese lo más de información: es lo menos lo que vemos; vivimos de fe ajena; es el oído la puerta segunda de la verdad, y principal de la mentira. La verdad ordinariamente se ve; extravagantemente se oye; raras veces llega en su elemento puro, y menos cuando viene de lejos; siempre trae algo de mixta, de los afectos por donde pasa; tiñe de sus colores la pasión cuanto toca, ya odiosa, ya favorable; tira siempre a impresionar: gran cuenta con quien alaba, mayor con quien vitupera. Es menester toda la atención en este punto para descubrir la intención en el que tercia, conociendo de antemano de qué pie se movió. Sea la reflexa contraste de lo falto[1] y de lo falso.

81

Usar el renovar su lucimiento. Es privilegio de fénix; suele envejecerse la excelencia y con ella la fama; la costumbre disminuye la admiración, y una mediana novedad suele vencer a la mayor eminencia envejecida. Usar, pues, del renacer en el valor, en el ingenio, en la dicha, en todo. Empeñarse con novedades de bizarría, amaneciendo muchas veces como el sol, variando teatros al lucimiento, para que, en el uno la privación y en el otro la novedad, soliciten aquí el aplauso, si allí el deseo.

[1] *Vide* Appendix, p. 306.

everything. 'A bit of nonsense now and then is relished by the wisest men,' and this characteristic of theirs wins general favour. Nevertheless, they always keep within the bounds of good sense and have due regard to the proprieties. Others find a quick way out of a difficulty with a joke, for there are certain things which you should take in fun which the other fellow sometimes takes seriously. A genial disposition is a sign of peaceableness, a charmer of hearts.

80

Be on your guard when collecting information. We live mainly by hearsay: what we see matters least; we live by the testimony of others; hearing is the side door of truth and the main entrance of falsehood. Truth is usually apprehended by the eyes; we hear it in a distorted form; it rarely reaches us in its pristine purity, and least of all when it comes from a distance; it always has some admixture of the feelings through which it is filtered; feeling tints with its own hue everything it touches, now in a repugnant, now in a pleasing fashion; it always strives to create an impression, an important consideration in the case of one who praises, and more important still in that of one who blames. In this matter, every care is needed in order to divine the intentions of an interlocutor; you should know beforehand what footing he is on. Let reflection assay what is defective and false.

81

Practise renewing your glory. It is the privilege of a genius; distinction usually grows stale and, with it, renown; with familiarity admiration is diminished, and a mediocre newcomer usually outshines the most outstanding genius grown old. Practise, then, renewing your valour, wit, fortune, everything. Enter the lists afresh with something new and startling, rising again and again like the sun, and changing the scene of your exploits, so that your absence from the former stage and your achievement on the new may provoke, respectively, regret and admiration.

82

Nunca apurar ni el mal ni el bien; a la moderación en todo
redujo la sabiduría toda un sabio.   El sumo derecho se hace
tuerto, y la naranja que mucho se estruja llega a dar lo amargo;
aun en la fruición nunca se ha de llegar a los extremos.   El mismo ingenio se agota, si se apura, y sacará sangre por leche el que
esquilmare a lo tirano.

83

Permitirse algún venial desliz; que un descuido suele ser tal vez
la mayor recomendación de las prendas.   Tiene su ostracismo la
invidia, tanto más civil cuanto más criminal; acusa lo muy
perfecto de que peca en no pecar; y por perfecto en todo, lo
condena todo.   Hácese Argos en buscarle faltas a lo muy bueno,
para consuelo siquiera.   Hiere la censura, como el rayo, los más
empinados realces.   Dormite, pues, tal vez Homero, y afecte
algún descuido en el ingenio o en el valor, pero nunca en la cordura; para sosegar la malevolencia: no reviente ponzoñosa.
Será como un echar la capa al toro de la invidia, para salvar la
inmortalidad.

84

Saber usar de los enemigos.   Todas las cosas se han de saber
tomar, no por el corte que ofenda,[1] sino por la empuñadura que
defienda;[2] mucho más la emulación.   Al varón sabio más le
aprovechan sus enemigos, que al necio sus amigos.   Suele
allanar una malevolencia montañas de dificultad, que desconfiara
de emprenderlas el favor.   Fabicáronles a muchos su grandeza
sus malévolos.   Más fiera es la lisonja que el odio, pues remedia
éste eficazmente las tachas que aquélla disimula.   Hace el cuerdo
espejo de la ojeriza, más fiel que el de la afición, y previene a la
detracción de los defectos, o los enmienda, que es grande el
recato cuando se vive en frontera de una emulación, de una
malevolencia.

[1] 1653 and 1659 have 'ofendan.'
[2] 1653 and 1659 have 'defiendan.'

82

Never drain either evil or good to the dregs: a sage once reduced the whole of wisdom to moderation in all things. Justice to excess becomes a wrong and the juice of an over-squeezed orange eventually becomes bitter to the taste: never go to extremes, even of enjoyment. Wit itself, if overstrained, becomes sterile; and if you milk a cow too hard you will draw blood.

83

Allow yourself some venial shortcoming: for a piece of careless-ness once in a while usually sets off good qualities to their best advantage. The envious have their own form of ostracism, the more vile, the more criminal; they accuse the highest per-fection of sinning in that it does not sin: and for being totally perfect it incurs total condemnation. The envious person be-comes an Argus in finding fault with excellence, if only for [his own] consolation. Censure, like a lightning flash, strikes at the highest points. Let, then, even Homer nod from time to time, and affect some lapse of wit or courage, but never of prudence; in order to appease malice, do not let it burst with its own venom. It will be, as it were, to throw your cloak to the bull of envy in order to preserve [the] immortality [of your name].

84

Know how to make use of your enemies. You should know how to take hold of everything, not by the blade, which wounds, but by the hilt, which protects; and this is more especially true of envy. Enemies are of more use to the wise man than friends are to the fool. Malice is wont to level mountains of difficulties, upon the scaling of which goodwill would hesitate to embark. Many owe their greatness to their malicious critics. Flattery is more deadly than hatred because it conceals those flaws for which hatred prompts us to find an efficacious remedy. The wise man turns spite into a mirror more faithful than that of affection, and he either forestalls the detraction aroused by his failings, or amends them; for extreme caution is required when one lives on the frontier of envy and malice.

85

No ser malilla.[1]   Achaque es de todo lo excelente que su mucho uso viene a ser abuso.   El mismo codiciarlo todo viene a parar en enfadar a todos; grande infelicidad ser para nada, no menor querer ser para todo; vienen a perder éstos por mucho ganar, y son después tan aborrecidos cuanto fueron antes deseados. Rózanse de estas malillas en todo género de perfecciones, que perdiendo aquella primera estimación de raras, consiguen el desprecio de vulgares.   El único remedio de todo lo extremado es guardar un medio en el lucimiento; la demasía ha de estar en la perfección, y la templanza en la ostentación; cuanto más luce una antorcha se consume más y dura menos; escaseces de apariencia se premian con logros de estimación.

86

Prevenir las malas voces.   Tiene el vulgo muchas cabezas, y así muchos ojos para la malicia y muchas lenguas para el descrédito.   Acontece correr en él alguna mala voz que desdora el mayor crédito, y si llegare a ser apodo vulgar, acabará con la reputación; dásele pie comúnmente con algún sobresaliente desaire, con ridículos defectos, que son plausible materia a sus hablillas.   Si bien hay desdoros echadizos de la emulación especial a la malicia común; que hay bocas de la malevolencia, y arruinan más presto una gran fama con un chiste que con un descaramiento.   Es muy fácil de cobrar la siniestra fama, porque lo malo es muy creíble y cuesta mucho de borrarse.   Excuse, pues, el varón cuerdo estos desaires, contrastando con su atención la vulgar insolencia; que es más fácil el prevenir que el remediar.

[1] *Vide* Appendix, p. 306.

85

Do not be a Jack-of-all-trades. It is a weakness of every good quality that its frequent exercise leads to its abuse. The very fact that every one covets it turns it into a source of general annoyance in the end; it is a great misfortune to be good for nothing, but it is no less disastrous to wish to be good at everything; those who fall within this last category lose in the end owing to the very extent of their gains, and they come to be as greatly loathed as they were previously sought out. These people are embarrassed by the possession of every kind of accomplishment; for, after losing their original reputation for being exceptional, they incur contempt as being vulgar. The only remedy for every kind of great ability is to show moderation in displaying it; extremes should be found in the talent and moderation in the manner of revealing it; the brighter a torch burns the more rapidly it is consumed and the less time it lasts; lack of outward display is rewarded by acquisition of esteem.

86

Forestall evil tongues. The multitude is many-headed and so has many eyes in the service of malice and many tongues in that of slander. Some evil report, capable of injuring the fairest name, happens to gain currency among the mob and, if it should end by getting you a vulgar nickname, it will destroy your reputation; the basis of these rumours is usually some outstanding shortcoming combined with ludicrous failings which provide plausible grounds for vulgar gossip. There are, indeed, imperfections which private envy cunningly exposes to the eyes of public spite; for there are spiteful tongues which destroy a good reputation with a jest more readily than with a barefaced insult. It is very easy to get a bad name because evil is readily believed and it is very hard to eradicate. The wise man, therefore, should avoid these mischances and counteract the insolence of the mob by the exercise of great vigilance; for prevention is easier than cure.

87

Cultura y aliño. Nace bárbaro el hombre; redímese de bestia,
cultivándose. Hace personas la cultura, y más cuanto mayor.
En fe de ella pudo Grecia llamar bárbaro a todo el restante
universo. Es muy tosca la ignorancia: no hay cosa que más
cultive que el saber. Pero aun la misma sabiduría fué grosera, si
desaliñada. No sólo ha de ser aliñado el entender; también el
querer, y más el conversar. Hállanse hombres naturalmente
aliñados de gala interior y exterior, en concepto y palabras, en los
arreos del cuerpo, que son como la corteza, y en las prendas del
alma, que son el fruto. Otros hay, al contrario, tan groseros,
que todas sus cosas y tal vez eminencias las deslucieron con un
intolerable bárbaro desaseo.

88

Sea el trato por mayor, procurando la sublimidad en él. El
varón grande no debe ser menudo en su proceder. Nunca se ha
de individuar mucho en las cosas, y menos en las de poco gusto;
porque aunque es ventaja notarlo todo al descuido, no lo es
quererlo averiguar todo de propósito. Hase de proceder de
ordinario con una hidalga generalidad, ramo de galantería. Es
gran parte del regir el disimular. Hase de dar pasada a las más
de las cosas entre familiares, entre amigos y más entre enemigos.
Toda nimiedad es enfadosa, y en la condición pesada. El ir y
venir a un disgusto es especie de manía, y comúnmente tal será
el modo de portarse cada uno, cual fuere su corazón y su capacidad.

89

Comprensión de sí. En el genio, en el ingenio, en dictámenes,
en afectos. No puede uno ser señor de sí, si primero no se
comprende. Hay espejos del rostro, no los hay del ánimo;

87

Culture and embellishment. Man is born a barbarian; he is saved from being a beast by acquiring culture. Culture, therefore, makes the man, and the greater his culture the greater the individual. By virtue of her culture, Greece was in a position to call the rest of the world barbarous. Ignorance is most uncouth; nothing refines so much as knowledge. But even knowledge itself is crude if it be unembellished. Not only must our understanding be refined: but our will, also, and especially our conversation. Some men are naturally cultured, both the inner and the outer man, in thought and in words, in their bodily appurtenances, which may be called the rind of their personality, and in their qualities of soul, which are the personality's fruit. On the other hand, some people are so uncouth that everything pertaining to them, and sometimes even their good qualities, is tarnished by an intolerable and savage boorishness.

88

Let your behaviour be your first concern. Try to excel in this matter. The great man ought not to be petty in his actions. He ought never to pry too closely into things, least of all when they are unpleasant; for although it is an advantage to keep a nonchalant eye on everything, it is not so to make a deliberate point of getting to the bottom of everything. One should normally behave with the polite indifference which is a kind of good manners. Dissimulation plays a large part in the art of ruling. Among relations, friends, and more especially enemies, most things should pass unnoticed. All fussiness is irritating, and fussiness of temperament intolerable. To dwell upon and continually revert to a grievance is a kind of obsession. Generally speaking, every one behaves as his qualities of heart and his abilities dictate.

89

Know yourself; your character, mind, judgment, passions. One cannot be master of oneself unless one first understands oneself. There are mirrors for the face, but none for the mind;

séalo la discreta reflexión sobre sí, y, cuando se olvidare de su imagen exterior, conserve la interior para emendarla, para mejorala. Conoce las fuerzas de su cordura y sutileza para el emprender; tantee la irascible para el empeñarse; tenga medido su fondo y pesado su caudal para todo.

90

Arte para vivir mucho. Vivir bien. Dos cosas acaban presto con la vida: la necedad o la ruindad. Perdiéronla unos por no saberla guardar, y otros por no querer. Así como la virtud es premio de sí misma, así el vicio es castigo de sí mismo. Quien vive aprisa en el vicio, acaba presto de dos maneras; quien vive aprisa en la virtud, nunca muere. Comunícase la entereza del ánimo al cuerpo, y no sólo se tiene por larga la vida buena en la intensión, sino en la misma extensión.

91

Obrar siempre sin escrúpulos de imprudencia. La sospecha de desacierto en el que ejecuta es evidencia ya en el que mira, y más si fuere émulo. Si ya al calor de la pasión escrupulea el dictamen, condenará después desapasionado a necedad declarada. Son peligrosas las acciones en duda de prudencia; más segura sería la omisión. No admite probabilidades la cordura; siempre camina al mediodía de la de la razón. ¿Cómo puede salir bien una empresa que, aun concebida, la está ya condenando el recelo? Y si la resolución más graduada con el *nemine discrepante* interior suele salir infelizmente, ¿qué aguarda la que comenzó titubeando en la razón y mal agorada del dictamen?

92

Seso trascendental, digo en todo. Es la primera y suma regla del obrar y del hablar; más encargada cuanto mayores y más altos los empleos; más vale un grano de cordura que arrobas de sutileza.

let discreet introspection be your mental looking-glass and, when the exterior image has been forgotten, preserve the interior one in order to amend it, to improve it. Know the powers of your mind and your skill in enterprise; take the measure of your wrath before you join battle; gauge the extent of your abilities and weigh up your capacity for all things.

90

The art of longevity. Live virtuously. Two things bring life quickly to an end: folly or vice. Some men lose their lives because they do not know how to preserve them, and others because they lack the will to do so. Just as virtue is its own reward, so vice is its own punishment. The man who lives a fast and vicious life, fast dies a double death; he who speeds along life's road accompanied by virtue, never dies. Integrity of soul is passed on to the body, and a good life may be regarded as long not only intensively but extensively.

91

Always set to work without misgivings on the score of imprudence. Fear of failure in the mind of a performer is, for an onlooker, already evidence of failure, especially if he should happen to be a rival. If, in the heat of passion, your judgment has scruples, it will later, when that heat is past, condemn plain folly. Actions are dangerous when there is doubt as to their wisdom; it would be safer to do nothing. Wisdom does not admit probabilities; it invariably walks in the noonday light of reason. How can an undertaking be successful when it is condemned by misgivings at its very conception? And if a resolution which has been passed *nem. con.* by the inner tribunal of the mind afterwards comes to naught, what lies in wait for one at which the reason boggled from the start, and which the judgment disapproves as ill-omened?

92

Good sense is all-important, in everything, I say. It is the first and highest rule of conduct and speech: it is the more in demand the higher and more responsible the position; a grain of common

Es un caminar [1] a lo seguro, aunque no tan a lo plausible; si bien la reputación de cuerdo es el triunfo de la fama. Bastará satisfacer a los cuerdos, cuyo voto es la piedra de toque a los aciertos.

93

Hombre universal. Compuesto de toda perfección, vale por muchos. Hace felicísimo el vivir, comunicando esta fruición a la familiaridad. La variedad con perfección es entretenimiento de la vida. Gran arte la de saber lograr todo lo bueno, y pues le hizo la naturaleza al hombre un compendio de todo lo natural por su eminencia, hágale el arte un universo por ejercicio y cultura del gusto y del entendimiento.

94

Incomprensibilidad de caudal. Excuse el varón atento sondarle el fondo, ya al saber, ya al valer, si quiere que le veneren todos: permítase al conocimiento, no a la comprensión. Nadie le averigüe los términos de la capacidad, por el peligro evidente del desengaño. Nunca dé lugar a que alguno le alcance todo: mayores afectos de veneración causa la opinión y duda de adonde llega el caudal de cada uno, que la evidencia de él por grande que fuere.

95

Saber entretener la expectación; irla cebando siempre: prometa más lo mucho, y la mejor acción sea envidar de mayores. No se ha de echar todo el resto al primer lance; gran treta es saberse templar en las fuerzas, en el saber, y ir adelantando el desempeño.

96

De la gran sindéresis: es el trono de la razón, base [2] de la prudencia, que en fe de ella cuesta poco el acertar. Es suerte del

---

[1] 1653 and 1659 have 'caminar.' Reyes has 'camino.'
[2] 1653 and 1659 have 'basa.'

sense is worth bushels of cunning. It is a road to security
although not, to the same extent, to praise; a reputation for
wisdom is, indeed, the triumph of renown. It will be enough
to satisfy the wise, whose vote is the touchstone of success.

93

The versatile man. A compound of all high qualities, he is a
host in himself. He leads an extremely happy life and com-
municates his *joie de vivre* to his intimates. Variety combined
with perfection is the delight of life. It is a great art to know
how to attain all that is good, and since Nature has, in virtue of his
noble qualities, made man a compendium of all her characteristics, so Art should make him a universe in himself by the
exercise and cultivation of his taste and his understanding.

94

Unfathomability of endowments. The cautious man, if he
wishes everybody to respect him, allows neither his knowledge
nor his worth to be completely fathomed: he permits them to
be recognized, but not to be fully grasped. Because of the
obvious risk of disillusionment, nobody must be allowed to
discover the limits of his capacity. He must never give anybody the chance to take his measure completely: surmise and
doubt as to how far a man's capacity extends excite deeper
feelings of respect than does evidence of it, however great that
capacity may be.

95

Know how to foster expectation; always keep on feeding it: let
much give promise of more, and let the finest deed be a pledge of
others to come. You must not go to the whole limit on the
first throw; it is an important device to know how to be moderate
in the use of your powers and your knowledge, and to further
the redemption of the pledge.

96

Concerning sound judgment: this is the throne of reason, the
foundation-stone of discretion, for, by virtue of it, success costs

E

cielo y la más deseada por primera y por mejor. La primera pieza del arnés, con tal urgencia que ninguna otra que le falte a un hombre le domina falto. Nótase más su menos. Todas las acciones de la vida dependen de su influencia, y todos solicitan su calificación, que todo ha de ser con seso. Consiste en una connatural propensión a todo lo más conforme a razón, casándose siempre con lo más acertado.

97

Conseguir y conservar la reputación es el usufructo de la fama. Cuesta mucho, porque nace de las eminencias, que son tan raras cuanto comunes las medianías. Conseguida, se conserva con facilidad. Obliga mucho y obra más. Es especie de majestad cuando llega a ser veneración, por la sublimidad de su causa y de su esfera; pero la reputación sustancial es la que valió siempre.

98

Cifrar la voluntad. Son las pasiones los portillos del ánimo. El más plático saber consiste en disimular. Lleva riesgo de perder el que juega a juego descubierto. Compite la detención del recato con la atención del advertido; a linces de discurso, jibias de interioridad. No se le sepa el gusto, porque no se le prevenga, unos para la contradicción, otros para la lisonja.

99

Realidad y apariencia. Las cosas no pasan por lo que son, sino por lo que parecen; son raros los que miran por dentro, y muchos los que se pagan de lo aparente. No basta tener razón con cara de malicia.

little. It is a lucky gift from heaven and the one most coveted, as being the chief and the best. It is the most important part of a man's equipment, and so necessary to him that the lack of it is far more significant than that of any other. Its absence is the more readily noticed. Every action in life depends upon its influence, and all solicit its favourable verdict, for all actions should be prompted by good sense. It consists in an innate tendency towards everything most in conformity with reason, and it is always wedded to the wisest course.

97

To win and keep your reputation is the usufruct of fame. A reputation is very costly to obtain because it arises from conspicuous abilities, which are as rare as mediocre gifts are common. Once a reputation is won it is easily preserved. It confers many obligations and fulfils even more. When, by virtue of the sublimity of its motives and lofty sphere of action, it comes to inspire veneration, it has a majestic quality about it; but the reputation which has the most substantial foundation is always the most valuable.

98

Conceal your purpose. The emotions are the breaches in the defences of the mind. The most practical kind of wisdom consists in dissimulation. The player who shows his hand risks losing the game. The reserve of caution combats the watchfulness of the curious; [pit the] cuttle-fish of intuition against the lynxes of logic. Do not allow your inclinations to be known, so that they will not be frustrated, some by opposition, others by flattery.

99

Reality and appearance. Things do not pass for what they are but for what they seem; few look within, and many are satisfied with appearances. It is not enough to be in the right if the outward appearance of your action is evil.

100

Varón desengañado, cristiano sabio,[1] *cortesano filósofo, mas no parecerlo:* menos afectarlo. Está desacreditado el filosofar, aunque el ejercicio mayor de los sabios. Vive desautorizada la ciencia de los cuerdos. Introdújola Séneca en Roma; conservóse algún tiempo cortesana; ya es tenida por impertinencia. Pero siempre el desengañado fué pasto de la prudencia, delicias de la entereza.

101

La mitad del mundo se está riendo de la otra mitad, con necedad de todos. O todo es bueno, o todo es malo, según votos. Lo que éste sigue, el otro persigue. Insufrible necio el que quiere regular todo objeto por su concepto. No dependen las perfecciones de un solo agrado. Tantos son los gustos como los rostros, y tan varios. No hay defecto sin afecto, ni se ha de desconfiar porque no agraden las cosas a algunos, que no faltarán otros que las aprecien. Ni aun el aplauso de éstos le sea materia al desvanecimiento, que otros lo condenarán. La norma de la verdadera satisfacción es la aprobación de los varones de reputación, y que tienen voto en aquel orden de cosas. No se vive de un voto solo, ni de un uso, ni de un siglo.

102

Estómago para grandes bocados de la fortuna. En el cuerpo de la prudencia no es la parte menos importante un gran buche, que de grandes partes se compone una gran capacidad. No se embaraza con las buenas dichas quien merece otras mayores; lo que es ahito en unos es hambre en otros. Hay muchos que se les gasta cualquier muy importante manjar por la cortedad de su natural, no acostumbrado ni nacido para tan sublimes empleos; acédaseles el trato, y con los humos que se levantan de la postiza honra, viene a desvanecérseles la cabeza; corren gran peligro en los lugares altos, y no caben en sí porque no cabe en ellos la suerte.

[1] 1653 and 1659 have a full stop after 'sabio.'

100

[Be] a man without illusions, a wise Christian, a courtier-philosopher, but do not look like one: much less pose as one. Philosophy is discredited, although it is the major intellectual exercise of the wise. The wisdom of the sages lacks authority. Seneca introduced it to Rome; it was kept alive at Court for a time; now it is regarded as folly. Nevertheless, wisdom is always nourished by disillusion, the delight of integrity.

101

One half of the world is laughing at the other half, and all its inhabitants are fools. Either everything is good, or everything is bad, by votes: what one man pursues another persecutes. The man who wants to regulate everything according to his own whim is an insufferable ass. Great attainments do not depend upon the pleasure they give to a single individual: there are as many fancies as there are faces, and they are as various. There is no failing which is not somebody's pet; nor need we lose hope because things as they are may displease some people, for there will be no lack of others to appreciate them. Yet neither should the approval of the latter give you cause to lose your head, for yet others will condemn their praise. The criterion of true competence is the approval of reputable men who have a right to express an opinion in the field concerned. Life does not depend upon any one vote, any one custom, or any one period.

102

A stomach for big mouthfuls of good fortune. In the body of wisdom not the least important organ is a big belly, for a great capacity is made up of great parts. Strokes of good luck do not worry the man who deserves further and still larger ones; one man's surfeit is another's hunger. There are many upon whom any very special dainty is wasted on account of their natural limitations. They are neither accustomed nor born to such high office; their affairs go sour on them, and the fumes which arise from their spurious honours eventually turn their heads; they run a great risk in high positions and cannot contain themselves because they cannot contain their good fortune. A great man

Muestre, pues, el varón grande que aún le quedan ensanches para cosas mayores, y huya[1] con especial cuidado de todo lo que puede dar indicio de angosto corazón.

103

Cada uno, la majestad en su modo. Sean todas las acciones, si no de un rey, dignas de tal, según su esfera, el proceder real, dentro de los límites de su cuerda suerte, sublimidad de acciones, remonte de pensamientos; y en todas sus cosas, represente un rey por méritos, cuando no por realidad. Que la verdadera soberanía consiste en la entereza de costumbres. Ni tendrá que envidiar a la grandeza quien pueda ser norma de ella. Especialmente a los allegados al trono péagueseles algo de la verdadera superioridad, participen antes de las prendas de la majestad que de las ceremonias de la vanidad, sin afectar lo imperfecto de la hinchazón, sino lo realzado de la sustancia.

104

Tener tomado el pulso a los empleos. Hay su variedad en ellos: magistral conocimiento, y que necesita de advertencia. Piden unos valor y otros sutileza. Son más fáciles de manejar los que dependen de la rectitud, y más difíciles los que del artificio. Con un buen natural, no es menester más para aquéllos; para éstos no basta toda la atención y desvelo. Trabajosa ocupación gobernar hombres, y más, locos o necios. Doblado seso es menester para con quien no le tiene. Empleo intolerable el que pide todo un hombre, de horas contadas y la materia cierta. Mejores son los libres de fastidio, juntando variedad con la gravedad, porque la alternación[2] refresca el gusto. Los más autorizados son los que tienen menos, o más distante, la dependencia; y aquél es el peor que, al fin, hace sudar en la residencia[3] humana, y más en la divina.

[1] 1653 has 'huiga,' 1659 has 'hulga,' both misprints. The context appears to demand 'huya.' Reyes has 'huelga.'
[2] 1653 and 1659 have 'alternación.' Reyes has 'alteración.'
[3] *Vide* Appendix, p. 306.

should, therefore, show that he still has room for greater things, and should take special care to avoid everything which may give any indication of mean-spiritedness.

103

Every one should be royal after his own fashion. Let all [your] actions, even though they are not those of a king, be, in their own sphere, worthy of one: let your behaviour be wise and kingly within the discreet limits of your lot. Be sublime in your actions, lofty in your thoughts; and in all your doings show that you deserve to be a king even though you are not one in reality. For integrity of conduct constitutes true sovereignty. Nor need he envy greatness who can serve as a model for it. Something of true nobility should, especially, cling to those around the throne; they should share in the high qualities of sovereignty rather than in its empty ceremonies; they should not delight in the defects of its vanity but share in its substantial worth.

104

Get to know the exigencies of different occupations. They vary from one to another: you need masterly skill and discernment to recognize them. Some demand courage, and others tact. It is easier to cope with those which depend upon integrity, and more difficult to handle those which demand craft. In the former, no more is required than a good character; in the latter, all one's care and vigilance may not be enough. Governing men is an arduous task, more especially idiots or fools. A double dose of sense is needed to deal with people who have none. A job which demands a man's whole attention hour after hour, and always to the same thing, is intolerable. Jobs which are free from boredom and which combine variety with responsibility are to be preferred, for a change refreshes the palate. The most reputable are those which involve very little dependence upon others; the worst job of all is that which makes us sweat in the courts of this world and even more in the heavenly ones.

105

No cansar. Suele ser pesado el hombre de un negocio y el de un verbo. La brevedad es lisonjera y más negociante. Gana por lo cortés lo que pierde por lo corto. Lo bueno, si breve, dos veces bueno. Y aun lo malo, si poco, no tan malo. Más obran quintas esencias que fárragos. Y es verdad común que, hombre largo, raras veces entendido: no tanto en lo material de la disposición, cuanto en lo formal del discurso. Hay hombres que sirven más de embarazo que de adorno del universo—alhajas perdidas, que todos las desvían. Excuse el discreto el embarazar; y mucho menos a grandes personajes, que viven muy ocupados, y sería peor desazonar uno de ellos que todo lo restante del mundo. Lo bien dicho se dice presto.

106

No afectar la fortuna. Más ofende el ostentar la dignidad que la persona. 'Hacer del hombre' es odioso: bastábale ser envidiado. La estimación se consigue menos cuanto se busca más. Depende del respeto ajeno, y así, no se la puede tomar uno, sino merecerla de los otros y aguardarla. Los empleos grandes piden autoridad ajustada a su ejercicio, sin la cual no pueden ejercerse dignamente. Conserve la que merece para cumplir con lo sustancial de sus obligaciones; no estrujarla, ayudarla sí. Y todos los que hacen del hacendado en el empleo dan indicio de que no lo merecían, y que viene sobrepuesta la dignidad. Si se hubiere de valer, sea antes de lo eminente de sus prendas que de lo adventicio; que hasta un rey se ha de venerar más por la personal que por la extrínseca soberanía.

107

No mostrar satisfacción de sí. Viva, ni descontento que es poquedad, ni satisfecho que es necedad. Nace la satisfacción en los más de ignorancia, y pára en una felicidad necia que, aunque

105

Do not be a bore. The man of one interest and one topic is generally dull. Brevity is agreeable and more profitable. It gains in courtesy what it loses in curtness. Good things, if brief, are doubly good. And even evil, where there is little of it, is not so bad. Pithiness is more effective than prolixity; and it is a generally accepted truth that a man 'full blown,' not so much in his physical make-up as, formally, in his discourse, is rarely sensible. There are some men who are more of a nuisance than an adornment to the world, worthless fellows whom every one avoids. A discreet man avoids being a nuisance, least of all to important people who live very busy lives, and it is more disastrous to annoy one of these than all the rest of the world put together. Well said is quickly said.

106

Do not give yourself airs in your position. It is more offensive to show off about your rank than about your personal qualities. It is hateful to pose as a 'somebody'; to be envied is surely enough. The more you seek esteem the less of it you will get. It depends upon the respect of others, so that it cannot be won by force, but must rather be deserved and awaited from others. High positions demand a degree of authority proportionate to their functions, without which the latter cannot be worthily discharged. Maintain, then, the authority to which you are entitled in order to fulfil your most important duties; protect it, by all means, but do not press it too far. All officious people show themselves to be unworthy of their office and that it is too big for them. If you must be appreciated, let it be because of the excellence of your qualities rather than for adventitious reasons; even a king should be honoured rather for his personal qualities than for his extrinsic sovereignty.

107

Do not appear self-satisfied. Be neither discontented, for that is mean-spirited, nor complacent, for that is foolish. In most people self-satisfaction is born of ignorance and ends in a stupid contentment which, although it pleases a man's fancy, does not

* E

entretiene el gusto, no mantiene el crédito.   Como no alcanza las superlativas perfecciones en los otros, págase de cualquiera vulgar medianía en sí.   Siempre fué útil, a más de cuerdo, el recelo: o para prevención de que salgan bien las cosas, o para consuelo cuando salieren mal; que no se le hace de nuevo el desaire de su suerte al que ya se lo temía.   El mismo Homero dormita tal vez, y cae Alejandro de su estado y de su engaño.   Dependen las cosas de muchas circunstancias, y la que triunfó en un puesto y en tal ocasión, en otra se malogra.   Pero la incorregibilidad de lo necio está en que se convirtió en flor la más vana satisfacción, y va brotando siempre su semilla.

108

Atajo para ser persona: saberse ladear.   Es muy eficaz el trato; comunícanse las costumbres y los gustos, pégase el genio y aun el ingenio sin sentir.   Procure, pues, el pronto juntarse con el reportado, y así en los demás genios; con [1] éste conseguirá la templanza sin violencia.   Es gran destreza saberse atemperar. La alternación de contrariedades hermosea el universo y le sustenta; y si causa armonía en lo natural, mayor en lo moral. Válgase de esta política advertencia en la elección de familiares y de famulares, que con la comunicación de los extremos, se ajustará un medio muy discreto.

109

No ser acriminador.   Hay hombres de genio fiero: todo lo hacen delito, y no por pasión, sino por naturaleza.   A todos condenan, a unos porque hicieron, a otros porque harán.   Indica ánimo peor que cruel, que es vil.   Y acriminan con tal exageración, que de los átomos hacen vigas para sacar los ojos.   Cómitres en cada puesto, que hacen galera de lo que fuera Elisio.   Pero

---

[1] 1653 and 1659 have 'con.'   Reyes has 'que en.'

uphold his reputation.   As it cannot attain to the superlative perfection of others, it delights in any poor, mediocre talent that it may itself possess.   Misgiving, in addition to being prudent, is always advantageous, either as a means of ensuring beforehand that things will turn out well, or as a consolation when they turn out badly; for bad luck is nothing new to the man who already feared it.   Even Homer himself nods at times, and Alexander fell from his high estate and was stripped of his illusions.   Things depend upon a large number of circumstances, and the man who succeeds in one position and on one occasion will fail in it on others.   But the incorrigibility of the fool resides in the fact that his emptiest ambition comes to flower, and that its seed is always sprouting.

108

A short cut to being a 'somebody': learn how to be a good mixer.   Social intercourse is very profitable; manners and tastes are communicated, character and even talent are unconsciously infectious.   Be quick, therefore, to frequent the company of the level-headed and, also, other [well-endowed] characters; for thus you may attain the golden mean without undue effort.   To know how to be accommodating is a great art.   The alternation of opposites embellishes and sustains the universe; and if it brings about harmony in the physical world, it does so all the more in the moral sphere.   Follow this wise counsel in your choice of associates and servants, for a very nice balance is to be adjusted by intercourse between extremes.

109

Do not be censorious.   There are men of a brutish disposition: they take offence at everything, and not so much out of perversity as from natural inclination.   They condemn everybody, some for what they have [already] done, others for what they may do in the future.   This is the mark of a worse than cruel nature; it is loathsome.   And so excessively censorious are these folk that from motes they build beams to gouge out one's eyes.   Hard taskmasters in every job, they would turn what might have been the Elysian fields into a prison.   If, moreover,

si media la pasión, de todo hacen extremos. Al contrario la ingenuidad: para todo halla[1] salida, si no de intención, de inadvertencia.

110

No aguardar a ser sol que se pone. Máxima es de cuerdos dejar las cosas antes que los dejen. Sepa uno hacer triunfo del mismo fenecer, que tal vez el mismo sol, a buen lucir, suele retirarse a una nube, porque no lo vean caer, y deja en suspension de si se puso o no se puso. Hurte el cuerpo a los acasos para no reventar de desaires; no aguarde a que le vuelvan las espaldas, que le sepultarán vivo para el sentimiento y muerto para la estimación. Jubila con tiempo el advertido al corredor caballo, y no aguarda a que cayendo levante la risa en medio la carrera; rompa el espejo con tiempo y con astucia la belleza, y no con impaciencia después al ver su desengaño.

111

Tener amigos. Es el segundo ser. Todo amigo es bueno y sabio para el amigo. Entre ellos todo sale bien. Tanto valdrá uno cuanto quisieren los demás; y para que quieran, se les ha de ganar la boca por el corazón. No hay hechizo como el buen servicio, y para ganar amistades, el mejor medio es hacerlas. Depende lo más y lo mejor que tenemos de los otros. Hase de vivir[2] o con amigos o con enemigos: cada día se ha de diligenciar uno, aunque no para íntimo, para aficionado; que algunos se quedan después para confidentes pasando por el acierto del delecto.

112

Ganar la pía afición: que aun la primera y suma causa en sus mayores asuntos la previene y la dispone. Éntrase por el afecto al concepto: algunos se fían tanto del valor que desestiman la diligencia; pero la atención sabe bien que es grande el rodeo de solos los méritos, si no se ayudan del favor: todo lo facilita y

---

[1] 1653 and 1659 have 'halla.' Reyes has 'haya.'
[2] 1653 and 1659 have 'vivir.' Reyes has 'servir.'

passion intervenes, they go to extremes in everything. The contrary is the case with the frank: they find a way out for everything, if not by direct excuse, then by turning a blind eye.

110

Do not wait for the sunset of your reputation. It is a maxim of the wise to leave things before things leave them. One should know how to convert even an eclipse into a victory; for the sun itself, when shining brilliantly, sometimes retires behind a cloud so that it may not be seen to sink, and thus leaves us in doubt whether it has set or not. Avoid occasions of misadventure so that you may not be irritated by rebuffs; do not wait until you are given the cold shoulder, for if you do you will be carried to your grave, a living object of pity, but dead to esteem. A wise owner puts a racehorse out to grass in time and does not wait until it provokes derision by collapsing in the middle of a race; a shrewd beauty should take care to smash her mirror in good time, and not too late, out of impatience at seeing her illusions shattered.

111

Have friends. A friend is a second self. Every friend is virtuous and wise in the eyes of his friend. Between friends, everything turns out well. Each man has the value which others may choose to put upon him; and to gain their regard he must win their lips through their hearts. There is no charm so efficacious as a good turn; and the best way to win friendship is to make friends. The greatest and best that we have depends upon others. We must live, among either friends or enemies: try to find a friend every day, if not as a boon companion, then as a well-wisher; for some of these will later become intimates when once you have contrived to win their regard.

112

Win affection: for thus even the first and sovereign cause of all things foresees and furthers its greatest objects. By winning men's affection you gain their esteem: some put so much faith in courage that they underrate diligence; but the heedful know very well that merits alone have a long and roundabout way to go if

suple la benevolencia; no siempre supone las prendas, sino que
las pone, como el valor, la entereza, la sabiduría, hasta la discreción; nunca ve las fealdades, porque no las querría ver: nace,
de ordinario, de la correspondencia material en genio, nación,
parentesco, patria y empleo. La formal es más sublime en
prendas, obligaciones, reputación, méritos: toda la dificultad es
ganarla, que con facilidad se conserva; puédese diligenciar y
saberse valer de ella.

113

Prevenirse en la fortuna próspera para la adversa. Arbitrio es
hacer en el estío provisión para el invierno, y con más comodidad;
van baratos entonces los favores, hay abundancia de amistades;
bueno es conservar para el mal tiempo, que es la adversidad cara
y falta de todo. Haya retén de amigos y de agradecidos, que
algún día hará aprecio de lo que ahora no hace caso. La
villanía nunca tiene amigos en la prosperidad, porque los des-
conoce; en la adversidad, la desconocen a ella.

114

Nunca competir. Toda pretensión con oposición daña el
crédito; la competencia tira luego a desdorar, por deslucir. Son
pocos los que hacen buena guerra; descubre la emulación los
defectos que olvidó la cortesía: vivieron muchos acreditados,
mientras no tuvieron émulos. El calor de la contrariedad aviva
o resucita las infamias muertas, desentierra hediondeces pasadas
y antepasadas. Comiénzase la competencia con manifiesto de
desdoros, ayudándose de cuanto puede y no debe; y aunque a
veces y las más no sean armas de provecho las ofensas, hace de
ellas vil satisfacción a su venganza, y sacude ésta con tal aire que
hace saltar a los desaires el polvo del olvido. Siempre fué
pacífica la benevolencia y benévola la reputación.

they are not assisted by favour: goodwill procures everything and expedites everything; this does not always imply the existence of high qualities in its object; rather does it supply those qualities, such as courage, integrity, wisdom, even discretion; it never notices failings because it does not want to see them; it usually arises from the possession of some material quality in common: temperament, nationality, kinship, common citizenship, and office. There is a higher, or formal kind of sympathy which arises out of a similarity of gifts, duties, reputation, merits: the whole difficulty lies in winning goodwill, for it is easy to preserve; it can be acquired with effort and you can learn how to profit by it.

113

In times of prosperity, prepare for adversity. It is a good idea, and easier, to make provision for the winter during the summer; favours are going cheap then and there are friends in abundance; it is a good thing to keep something aside for bad times, for adversity costs dear and is lacking in everything. Let there be a reserve of friends and grateful debtors, for one day you will appreciate what is of no importance to you at the moment. In times of prosperity, a mean fellow never has friends because he disowns them; in adversity, they disown him.

114

Never compete. Every claim which encounters opposition damages your reputation; your rivals at once aim at belittling you in order to tarnish your good name. Those who wage war honourably are few in number; envy discloses faults which courtesy has forgotten: many have enjoyed a good reputation while they had no rivals. The heat of conflict revives, or resurrects, dead infamies; it digs up old, long-buried filth. Rivalry starts with the disclosure of failings by every possible means, legitimate and illegitimate, and although, sometimes, and in the majority of cases, insults are not satisfactory weapons, a rival will use them to wreak his ill-conditioned vengeance, and beat about with such fury that he shakes the dust of oblivion from our discreditable behaviour. Men of goodwill are always peaceable, and those of good repute always well-disposed.

115

Hacerse a las malas condiciones de los familiares, así como a los malos rostros.   Es conveniencia donde tercia dependencia.   Hay fieros genios que no se puede vivir con ellos, ni sin ellos.   Es, pues, destreza irse acostumbrando como a la fealdad, para que no se hagan de nuevo en la terribilidad de la ocasión.   La primera vez espantan; pero poco a poco se les viene a perder aquel primer horror; y la reflexa previene los disgustos o los tolera.

116

Tratar siempre con gente de obligaciones.   Puede empeñarse con ellos y empeñarlos.   Su misma obligación es la mayor fianza de su trato, aun para barajar, que obran como quien son; y vale más pelear con gente de bien que triunfar de gente de mal.   No hay buen trato con la ruindad, porque no se halla obligada a la entereza; por eso entre ruines nunca hay verdadera amistad, ni es de buena ley la fineza aunque lo parezca, porque no es en fe de la honra.   Reniegue siempre de hombre sin ella, que quien no la estima, no estima la virtud; y es la honra el trono de la entereza.

117

Nunca hablar de sí.   O se ha de alabar que es desvanecimiento, o se ha de vituperar, que es poquedad: y siendo culpa de cordura en el que dice, es pena de los que oyen.   Si esto se ha de evitar en la familiaridad, mucho más en puestos sublimes, donde se habla en común, y pasa ya por necedad cualquier apariencia de ella.   El mismo inconveniente de cordura tiene el hablar de los presentes, por el peligro de dar en uno de dos escollos de lisonja o vituperio.

115

Get used to ill nature in your domestic circle, just as you do to ugly faces.   It is convenient to do so, where mutual dependence is involved.   There are some turbulent characters whom you can neither live with nor live without.   It is, therefore, a shrewd scheme to get used to them as you do to ugliness, so that they do not repel you again and again on every fresh occasion of your meeting with them.   They horrify you at first; but they gradually lose their original repulsiveness; and upon reflection, disgust is either forestalled or tolerated.

116

Always deal with men of honour.   You can enter into mutually binding agreements with them.   Their word is itself the best guarantee of their conduct, even in disputes, for they act according to their nature; and it is better to fight with men of honour than to triumph over rogues.   You cannot have satisfactory dealings with worthless people because they do not regard themselves as bound by the laws of honour; thus there is no true friendship among rogues; nor, despite appearances, is courtesy among them genuine, for it is not rooted in honesty.   Always avoid the company of a dishonourable person: for he who has no regard for honour has none for virtue; and honour is the throne of integrity.

117

Never talk about yourself.   [If you do,] you must either praise yourself, which is vain, or belittle yourself, which is mean-spirited: and indiscretion on the part of the speaker is a source of vexation to his hearers.   If this fault should be avoided in ordinary conversation, it is much more to be eschewed in high positions, which involve public speaking, and in which every semblance of folly is at once regarded as folly itself.   The same lack of discretion is evinced by talking about people in their presence, on account of the risk you run of foundering upon one of two reefs: that of flattery or that of censoriousness.

118

Cobrar fama de cortés, que basta a hacerle plausible.   Es la
cortesía la principal parte de la cultura, especie de hechizo; y así
concilia la gracia de todos, así como la descortesía el desprecio y
enfado universal.   Si ésta nace de soberbia, es aborrecible; si
de grosería, despreciable.   La cortesía siempre ha de ser más que
menos, pero no igual, que degeneraría en injusticia: tiénese por
deuda entre enemigos.   Para que se vea su valor, cuesta poco y
vale mucho; todo honrador es honrado.   La galantería y la
honra tienen esta ventaja, que se quedan, aquélla en quien la usa,
ésta en quien la hace.

119

No hacerse de mal querer.   No se ha de provocar la aversión,
que aun sin quererlo, ella se adelanta.   Muchos hay que aborrecen de balde, sin saber el cómo ni por qué.   Previene la
malevolencia a la obligación.   Es más eficaz y pronta para el
daño la irascible, que la concupiscible para el provecho.   Afectan
algunos ponerse mal con todos, por enfadoso o por enfadado
genio: y si una vez se apodera el odio, es, como el mal concepto,
dificultoso de borrar.   A los hombres juiciosos los temen; a los
maldicientes aborrecen; a los presumidos asquean; a los fisgones
abominan; a los singulares los dejan.   Muestre, pues, estimar
para ser estimado: y el que quiere hacer casa hace caso:

120

Vivir a lo plático.   Hasta el saber ha de ser al uso; y donde no
se usa, es preciso saber hacer del ignorante.   Múdanse a tiempos
el discurrir y el gustar.   No se ha de discurrir a lo viejo, y se ha
de gustar a lo moderno.   El gusto, de las cabezas[1] hace voto en

---

[1] *Vide* Appendix, p. 306.

118

Acquire a reputation for being polite, for it suffices to make you agreeable. Politeness is the chief ingredient of culture, a kind of witchery; and it thus wins the regard of all, just as discourtesy [fosters] universal contempt and irritation. If rudeness springs from arrogance it is detestable; if from ill breeding, contemptible. Too much politeness is always better than too little, but courtesy should not always be exhibited to the same degree, for it would [then] degenerate into injustice: between enemies, it is a duty. So that its value may be apparent, it costs little and is worth much; every one who pays respect is worthy of it. Courtesy and honour have this advantage, that each becomes a personal attribute, the former of those who show it, the latter of those who confer it.

119

Do not get yourself disliked. You must not provoke aversion, for it comes quickly enough without being sought for. There are many who hate for no reason at all, without knowing the why or wherefore of their detestation. Malevolence forestalls the duty [to please]. Ill-natured people are better able and more ready to do harm to others than they are eager in the furtherance of their own interests. Some like to be on bad terms with everybody, either because they are contentious, or because they have an irritable disposition: and if once hatred has taken root it is, like ill repute, difficult to remove. Men of good sense are feared; slanderers are detested; the presumptuous arouse disgust; Paul Prys are loathed; eccentrics are left alone. Show respect, therefore, in order that you may be respected: the man who wants to establish himself in the world takes this into account.

120

Live practically. Even knowledge must be in the fashion; and when it is not, you must know how to affect ignorance. Conversation and tastes change with the times. Do not be old-fashioned in your manner of speech, and let your tastes be up to date. Fashion, in every sphere, is determined by the vote of the

cada orden de cosas. Ese se ha de seguir por entonces y adelantar a eminencia : acomódese el cuerpo a lo presente, aunque le parezca mejor lo pasado, así en los arreos del alma como del cuerpo. Sólo en la bondad no vale esta regla de vivir, que siempre se ha de platicar la virtud. Desconócese ya, y parece cosa de otros tiempos el decir verdad, el guardar palabra, y los varones buenos parecen hechos al buen tiempo, pero siempre amados, de suerte, que si algunos hay, no se usan ni se imitan. ¡Oh, grande infelicidad del siglo nuestro que se tenga la virtud por extraña y la malicia por corriente! Viva el discreto como puede, si no como querría. Tenga por mejor lo que le concedió la suerte que lo que le ha negado.

121

No hacer negocio del no negocio. Así como algunos todo lo hacen cuento, así otros todo negocio. Siempre hablan de importancia, todo lo toman de veras, reduciéndolo a pendencia y a misterio. Pocas cosas de enfado se han de tomar de propósito, que sería empeñarse sin él. Es trocar los puntos tomar a pechos lo que se ha de echar a las espaldas. Muchas cosas que eran algo, dejándolas, fueron nada ; y otras que eran nada, por haber hecho caso de ellas, fueron mucho. Al principio es fácil dar fin a todo ; que después, no. Muchas veces hace la enfermedad el mismo remedio ; ni es la peor regla del vivir el dejar estar.

122

Señorío en el decir y en el hacer. Hácese mucho lugar en todas partes, y gana de antemano el respeto. En todo influye : en el conversar, en el orar, hasta en el caminar y aún el mirar ; en el querer. Es gran victoria coger los corazones ; no nace de una necia intrepidez, ni del enfadoso entremetimiento ;[1] sí en una decente autoridad, nacida del genio superior y ayudada de los méritos.

[1] *Vide* Appendix, p. 306.

élite.   It must then be followed for the time and assist you [on the road] to eminence: even though the past may appear better to you, come to terms with the present in both your mental and physical make-up.   This rule of life is alone inapplicable to virtue, for virtue must always be practised.   The habit of telling the truth and keeping one's word is unknown to-day and seems to belong to a bygone age; and good men, though always loved, appear to belong rather to the good old days, so that if any now exist they are not in the fashion and nobody follows their example.   What a misfortune it is for our age that it should look upon virtue as peculiar and vice as normal!   Let the sensible man live as best he can if he cannot live as he would wish. Regard what Fortune has bestowed upon you as being better than what she has denied you.

121

Avoid much ado about nothing.   As some make gossip out of everything, so others make much ado about everything.   They are always talking big, [and] take everything seriously, making a quarrel and a mystery of it.   You should take very few grievances to heart, for to do so is to give yourself groundless worry. It is a topsyturvy way of behaving to take to heart cares which you ought to throw over your shoulder.   Many things which seemed important [at the time] turn out to be of no account when they are ignored; and others, which seem trifling, appear formidable when you pay attention to them.   Things can easily be settled at the outset, but not so later on.   In many cases, the remedy itself is the cause of the disease: to let things be is not the least satisfactory of life's rules.

122

Authority in word and deed.   This creates a strong position everywhere, and wins respect in advance.   Its influence is apparent in everything: in conversation, public speaking, even in gait and glance; and in your affections.   It is a great victory to capture men's hearts; it does not arise out of foolish intrepidity, nor offensive behaviour, but by wearing that modest air of authority which is born of superior talent supported by merit.

123

Hombre desafectado.   A más prendas menos afectación, que suele ser vulgar desdoro de todas.   Es tan enfadosa a los demás, cuan penosa al que la sustenta, porque vive mártir del cuidado y se atormenta con la puntualidad.   Pierden su mérito las mismas eminencias con ella, porque se juzgan nacidas antes de la artificiosa violencia que de la libre naturaleza, y todo lo natural fué siempre más grato que lo artificial.   Los afectados son tenidos por extranjeros en lo que afectan: cuanto mejor se hace una cosa se ha de desmentir la industria, porque se vea que se cae de su natural la perfección.   Ni por huir la afectación se ha de dar en ella, afectando el no afectar; nunca el discreto se ha de dar por entendido de sus méritos, que el mismo descuido despierta en los otros la atención.   Dos veces es eminente el que encierra todas las perfecciones en sí, y ninguna en su estimación, y por encontrada senda llega al término de la plausibilidad.

124

Llegar a ser deseado.   Pocos llegaron a tanta gracia de las gentes; y si de los cuerdos, felicidad.   Es ordinaria la tibieza con los que acaban.   Hay modos para merecer este premio de afición: la eminencia en el empleo y en las prendas es segura, el agrado eficaz.   Hácese dependencia de la eminencia, de modo que se note que el cargo le hubo menester a él, y no él al cargo: honran unos los puestos, a otros honran.   No es ventaja que le haga bueno el que sucedió malo, porque eso no es ser deseado absolutamente, sino ser el otro aborrecido.

125

No ser libro verde.[1]   Señal de tener gastada la fama propia es cuidar de la infamia ajena: querrían algunos con las manchas de

[1] *Vide* Appendix, p. 306.

123

The unaffected man.   The more numerous the gifts, the less affectation there should be, for that is wont to be a vulgar blot upon all talents.   Affectation is as vexatious to others as it is troublesome to the one who fosters it, because he lives a martyr to care and torments himself over punctilios.   Even high qualities lose their merit is accompanied by affectation, for they are judged to arise from artificial effort rather than from spontaneous inclination and everything natural is always more pleasing than the artificial.   Affected persons are held to be lacking in the qualities they affect: the better you do a thing, the more necessary it is to conceal the effort you make to do it, so that your ability may appear to spring from your natural gifts.   Nor should you be guilty of affectation by avoiding it, by affecting to be unaffected; the wise man should never appear to be conscious of his merits, for his very disregard of them attracts the attention of others. The man who enshrines within himself all the talents while believing himself to possess none, and who reaches the goal of esteem by the road leading in the opposite direction, is doubly distinguished.

124

Come to be sought after.   Few attain to such favour among men; and if they do so in the eyes of the wise they are lucky. Those who are at the end of their career usually command but lukewarm respect.   There are ways of meriting this prize of regard: distinction in office and in talents is a sure means, and an agreeable manner is effective.   See that your position depends upon your endowments, so that it may be observed that your job was in need of your abilities and not your abilities of your job: some are honoured by their positions, others do honour to them.   It is of no advantage to you to appear good because of your successor's shortcomings, for that is not to be wanted for your own sake, but rather because the other fellow is detested.

125

Do not be a scandalmonger.   To concern yourself with the disreputability of others is a sign that your own reputation is in a

los otros disimular, si no lavar las suyas; o se consuelan, que es el consuelo de los necios. Huéleles mal la boca a éstos, que son los albañares de las inmundicias civiles. En estas materias, el que más escarba más se enloda; pocos se escapan de algún achaque original, o al derecho o al través. No son conocidas las faltas en los poco conocidos: huya el atento de ser registro de infamias, que es ser un aborrecido padrón; y aunque vivo, desalmado.

126

No es necio el que hace la necedad, sino el que hecha, no la sabe encubrir. Hanse de sellar los afectos, cuanto más los defectos. Todos los hombres yerran, pero con esta diferencia, que los sagaces desmienten las hechas, y los necios mientan las por hacer.[1] Consiste el crédito en el recato, más que en el hecho, que si no es uno casto sea cauto. Los descuidos de los grandes hombres se observan más como eclipses de las lumbreras mayores. Sea excepción de la amistad el no confiarla los defectos, ni aun, si ser pudiese, a su misma identidad; pero puédese valer aquí de aquella otra regla del vivir, que es saber olvidar.

127

El despejo en todo. Es vida de las prendas, aliento del decir, alma del hacer, realce de los mismos realces. Las demás perfecciones son ornato de la naturaleza; pero el despejo lo es de las mismas perfecciones. Hasta en el discurrir se celebra. Tiene de privilegio lo más; debe al estudio lo menos, que aun a la disciplina es superior; pasa de facilidad, y adelántase a bizarría; supone desembarazo y añade perfección; sin él, toda belleza es muerta y toda gracia, desgracia; es trascendental al valor, a la discreción, a la prudencia, a la misma majestad. Es político atajo en el despacho, y un culto salir de todo empeño.

[1] *Vide* Appendix, p. 306.

bad way: some people would like to conceal, if not wash out, the stains upon their own character by means of the shortcomings of others: or they console themselves with the latter, and that is the consolation of fools. Those who are sewers for the filth of the town have a stinking breath. In these matters, the more a man pokes about the filthier he gets. In one way or another, few are free from some natural failing. The faults of the little known pass unnoticed; let the cautious man avoid becoming a registrar of scandals, for that is to be a detested token of infamy and, though alive, to be without a soul.

126

The man who does a foolish thing is not a fool; rather is he a fool who, having done it, is incapable of concealing it. You should keep your emotions under the seal of secrecy, still more your failings. All men make mistakes, but with this distinction, that the wise conceal the blunders they have made while fools proclaim those which they are about to make. Your good name depends not so much upon what you do as upon the discreet way in which you do it. If you can't be good be careful. The slips of great men are more closely observed [than those of others], as are the eclipses of the larger luminaries. Do not confide your failings even to your friends, nor, if that be possible, admit them even to yourself: but here you can abide by another rule of life, namely: know how to forget.

127

Charm in everything. Charm is the life of natural endowments, the breath of speech, the soul of action, the adornment of adornments themselves. Other gifts are a natural embellishment; but charm is the adornment of perfection itself. It is appreciated even in discourse. It is, in the main, a gift; it owes least to study and even rises above discipline; it is more than ease of deportment, and is superior to gallantry; it implies a natural manner and adds the finishing touch [to everything]; without it all beauty is lifeless and all grace, disgrace; it surpasses courage, discretion, prudence, sovereignty itself. It provides a polite and speedy means to the achievement of one's ends, and an urbane way out of every tight corner.

128

Alteza de ánimo. Es de los principales requisitos para héroe, porque inflama a todo género de grandeza: realza el gusto, engrandece el corazón, remonta el pensamiento, ennoblece la condición y dispone la majestad. Dondequiera que se halla descuella, y aun tal vez desmentida de la envidia de la suerte, revienta por campear, ensánchase en la voluntad, ya que en la posibilidad se violente. Reconócenla por fuente la magnanimidad, la generosidad, y toda heroica prenda.

129

Nunca quejarse. La queja siempre trae descrédito: más sirve de ejemplar de atrevimiento a la pasión, que de consuelo a la compasión; abre el paso a quien la oye para lo mismo, y es la noticia del agravio del primero, disculpa del segundo. Dan pie algunos con sus quejas de las ofensiones pasadas, a las venideras, y pretendiendo remedio o consuelo, solicitan la complacencia, y aun el desprecio. Mejor política es celebrar obligaciones de unos para que sean empeños de otros; y el repetir favores de los ausentes es solicitarlos de los presentes, es vender crédito de unos a otros; y el varón atento nunca publique ni desaires ni defectos: sí estimaciones, que sirven para tener amigos y de contener enemigos.

130

Hacer, y hacer parecer. Las cosas no pasan por lo que son, sino por lo que parecen. Valer y saberlo mostrar, es saber dos veces: lo que no se ve es como si no fuese. No tiene su veneración la razón misma, donde no tiene cara de tal. Son muchos más los engañados que los advertidos; prevalece el engaño y júzganse las cosas por fuera; hay cosas que son muy otras de lo que parecen. La buena exterioridad es la mejor recomendación de la perfección interior.

128

High courage. This is one of the chief requisites for a hero, for it spurs him on to all kinds of great exploits: it improves the taste, exalts the heart, elevates the mind, ennobles the character, and is conducive to majesty. It stands out wherever it is found, and although it is sometimes belied by the envy of fortune, it is eager to excel and widens the scope of the will, since it may overcome disinclination to act. Magnanimity, generosity, and every heroic quality recognize it as their source.

129

Never complain. Complaint always brings discredit in its train: it serves rather to stimulate the audacity of the hostile than to prompt the compassionate to console you; it opens the way for those who hear it to behave in the same fashion, and the disclosure of the insult to the first party provides an excuse for another, by the second. Some people open the way to future injuries by complaining of others in the past, and in seeking a remedy or consolation they court condescension and even contempt. It is better policy to proclaim the benefits you have received from some people, and thereby prompt others to favour you likewise; and to recount favours granted by the absent is to solicit them from those who are present; it is to sell to the latter the credit you have with the former. And a sensible man should never broadcast either his disappointments or his failings, but rather the marks of consideration he has received, for the latter serve to retain friends and contain enemies.

130

Act, and let it be seen that you are doing so. Things do not pass for what they are but for what they seem. To be worthy and to know how to show your worth is to be doubly wise: what is not seen is as though it did not exist. Even reason itself is not revered when it lacks the semblance of reason. Those who are deceived by appearances are far more numerous than the observant; deceit prevails, and things are judged by their outward seeming; some things are very different from what they appear to be. A good exterior is the best witness to interior perfection.

131

Galantería de condición. Tienen su bizarría las almas, gallardía del espíritu, con cuyos galantes actos queda muy airoso un corazón. No cabe en todos, porque supone magnanimidad. Primer[1] asunto suyo es hablar bien del enemigo y obrar mejor; su mayor lucimiento libra en los lances de la venganza. No se los quita, sino que se los mejora, convirtiéndola, cuando más vencedora, en una impensada generosidad. Es política también, y aun la gala de la razón de Estado. Nunca afecta vencimientos, porque nada afecta; y cuando los alcanza el merecimiento, los disimula la ingenuidad.

132

Usar del reconsejo. Apelar a la revista es seguridad, y más donde no es evidente la satisfacción. Tomar tiempo, o para conceder o para mejorarse. Ofrécense nuevas razones para confirmar y corroborar el dictamen: si es en materia de dar, se estima más el don en fe de la cordura que en el gusto de la presteza: siempre fué más estimado lo deseado: si se ha de negar, queda[2] lugar al modo, y para madurar el no, que sea más sazonado. Y las más veces, pasado aquel primer calor del deseo, no se siente después a sangre fría el desaire del negar. A quien pide aprisa, conceder tarde, que es treta para desmentir la atención.

133

Antes loco con todos que cuerdo a solas, dicen políticos. Que si todos lo son, con ninguno perderá; y si es sola la cordura, será tenida por locura. Tanto importará seguir la corriente: es el mayor saber a veces no saber, o afectar no saber. Hase de vivir con los otros, y los ignorantes son los más. Para vivir a solas ha

---

[1] 1653 and 1659 have 'primero.'
[2] 1653 and 1659 have 'que da.'

131

A chivalrous nature. There is a generosity of soul, a nobility of spirit, which prompts us to gallant deeds by virtue of which the heart becomes very gracious. It is not to be found in every one, for it implies magnanimity. Its chief concern is to speak well of an enemy and to behave even better; it is seen at its best when occasions for revenge arise: not merely does it let such opportunities pass by, but improves upon them, turning revenge, at its most alluring, into unexpected generosity. It is good policy, too, and the acme of statecraft. It makes no pretence to conquests because it pretends to nothing; and when its merit wins victories its modesty conceals them.

132

Make use of reconsideration. To have recourse to reconsideration is a safe policy, especially when there is no obvious and satisfactory solution to a problem. Take time, both in granting favours and in improving your position. New arguments present themselves to confirm and corroborate your judgment: if it is a matter of giving, the gift is prized rather by virtue of the discernment [of the donor] than on account of the pleasure derived from its speedy bestowal. What is coveted is always most highly valued; if you must refuse, room remains for consideration of the manner of your refusal, so that it may be, as it were, mature, and thus more palatable. And, in the majority of cases, once the first heat of desire has subsided, the disappointment occasioned by a refusal is not felt, in cold blood. When a pressing request is made, do not be in a hurry to grant it, for [the urgency of the demand] is a trick to disarm your caution.

133

Better mad with the mob than sane by yourself, say the politicians. For if every one is mad, you will be no worse off than anybody else; and if sanity is unique, it will be regarded as folly. So important is it to swim with the stream: not to know, or to pretend not to know, is sometimes the highest form of knowledge. You are obliged to live with other people, and most of them are fools. 'To live alone you must be either very much like God,

de tener o mucho de Dios, o todo de bestia; mas yo moderaría el aforismo, diciendo: 'Antes cuerdo con los demás, que loco a solas.' Algunos quieren ser singulares en las quimeras.

134

Doblar los requisitos de la vida. Es doblar el vivir. No ha de ser única la dependencia, ni se ha de estrechar a una cosa sola, aunque singular: todo ha de ser doblado, y más las causas del provecho, del favor, del gusto. Es trascendente la mutabilidad de la luna, término de la permanencia, y más las cosas que dependen de la humana voluntad, que es quebradiza. Valga contra la fragilidad el retén, y sea gran regla del arte del vivir doblar las circunstancias del bien y de la comodidad. Así como dobló la naturaleza los miembros más importantes y más arriesgados, así el arte los de la dependencia.

135

No tenga espíritu de contradicción, que es cargarse de necedad y de enfado. Conjurarse ha contra él la cordura: bien puede ser ingenioso el dificultar en todo, pero no se escapa de necio lo porfiado. Hacen éstos guerrilla de la dulce conversación, y así son enemigos más de los familiares que de los que no les tratan. En el más sabroso bocado se siente más la espina que se atraviesa, y eslo la contradicción de los buenos ratos: son necios, perniciosos, que añaden lo fiera a lo bestia.

136

Ponerse bien en las materias; tomar el pulso luego a los negocios. Vanse muchos, o por las ramas de un inútil discurrir, o por las hojas de una cansada verbosidad, sin topar con la sustancia del caso; dan cien vueltas rodeando un punto, cansándose y cansando, y nunca llegan al centro de la importancia.

or altogether like a beast'; but I would modify the aphorism and say: 'Better sane with the other fellows than crazy on your own.' Some people like to be notorious on account of their fads.

134

Have a double store of the necessities of life. This is to live two lives. You must not depend upon one thing only, nor must you confine yourself to one thing only, though its value be unique: there should be a double supply of everything, and more especially of those things which are the source of profit, favour, and delight. The mutability of the moon is all-pervasive and puts a term to all existence, especially to those things which depend upon our human will, which is frail. Let your reserves protect you against this frailty, and let it be a fundamental rule of the art of living to duplicate your store of those things which provide comfort and well-being. Just as nature has duplicated the most important of our limbs, to wit, those most exposed to danger, so the shrewd should deal with those qualities upon which their well-being depends.

135

Do not be of a contentious turn of mind, for that is to burden yourself with folly and vexation. Wisdom should conspire against this attitude of mind: it may well be clever to make difficulties about everything, but opinionated folk are, inescapably, fools. They turn agreeable conversation into guerilla warfare, and are thus enemies of their intimates rather than of those who have no truck with them. The tastier the morsel, the more conscious one is of the bone which runs through it, and contention is the bone of agreeable moments: those who pile violence upon stupidity are fools, and pernicious fools at that.

136

Be well informed; feel the pulse of affairs right away. Many wander off either into the ramifications of futile discussion or the exfoliations of a wearisome verbosity and never come to the heart of the matter; they wander around the point a hundred times, wearying both themselves and others, and never get to the

Procede de entendimientos confusos que no se saben desembarazar. Gastan el tiempo y la paciencia en lo que habían de dejar, y después no la hay para lo que dejaron.

137

Bástese a sí mismo el sabio. El será todas sus cosas, y llevándose a sí lo llevaba todo. Si un amigo universal basta hacer Roma, y todo lo restante del universo, séase uno ese amigo de sí propio y podrá vivirse a solas. ¿Quién le podrá hacer falta, si no hay ni mayor concepto ni mayor gusto que el suyo? Dependerá de sí solo, que es felicidad suma semejar a la entidad suma. El que puede pasar así a solas, nada tendrá de bruto, sino mucho de sabio y todo de Dios.

138

Arte de dejar estar, y más cuando más revuelta la común mar o la familiar. Hay torbellinos en el humano trato, tempestades de voluntad: entonces es cordura retirarse al seguro puerto del dar vado. Muchas veces empeoran los malos con los remedios. Dejar hacer a la naturaleza allí, y aquí a la moralidad: tanto ha de saber el sabio médico para recetar como para no recetar, y a veces consiste el arte más en el no aplicar remedios. Sea modo de sosegar vulgares torbellinos el alzar la mano y dejar sosegar; ceder al tiempo ahora, será vencer después. Una fuente con poca inquietud se enturbia; ni se volverá a serenar procurándolo, sino dejándola. No hay mejor remedio de los desconciertos que dejarlos correr, que así caen de sí propios.

139

Conocer el día aciago, que los hay. Nada saldrá bien, y aunque se varíe el juego, pero no la mala suerte. A dos lances,

root of the matter in hand. This arises out of a confusion of mind from which they are unable to extricate themselves. They waste both time and patience upon what they should have left alone, and afterwards have no patience [left] for what they have neglected.

137

The wise man should be self-sufficient. He will be all in all to himself and, possessing himself, will possess everything. If to have a friend of parts is to possess Rome itself and all the world besides, let a man be such a friend to himself and he will be able to live alone. Of whom can such a man be in need if there is no understanding or taste higher than his own? He will depend upon himself alone and it is the highest form of happiness to resemble the highest form of being. He who can thus contrive to pass [his days] alone will have nothing of the brute about him, but much of the sage, and will be, in every way, like God.

138

It is a shrewd device to let things be, and more especially when the seas of public or domestic life are at their stormiest. There are whirlwinds in the affairs of men, tempests of the will: it is then wise to retire to a safe harbour and ride at anchor. Evils are often aggravated by remedies. In the case of the former, you should leave things to the moral sense, and, in that of the latter, to nature; the clever doctor must know just as much in order not to prescribe as to prescribe, and there are times when skill lies rather in applying no remedies. Let it be your way to still the whirlwinds of the mob to hold your hand and allow them to subside; to yield to the storm now will be to conquer later on. A spring needs but little stirring to make it turbid; nor will it be calmed again by effort, but by leaving it alone. There is no better cure for disorders than to let them run [their course], for in this way they vanish of their own accord.

139

Know your unlucky days, for there are such. Nothing will go well [on such days] and, although you may vary your [mode of] play, your bad luck will not change. After [one or] two throws,

F

convendrá conocerla y retirarse, advirtiendo si está de día o no lo está.   Hasta en el entendimiento, hay vez, que ninguno supo a todas horas.   Es ventura acertar a discurrir, como el escribir bien una carta.   Todas las perfecciones dependen de sazón.   Ni siempre la belleza está de vez.   Desmiéntese la discreción a sí misma, ya cediendo, ya excediendo; y todo, para salir bien, ha de estar de día.   Así como en unos todo sale mal, en otros todo bien y con menos diligencias.   Todo se lo halla uno hecho: el ingenio está de vez, el genio de temple y todo de estrella.   Entonces conviene lograrla, y no despreciar la menor partícula.   Pero el varón juicioso, no por un azar que vió sentencie definitivamente de malo, ni al contrario, de bueno; que pudo ser aquéllo desazón, y esto ventura.

140

Topar luego con lo bueno en cada cosa.   Es dicha del buen gusto. Va luego la abeja a la dulzura para el panal, y la víbora a la amargura para el veneno.   Así los gustos; unos a lo mejor y otros a lo peor; no hay cosa que no tenga algo bueno, y más si es libro, por lo pensado.   Es, pues, tan desgraciado el genio de algunos, que entre mil perfecciones toparán con sólo un defecto que hubiere, y ése lo censuran y lo celebran; recogedores de las inmundicias de voluntades y de entendimientos, cargando de notas de defectos, que es más castigo de su mal delecto que empleo de su sutileza. Pasan mala vida, pues siempre se ceban de amarguras y hacen pasto de imperfecciones.   Más feliz es el gusto de otros, que entre mil defectos toparán luego con una sola perfección que se le cayó a la ventura.

it will be advisable to recognize this, retire, and find out whether it is your lucky day or not. Even the mind has its seasons, for nobody is wise all the time. Chance plays its part in successful conversation, as it does in the writing of a good letter. All high qualities depend upon their times and seasons. Even beauty is not always up to the mark. Discretion betrays itself, sometimes by yielding, sometimes by going too far ; and everything, if it is to have a happy issue, must be done on a propitious day. Just as on some days everything goes badly, so on others all goes well, and with less effort on our part. Everything seems to be already done for us : wit rises to the occasion, we are in a good mood and our lucky star is everywhere in the ascendant. At such times, we must profit by the opportunity and must not neglect the slightest detail. Nevertheless, a shrewd man should not finally judge a day to be ill-omened or, on the contrary, auspicious, merely on account of one chance happening, for the latter might be no more than a stroke of luck, bad or good.

140

Hit upon the good in everything from the start. To do so is the good fortune of good taste. The bee goes straight to the sweet [flower] for its honey, and the viper to the gall for its venom. So it is with tastes ; some seek the best, others the worst ; there is nothing that has not some good in it, especially if it is a book, for a book provides food for thought. Some folk, moreover, are by nature so miserable that, among a thousand good qualities, they will hit upon one solitary defect, if such exists, and this they censure and proclaim from the house tops ; they are the scavengers of unclean wills and minds, burdening themselves with records of shortcomings, an occupation which is rather a punishment for their low taste than an exercise of their skill. They lead a wretched life, for they are always gorging themselves with bitterness and battening upon imperfections. Those others have a happier disposition who, among a thousand blemishes, will hit at once upon a single good quality, which they have come upon by mere chance.

141

No escucharse.   Poco aprovecha agradarse a sí, si no contenta a los demás; y de ordinario castiga el desprecio común
la satisfacción particular.   Débese a todos el que se paga de sí
mismo.   Querer hablar y oirse no sale bien; y si hablarse a solas
es locura, escucharse delante de otros será doblada..   Achaque de
señores es hablar con el bordón del '¿digo algo?' y aquel '¿eh?'
que aporrea a los que le escuchan: a cada razón orejean[1] la aprobación o la lisonja, apurando la cordura.   También los hinchados
hablan con eco, y como su conversación va en chapines de entono,
a cada palabra solicita el enfadoso socorro del necio '¡bien dicho!'

142

Nunca por tema seguir el peor partido, porque el contrario se
adelantó y escogió el mejor.   Ya comienza vencido, y así será
preciso ceder desairado.   Nunca se vengará bien con el mal: fué
astucia del contrario anticiparse a lo mejor, y necedad suya
oponérsele tarde con lo peor.   Son éstos porfiados de obra, más
empeñados que los de palabra, cuanto va más riesgo del hacer al
decir: vulgaridad de temáticos no reparar en la verdad por
contradecir, ni en la utilidad por litigar.   El atento siempre está
de parte de la razón, no de la pasión, o anticipándose antes o
mejorándose después; que si es necio el contrario, por el mismo
caso mudará de rumbo, pasándose a la contraria parte, con que
empeorará de partido.   Para echarle de lo mejor es único remedio
abrazar lo propio, que su necedad le hará dejarlo, y su tema le será
desempeño.

[1] 1659 has 'orejan.'

141

Do not listen to yourself. It is of little use to please yourself if you do not please others; and general contempt is, as a rule, the punishment of self-satisfaction. The man who is pleased with himself is in everybody's debt. The desire to talk and, at the same time, to hear yourself talking, is futile; and, if it is crazy to talk to yourself, it is doubly foolish to listen to yourself talking in the presence of others. It is a weakness of the great to interlard their remarks with the refrain 'What was I saying?' and that 'Eh?' which is a torture to their hearers: with every word they utter such people prick up their ears to catch the sound of applause or flattery, exhausting [the patience of] sensible men. The pompous also speak with an echo and, as their conversation clatters along in the clogs of arrogance, they solicit with every word the irritating endorsement of a fatuous 'Well said!'

142

Never, out of obstinacy, champion the worse cause, because your opponent has forestalled you and chosen the better one. You begin the fight already beaten, and so will be obliged to surrender, discomfited. You can never avenge good with evil: it was clever of your opponent to champion the better cause first, and stupid of you to be left to oppose him later as a supporter of the worse. The obstinate in deed have more to cope with than the obstinate in word, for there is more risk involved in action than in speech: it is a common failing of the stubborn to miss the truth through contrariness, and their own advantage through contentiousness. The cautious man is always on the side of reason, never on that of emotion; either he gets his blow in first, or improves his position later; for, if the enemy is a fool, he will, on that account, change his front and go over to the other side, and so his cause will deteriorate. The only way to deprive your antagonist of the better cause is to support it yourself, for his stupidity will force him to abandon it, and his stubbornness will provide you with a way out of your difficulty.

143

No dar en paradojo por huir de vulgar. Los dos extremos son del descrédito. Todo asunto que desdice de la gravedad es ramo de necedad. Lo paradojo es un cierto engaño plausible a los principios, que admira por lo nuevo y por lo picante, pero después, con el desengaño del salir tan mal, queda muy desairado. Es especie de embeleco, y en materias politicas, ruina de los estados. Los que no pueden llegar, o no se atreven a lo heroico por el camino de la virtud, echan por lo paradojo, admirando necios y sacando verdaderos a muchos cuerdos. Arguye destemplanza en el dictamen, y por eso tan opuesto a la prudencia; y si tal vez no se funda en lo falso, por lo menos en lo incierto, con gran riesgo de la importancia.

144

Entrar con la ajena para salir con la suya. Es estratagema del conseguir; aun en las materias del cielo encargan esta santa astucia los cristianos maestros. Es un importante disimulo, porque sirve de cebo la concebida utilidad para coger una voluntad: parécele que va delante la suya, y no es más de para abrir camino a la pretensión ajena: nunca se ha de entrar a lo desatinado, y más donde hay fondo de peligro. También con personas cuya primera palabra suele ser el 'no' conviene desmentir el tiro, porque no se advierta la dificultad del conceder; mucho más cuando se presiente la aversión.[1] Pertenece este aviso a los de segunda intención, que todos son de la quinta sutileza.

145

No descubrir el dedo malo, que todo topará allí. No quejarse de él, que siempre sacude la malicia adonde le duele a la flaqueza. No servirá el picarse uno, sino de picar el gusto al entremetimiento:[2] va buscando la mala intención el achaque de hacer saltar;

---

[1] *Vide* Appendix, p. 306.   [2] *Vide* Appendix, p. 306.

143

Do not indulge in paradox in order to avoid the trite. Both extremes are discreditable. Every topic unbecoming to gravity is an offshoot of folly. Paradox is a species of deception, plausible at first and evoking admiration on account of its novelty and spiciness; later, however, with the disillusionment which follows conspicuous failure, it is regarded with total contempt. It is a kind of fraud, and in political matters proves the undoing of states. Those who cannot attain, or who do not dare to attempt, the heroic by following the path of virtue, resort to paradox; they are admired by fools, and [so] show many wise men to have been accurate in their judgment. Paradox reveals a lack of balance in the judgment and is, therefore, very much at loggerheads with discretion; and if it is not invariably founded upon falsehood, it is at least based upon uncertainty, to the great danger of your status.

144

Begin by furthering another's interest in order that you may get your own way in the end. This is a ruse for achieving your objects; even in spiritual matters Christian teachers recommend this holy cunning. It is an important kind of dissimulation, because an imagined advantage serves as a bait to capture a man's will: to him it seems that his affairs are going forward well, and this but serves to open the way to the ambitions of someone else: you should never embark upon a project recklessly, and more especially where there is an undercurrent of danger. In the case of people whose first word is usually 'No,' it is also advisable to conceal your aim in such a way that the difficulty of making a concession is not apparent to them; more especially when a rabuff is foreseen. This warning applies to ulterior motives which are, all of them, the quintessence of subtlety.

145

Do not expose your sore finger, for everything will knock up against it. Do not complain about it, for the malicious always attack the weak where it hurts most. To get annoyed will only serve to encourage the meddlesome: the malicious go in search of

arroja varillas para hallarle el sentimiento; hará la prueba de mil modos hasta llegar al vivo.   Nunca el atento se dé por entendido, ni descubra su mal, o personal o heredado, que hasta la fortuna se deleita a veces de lastimar donde más ha de doler.   Siempre mortifica en lo vivo: por esto no se ha de descubrir, ni lo que mortifica ni lo que vivifica: uno para que se acabe, otro para que dure.

146

Mirar por dentro.   Hállanse de ordinario ser muy otras las cosas de lo que parecían, y la ignorancia que no pasó de la corteza, se convierte en desengaño cuando se penetra al interior.   La mentira es siempre la primera en todo; arrastra necios por vulgaridad continuada.   La verdad siempre llega la última y tarde, cojeando con el tiempo.   Resérvanle los cuerdos la otra mitad de la potencia que sabiamente duplicó la común madre.   Es el engaño muy superficial, y topan luego con él los que lo son.   El acierto vive retirado a su interior, para ser más estimado de sus sabios y discretos.

147

No ser inaccesible.   Ninguno hay tan perfecto que alguna vez no necesite de advertencia.   Es irremediable de necio el que no escucha.   El más exento ha de dar lugar al amigable aviso; ni la soberanía ha de excluir la docilidad.   Hay hombres irremediables por inaccesibles, que se despeñan porque nadie osa llegar a detenerlos.   El más entero ha de tener una puerta abierta a la amistad, y será la del socorro.   Ha de tener lugar un amigo, para poder con desembarazo avisarle y aun castigarle.   La satisfacción le ha de poner en esta autoridad, y el gran concepto de su fidelidad y prudencia.   No a todos se les ha de facilitar el

your tender spot in order to make you jump; they throw darts to probe your feelings; they will try you in a thousand ways until they reach the quick.   The careful man never appears to notice [insults], nor does he disclose his troubles, personal or inherited, for even Fortune sometimes delights in hitting us where it will hurt most.   She always cuts to the quick: it is for this reason that no source either of mortification or of joy should ever be revealed, if you want the former to vanish and the latter to endure.

146

Look within.   Things are usually very different from what they seemed, and ignorance, which never looks beneath the surface, becomes disillusion when it penetrates within.   In everything, falsehood is always first in the field; it drags fools along with [the strength of] their own obstinate vulgarity.   Truth is always the last to arrive, limping along on the arm of time.[1]   For truth, the wise reserve the other half of the gift [of hearing] which we have received from our wise mother Nature in twofold endowment.   Deceit is very superficial, and the superficial soon come up against it.   Clear judgment lives an interior life apart, so that it may be the more highly esteemed by the wise and the discreet.

147

Do not be unapproachable.   There is no one so perfect that he may not sometimes need advice.   The man who does not listen is an incorrigible idiot.   The most independent person should find a place for friendly advice; even sovereignty should not exclude readiness to learn.   Some men are incurably aloof; they hurl themselves over precipices because nobody dares to hold them back.   The soundest of men should leave a door open to friendship, and it will be the gate of succour.   A friend must be at liberty to advise, and even to reprove you, without feeling embarrassment.   The pleasure which you derive from his friendship, and your lofty conception of his fidelity and wisdom, should entitle him to such a position of authority.   We must not too readily accord respect, nor even give credit to

[1] (J).

*F

respeto, ni aun el crédito; pero tenga en el retrete de su recato un fiel espejo[1] de un confidente, a quien deba y estime la corrección en el desengaño.

148

Tener el arte de conversar, en que se hace muestra de ser persona. En ningún ejercicio humano se requiere más la atención, por ser el más ordinario del vivir; aquí es el perderse o el ganarse, que si es necesaria la advertencia para escribir una carta, con ser conversación de pensado y por escrito, ¿cuánto más en la ordinaria, donde se hace examen pronto de la discreción? Toman los péritos el pulso al ánimo en la lengua, y en fe de ella dijo el sabio: 'Habla, si quieres que te conozca.' Tienen algunos por arte en la conversación el ir sin ella, que ha de ser holgada como el vestir; entiéndese entre muy amigos, que cuando es de respeto ha de ser más substancial y que indique la mucha substancia de la persona. Para acertarse, se ha de ajustar al genio y al ingenio de los que tercian; no ha de afectar el ser censor de las palabras, que será tenido por gramático; ni menos fiscal de las razones, que le hurtarán todos el trato y le vendarán la comunicación. La discreción en el hablar importa más que la elocuencia.

149

Saber declinar a otro los males: tener escudos contra la malevolencia; gran treta de los que gobiernan. No nace de incapacidad, como la malicia piensa, sí de industria superior, tener en quien recaiga la censura de los desaciertos y el castigo común de la murmuración. No todo puede salir bien, ni a todos se puede contentar. Haya, pues, un testa de hierros,[2] terrero de infelicidades, a costa de su misma ambición.

---

[1] 1653 and 1659 have 'espejo.' Reyes has 'consejo.'
[2] *Vide* Appendix, p. 306.

every one; but, in the innermost chamber of his reserve, a man should have the trusty counsel of some close friend, to whom he should be gladly indebted for correction in times of disillusionment.

148

Possess the art of conversation, by which you show yourself to be an individual. In no human activity is care more required, for it is the commonest in life; by it you either lose or gain, for, if it needs care to write a letter, which is conversation thought out and set down in writing, how much more is required by ordinary talk, in which discretion is put to a sudden test! Those skilled in this art take the pulse of a man's intelligence from his tongue, wherefore the sage said: 'Speak, if you want me to know you.' Some maintain that the art of conversation resides in its very artlessness, that it should be easy, like clothing; this is understood where intimate friends are concerned, but in the company of those to whom you owe respect it should be more substantial, in keeping with the high importance of the person to whom you are talking. To be successful, it should be adapted to the temperament and wit of those who share in it; do not pose as a censor of words for if you do so you will be regarded as a pedant; and do not criticize the utterances of others, for if you do every one will ostracize you and avoid dealings with you. In talking, discretion is of more importance than eloquence.

149

Know how to put your troubles on someone else's shoulders: provide yourself with shields against ill will; it is a very skilful device of rulers. To have someone upon whom the blame for mistakes and the universal flail of gossip may fall is not, as the malicious think, the outcome of incapacity, but, rather, of superior shrewdness. Everything cannot turn out well, nor can you please every one. So have a scapegoat who, at the cost of his own ambition, will be a target for your misfortunes.

150

Saber vender sus cosas.   No basta la extrínseca bondad de ellas; que no todos muerden la substancia ni miran por dentro. Acuden los más adonde hay concurso: van porque ven ir a otros. Es gran parte del artificio saber acreditar unas veces celebrando, que la alabanza es solicitadora del deseo, otras dando buen nombre, que es un gran modo de sublimar, desmintiendo siempre la afectación. El destinar para solos los entendidos es picón general, porque todos se lo piensan, y cuando no, la privación espoleará el deseo. Nunca se han de acreditar de fáciles ni de comunes los asuntos, que más es vulgarizarlos que facilitarlos; todos pican en lo singular, por más apetecible, tanto al gusto como al ingenio.

151

Pensar anticipado.   Hoy para mañana, y aun para muchos días. La mayor providencia es tener horas de ella; para prevenidos no hay acasos, ni para apercibidos aprietos. No se ha de aguardar el discurrir para el ahogo, y ha de ir de antemano; prevenga con la madurez del reconsejo el punto más crudo. Es la almohada sibila muda, y el dormir sobre los puntos vale más que el desvelarse debajo de ellos. Algunos obran y después piensan; aquéllo más es buscar excusas que consecuencias; otros, ni antes ni después. Toda la vida ha de ser pensar para acertar el rumbo; el reconsejo y providencia dan arbitrio de vivir anticipado.

152

Nunca acompañarse con quien le pueda deslucir, tanto por más cuanto por menos.   Lo que excede en perfección excede en estimación; hará el otro el primer papel siempre, y él el segundo, y si le alcanzase algo de aprecio, serán las sobras de aquél.

150

Know how to sell your accomplishments. Their extrinsic merits are not enough, for not every one bites down to the marrow or looks within. The majority put in an appearance wherever there is a crowd: they go because they see others going. Craft consists to a great extent in knowing how to bring things into repute, sometimes by praising them, for praise courts desire, sometimes by giving them an attractive name, which is a good way to extol them, provided always that this be done without affectation. To label your wares 'for connoisseurs only' is an inducement to every one, for all regard themselves as such and, if they do not, the feeling of being 'out of it' will stimulate appetite. Things should never be commended as easy or common, for that is to depreciate them rather than make them accessible; every one runs after the unusual, as being more attractive, both to the taste and the intelligence.

151

Think ahead. To-day for to-morrow, and even for many days [after that]. Supreme foresight consists in determining the time at which foresight is necessary; for the forewarned, there are no accidents, for the alert, no difficulties. You must not wait until you are drowning before you begin to think [about your plight]; you must take precautions in advance; forestall the most awkward situation by mature reflection. The pillow is a silent Sybil and it is better to sleep on things than lie awake under their load. Some act, and think afterwards; that is to look to excuses rather than consequences; others reflect neither before nor after. All our life long we must think things out in order to hit upon the right course [to take]; consideration and foresight supply the judgment which enables us to live in advance.

152

Never associate with anybody who can put you in the shade; the more he does so the less desirable a companion he is. The more accomplished he is, the more highly esteemed he will be; he, the other fellow, will always play first fiddle and you second, and if you get any appreciation it will be [from] your companion's

Campea la luna mientras una entre las estrellas, pero en saliendo el sol, o no parece o desaparece. Nunca se arrime a quien le eclipse, sino a quien le realce. De esta suerte pudo parecer hermosa la discreta Fabulla[1] de Marcial: 'y lució entre la fealdad o el desaliño de sus doncellas.' Tampoco ha de peligrar de mal de lado, ni honrar a otros a costa de su crédito. Para hacerse vaya con los eminentes, para hecho entre los medianos.

153

Huya de entrar a llenar grandes vacíos, y si se empeña, sea con seguridad del exceso. Es menester doblar el valor para igualar al del pasado. Así como es ardid que el que se sigue sea tal que le haga deseado, así es sutileza que el que acabó no le eclipse. Es dificultoso llenar un gran vacío, porque siempre lo pasado pareció mejor, y aun la igualdad no bastará, porque está en posesión de primero. Es, pues, necesario añadir prendas para echar a otro de su posesión en el mayor concepto.

154

No ser fácil ni en creer, ni en querer. Conócese la madurez en la espera de la credulidad: es muy ordinario el mentir, sea extraordinario el creer. El que ligeramente se movió, hállase después corrido; pero no se ha de dar a entender la duda de la fe ajena, que pasa de descortesía a agravio, porque se le trata al que contesta de engañador o engañado. Y aun no es ése el mayor inconveniente, cuanto que el no creer es indicio del mentir; porque el mentiroso tiene dos males: que ni cree ni es creído. La suspensión del juicio es cuerda en el que oye, y remítase de fe al autor aquél que dice: 'También es especie de imprudencia la

---

[1] Reyes has 'Fábula.'

leavings. While she is alone, the moon shines out brightly among the stars, but when the sun appears she either fades or becomes invisible. Never associate with one who may eclipse you but, rather, with someone who may enhance your brilliance. In this way Martial's discreet Fabulla was able to appear beautiful: 'she was resplendent amid the ugliness or slovenliness of her handmaidens.' Neither must you run the risk of contamination by bad companions, nor honour others at the expense of your own reputation. In order to get on in life, mix with the eminent and, once you have arrived, with mediocrities.

153

Avoid stepping into a great man's shoes, and, if you are obliged to do so, be quite sure of excelling him. You will have to be worth twice as much as he was even to equal your predecessor. Just as it is a clever device so to contrive it that your successor may cause you to be regretted, so it is also good policy to make sure that your predecessor does not outshine you. It is difficult to step into a great man's shoes because the past always seems better than the present and even equality of worth will not be enough because your predecessor was first in the field. You must, therefore, possess additional high qualities in order to oust the other fellow from his higher place in esteem.

154

Do not be too ready either to believe or to like people. Waiting upon belief is a sign of maturity: lying is very common, [so] let belief be exceptional. The man who is easily persuaded finds himself discomfited later on. You should not, however, reveal your doubts as to the good faith of other people, for that adds insult to injury: for you make out your interlocutor to be either a liar or a simpleton. And even that is not the greatest drawback; inasmuch as lack of belief is a sign of lying, the liar suffers from two disadvantages; for he neither believes, nor is believed. It is wise in the hearer to suspend his judgment, and he may confidently refer to that author who says: 'Readiness to like

facilidad en el querer'; que si se miente con la palabra, también con las cosas; y es más pernicioso este engaño, por la obra.

155

Arte en el apasionarse.   Si es posible, prevenga la prudente reflexión la vulgaridad del ímpetu; no le será dificultoso al que fuere prudente.   El primer paso del apasionarse es advertir que se apasiona, que es entrar con señorío del afecto, tanteando la necesidad hasta tal punto de enojo y no más; con esta superior reflexa entre y salga en una ira.   Sepa parar bien y a su tiempo, que lo más dificultoso del correr está en el parar.   Gran prueba de juicio conservarse cuerdo en los trances de locura: todo exceso de pasión degenera de lo racional, pero con esta magistral atención nunca atropellará la razón, ni pisará los términos de la sindéresis. Para saber hacer mal a una pasión es menester ir siempre con la rienda en la atención; y será el primer cuerdo a caballo, si no el último.

156

Amigos de elección.   Que lo han de ser a examen de la discreción y a prueba de la fortuna; graduados no sólo de la voluntad, sino del entendimiento.   Y con ser el más importante acierto del vivir, es el menos asistido del cuidado.   Obra el entretenimiento en algunos y el acaso en los más; es definido uno por los amigos que tiene, que nunca el sabio concordó con ignorantes; pero el gustar de uno no arguye intimidad, que puede proceder más del buen rato de su graciosidad que de la confianza de su capacidad.   Hay amistades legítimas y otras adulterinas; éstas para la delectación, aquéllas para la fecundidad de aciertos. Hállanse pocos de la persona, y muchos de la fortuna.   Más aprovecha un buen entendimiento de un amigo que muchas buenas voluntades de otros: haya, pues, elección y no suerte.

[people] is also a species of imprudence'; for if words can lie, so can deeds, and this kind of deception, by deeds, is the more pernicious.

155

The art of getting into a rage. If possible, let prudent reflection forestall vulgar impetuosity; this will not be difficult for the man who is discreet. The first step in losing your temper is to realize that you are losing it, for you thus have your emotions under control from the start, gauging the precise degree of rage that is necessary, and not going beyond it; you should lose and recover your temper with the aid of this higher type of reflection. You should know the proper time to calm down, for the most difficult thing about running is coming to a standstill. It is an outstanding sign of wisdom to keep a cool head during fits of rage: all extremes of feeling are a falling away from reason, but with this masterly caution you will never ride rough-shod over it nor overstep the bounds of sound judgment. To curb an emotion you must always keep the reins of caution firmly in your hands, and he who can do this will be the first man to be 'wise on horseback,' if not the last.

156

The friends of one's choice. Such friends must pass the test of discretion and the examination of fortune; their degrees must be granted not only by the will but also by the understanding. And although the ability to choose friends is the most important accomplishment in life, it is the one which is fostered with least care. For some, diversion is the motive, for the majority, chance; a man is known by the friends he has, for a wise man never associates with the ignorant; but to enjoy a man's company does not imply intimacy, for the satisfaction may proceed from the good times his wit may provide rather than from confidence in his abilities. Some friendships are legitimate, and others illicit; the latter are for pleasure, the former conducive to success in abundance. A man has few friends who love him for himself, and many who love him for his money. The cordial understanding of one friend is worth more than masses of goodwill from others: so make your friends by choice and not by chance.

Un sabio sabe excusar pesares, y el necio amigo los acarrea.   Ni desearles mucha fortuna, si no los quiere perder.

157

No engañarse en las personas, que es el peor y más fácil engaño. Más vale ser engañado en el precio que en la mercadería, ni hay cosa que más necesite mirarse por dentro.   Hay diferencia entre el entender las cosas y conocer las personas, y es gran filosofía alcanzar los genios y distinguir los humores de los hombres: tanto es menester tener estudiados los sujetos como los libros.

158

Saber usar de los amigos.   Hay en esto su arte de discreción: unos son buenos para de lejos y otros para de cerca, y el que tal vez no fué bueno para la conversación, lo es para la correspondencia.   Purifica la distancia algunos defectos que eran intolerables a la presencia.   No sólo se ha de procurar en ellos conseguir el gusto, sino la utilidad, que ha de tener las tres calidades del bien.   Otros dicen las del ente: uno, bueno y verdadero, porque el amigo es todas las cosas.   Son pocos para buenos, y el no saberlos elegir los hace menos.   Saberlos conservar es más que el hacerlos amigos.   Búsquense tales que hayan de durar, y aunque al principio sean nuevos, baste para satisfacción que podrán hacerse viejos.   Absolutamente, los mejores son los muy salados, aunque se gaste una hanega en la experiencia.   No hay desierto como vivir sin amigos: la amistad multiplica los bienes y reparte los males; es único remedio contra la adversa fortuna, y un desahogo del alma.

159

Saber sufrír necios.   Los sabios siempre fueron mal sufridos, que quien añade ciencia añade impaciencia.   El mucho conocer

A wise friend can ward off troubles, and a foolish one occasion them. And do not wish your friends much good fortune, if you do not want to lose them.

157

Do not be mistaken in people, for it is the worst, and easiest, mistake [to make]. It is better to be cheated over the price of goods than over the goods themselves, nor is there any matter where insight is more needful. There is a difference between understanding things and knowing people, and it is profound philosophy to understand characters and distinguish between different temperaments: it is just as necessary to study persons as it is to study books.

158

Know how to make use of your friends. Skill and discretion are needed in this matter: some people are good friends at a distance, others near at hand, and a friend who may possibly be no good at conversation can be a good correspondent. Distance purges certain failings which would be intolerable at close quarters. One should not endeavour to obtain pleasure, merely, from one's friends, but also profit, which ought to have the three qualities of the good, or as others say, of Being: unity, goodness, and truth; for a friend is all in all. Only a few are capable of being good friends and the fact that men do not know how to choose them makes good friends rare. It is more important to know how to keep than to make friends. Seek out those whose friendship is likely to endure, and, if they are new at first, the fact that they may become old friends should be enough. Well-tried friends are definitely the best friends, though we may have to eat a whole bushel of salt with them first. There is no wilderness like a life without friends: friendship multiplies blessings and divides misfortunes; it is a unique remedy against adversity, and a balm to the soul.

159

Know how to suffer fools gladly. The wise are always impatient, for he who grows in knowledge grows in impatience.

es dificultoso de satisfacer.   La mayor regla del vivir, según Epicteto, es el sufrir, y a esto redujo la mitad de la sabiduría.   Si todas las necedades se han de tolerar, mucha paciencia será menester.   A veces sufrimos más de quien más dependemos, que importa para el ejercicio del vencerse.   Nace del sufrimiento la inestimable paz, que es la felicidad de la tierra; y el que no se hallare con ánimo de sufrir, apele al retiro de sí mismo, si es que aun a sí mismo se ha de poder tolerar.

160

Hablar de atento; con los émulos por cautela, con los demás por decencia.   Siempre hay tiempo para enviar la palabra, pero no para volverla.   Hase de hablar como en testamento; que a menos palabras, menos pleitos.   En lo que no importa se ha de ensayar uno para lo que importare: la arcanidad tiene visos de divinidad: el fácil a hablar cerca está de ser vencido y convencido.

161

Conocer los defectos dulces.   El hombre más perfecto no se escapa de algunos, y se casa y se amanceba con ellos.   Haylos en el ingenio, y mayores en el mayor, o se advierten más.   No porque no los conozca el mismo sujeto, sino porque los ama. Dos males juntos: apasionarse, y por vicios.   Son lunares de la perfección; ofenden tanto a los de afuera, cuanto a los mismos les suenan bien.   Aquí es el gallardo vencerse y dar esta felicidad a los demás realces: todos topan allí, y cuando habían de celebrar lo mucho bueno que admirar, se detienen donde reparan, afeando aquéllo por desdoro de las demás prendas.

It is difficult to satisfy those who know a great deal. The greatest rule of life, according to Epictetus, is endurance, and to this he reduced the moiety of wisdom. If folly is to be tolerated in all its forms we shall need a great deal of patience. We often have most to put up with at the hands of the person upon whom we most depend, a fact which it is important to remember for the practice of self-control. Of patience is born peerless peace, which is the joy of the world; and let him who has no stomach for patience retire into the sanctuary of his own heart, if, that is, he can put up even with himself.

160

Be careful when you talk; to your rivals, from caution, to others for propriety's sake. There is always time to utter a word, but not to withdraw one. We should speak as we do in our will and testament; for the fewer the words the fewer the disputes. Try yourself out on trivialities as a preparation for what may be serious matters: secrecy has something of the lustre of the divine about it: the man who is readiest of tongue is readily conquered and convinced.

161

Know your pet failings. The most perfect man is not free from some of these, and he stands to them in the relation of both husband and lover. There are faults of the understanding, and the greater the understanding, the greater, or the more obvious, the faults. This is not because their possessor is himself unaware of them but because he cherishes them. [In this case, we have] two evils conjoined: infatuation with, and obsession by, vices. These failings are blemishes upon [the fair face of] perfection; they offend observers to the same extent as they seem good to their possessors themselves. In this matter it is a fine thing to conquer yourself and so give your other, your good qualities, a favourable opportunity [to display themselves]: [for] every one concentrates upon your failing, and while they should be praising the many good points to be admired [in you], they linger upon the one weak spot which they have discovered and blacken that to the disadvantage of your other qualities.

162

Saber triunfar de la emulación y malevolencia. Poco es ya el desprecio aunque prudente, más es la galantería. No hay bastante aplauso a un decir bien del que dice mal, no hay venganza más heroica que con méritos y prendas, que vencen y atormentan a la envidia. Cada felicidad es un apretón de cordeles al mal afecto, y es un infierno del émulo la gloria del emulado. Este castigo se tiene por el mayor: hacer veneno de la felicidad. No muere de una vez el envidioso, sino tantas cuantas vive a voces de aplausos el envidiado, compitiendo la perennidad de la fama del uno con la penalidad del otro: es inmortal éste para sus glorias y aquél para sus penas. El clarín de la fama que toca a inmortalidad al uno publica muerte para el otro, sentenciándole al suspendio de tan envidiosa suspensión.

163

Nunca por la compasión del infeliz se ha de incurrir en la desgracia del afortunado. Es desventura para unos la que suele ser ventura para otros; que no fuera uno dichoso si no fueran muchos otros desdichados. Es propio de infelices conseguir la gracia de las gentes, que quiere recompensar ésta con su favor inútil los disfavores de la fortuna; y vióse tal vez que el que en la prosperidad fué aborrecido de todos, en la adversidad compadecido de todos. Trocóse la venganza de ensalzado en compasión de caído. Pero el sagaz atienda al barajar de la suerte. Hay algunos que nunca van sino con los desdichados, y ladean hoy por infeliz al que huyeron ayer por afortunado; arguye tal vez nobleza del natural, pero no sagacidad.

162

Know how to triumph over envy and malice. Here contempt, although prudent, counts, indeed, for little; magnanimity is better. A good word concerning one who speaks evil cannot be praised too highly: there is no revenge more heroic than that brought about by those merits and attainments which frustrate and torment the envious. Every stroke of good fortune is a further twist of the rope round the neck of the ill-disposed and the heaven of the envied is hell for the envious. To convert [your] good fortune into poison [for your enemies] is held to be the most severe punishment you can inflict on them. The envious man dies not only once but as many times as the person he envies lives to hear the voice of praise; the eternity of the latter's fame is the measure of the former's punishment: the one is immortal in his glory, the latter in his misery. The trumpet of fame which sounds immortality for the one heralds death for the other, sentencing him to the suspense of hoping, in vain, that the cause of his pains will cease.

163

Never allow your compassion for the wretched to incur the hostility of the fortunate. One man's misfortune is usually another man's good luck; for one person would not be fortunate unless many others were unlucky. It is characteristic of the unfortunate to win the goodwill of people who wish, by granting them bootless favours, to compensate them for the unkind blows of fate; and it has sometimes been observed that a man whom every one detested in his prosperity is pitied by every one in his adversity. The desire to take it out of a man in an important position is turned into compassion when he has fallen from his high estate. The sensible person, however, pays heed to the shuffling of Fortune's cards. There are some people who associate only with the unfortunate and who, to-day, because he has fallen upon bad times, rub shoulders with the very person whom they previously shunned because he was prosperous: this is, perhaps, a mark of a noble nature, but not of wisdom.

164

Echar al aire algunas cosas.   Para examinar la aceptación, un
ver cómo se reciben, y más las sospechosas de acierto y de agrado.
Asegúrase el salir bien, y queda lugar o para el empeño o para el
retiro.   Tantéanse las voluntades de esta suerte, y sabe el atento dónde tiene los pies: prevención máxima del pedir, del querer
y del gobernar.

165

Hacer buena guerra.   Puédenle obligar al cuerdo a hacerla,
pero no mala: cada uno ha de obrar como quien es, no como le
obligan.   Es plausible la galantería en la emulación: ha de pelear
no sólo para vencer en el poder, sino en el modo.   Vencer a lo
ruin no es gloria, sino rendimiento.   Siempre fué superioridad
la generosidad: el hombre de bien nunca se vale de armas
vedadas, y sonlo las de la amistad acabada para el odio comenzado, que no se ha de valer de la confianza para la venganza.
Todo lo que huele a traición inficiona el buen nombre.   En
personajes obligados se extraña más cualquier átomo de bajeza;
han de distar mucho la nobleza de la vileza.   Préciese de que, si
la galantería, la generosidad y la fidelidad se perdiesen en el
mundo, se habían de buscar en su pecho.

166

Diferenciar el hombre de palabras del de obras.   Es única pre-
cisión, así como la del amigo, de la persona o del empleo, que son
muy diferentes.   Malo es no teniendo palabra buena no tener
obra mala; peor no teniendo palabra mala no tener obra buena.
Ya no se come de palabras, que son viento, ni se vive de cortesias,
que es un cortés engaño.   Cazar las aves con luz es el verdadero

164

Fire a few random shots in the air. In order to find out to what extent your proposals are acceptable, to discover how they are received, especially those of which the success and favourable reception are doubtful. This ensures a happy issue out of your affairs and leaves you the choice either of committing yourself or of withdrawing. In this way intentions are probed, and the wise man gets to know the footing upon which he stands: such foresight is of the greatest importance in petitioning, resolving, and governing.

165

Wage war honourably. A good man may be obliged to wage war, but not to wage it dishonourably: every one must act according to his own nature, not as others would have him be. Gallantry towards a rival is praiseworthy: one must fight not merely to win by force but also by the way in which one employs it. To conquer by dishonourable means brings no glory but, rather, humiliation. Magnanimity always comes out on top: an honourable man never has recourse to forbidden weapons, and among these is the use of a quondam friendship to serve the purposes of a new-born hate; for one should not make use of intimacy in order to wreak vengeance. Everything which smells of treason infects our good name. The slightest trace of a mean spirit is the more out of place in those holding responsible positions; the noble and the ignoble must be poles apart. Let it be your boast that if gallantry, magnanimity, and loyalty should perish from the earth, they could be sought out in your own heart.

166

Distinguish the man of words from the man of deeds. [To do so] is uniquely necessary in the case of friends, personalities, and jobs, which differ greatly from one another. It is bad to say no good words and do no bad deeds: it is worse to say no bad words and do no good deeds. For one does not feed on words, which are [nothing more than] wind, nor live upon courtesy, which is polite deception. To hunt for birds with a

encandilar. Los desvanecidos se pagan del viento; las palabras han de ser prendas de las obras, y así han de tener el valor. Los árboles que no dan fruto, sino hojas, no suelen tener corazón. Conviene conocerlos, unos para provecho, otros para sombra.

167

Saberse ayudar. No hay mejor compañía en los grandes aprietos que un buen corazón; y cuando flaqueare, se ha de suplir de las partes que le están cerca. Hácensele menores los afanes a quien se sabe valer. No se rinda a la fortuna, que se le acabará de hacer intolerable. Ayúdanse poco algunos en sus trabajos, y dóblanlos con no saberlos llevar. El que ya se conoce, socorre con la consideración a su flaqueza; y el discreto de todo sale con victoria, hasta de las estrellas.

168

No dar en monstruos de la necedad. Sonlo todos los desvanecidos, presuntuosos, porfiados, caprichosos, persuadidos, extravagantes, figureros, graciosos, noveleros, paradojos, sectarios y todo género de hombres destemplados, monstruos todos de la impertinencia. Toda monstruosidad del ánimo es más disforme que la del cuerpo, porque desdice de la belleza superior. Pero ¿quién corregirá tanto desconcierto común? Donde falta la sindéresis no queda lugar para la dirección, y la que había de ser observación refleja de la irrisión, es una mal concebida presunción de aplauso imaginado.

169

Atención a no errar una, más que a acertar ciento. Nadie mira al sol resplandeciente; y todos, eclipsado. No le contará la nota vulgar las que acertare, sino las que errare. Más conocidos son los malos para murmurados que los buenos para aplaudidos; ni

light is the best way of dazzling them. The vain are satisfied with wind; words should be guarantors of deeds, and in that their [true] value should lie. Trees which bear no fruit, but only leaves, usually have no pith. It is advisable to recognize them for what they are; so that you may enjoy the fruit of those that bear it and rest in the shade of the others.

167

Know how to look after yourself. In very tight corners there is no better company than a stout heart; and, should this weaken, the neighbouring organs must do its work for it. For the man who knows how to look after himself, worries diminish. Do not give in to Fortune, for, if you do, she will become unbearable in the end. Some people do very little to help themselves in their troubles and multiply them because they are unable to endure them. The man who already knows himself gives succour, by reflection, to his own weakness; and the prudent man emerges victorious over everything, even his stars.

168

Have no truck with monsters of stupidity. Such are all conceited, presumptuous, pig-headed, capricious, self-opinionated, extravagant, eccentric, clowning, cranky, paradoxical, bigoted persons and all kinds of unbalanced folk, monsters of folly, all of them. Every deformity of the mind is more grotesque than any physical defect, for it betrays a higher loveliness. Who, nevertheless, is able to adjust a lack of balance so great and so universal? Where judgment is lacking there is no room for guidance, and instead of reflecting upon the ridicule [which they have earned], such people make an ill-founded assumption and imagine that they are admired.

169

Take more care not to miss once than to hit the mark a hundred times. Nobody looks at the sun when it is shining; everybody stares at it when it is in eclipse. Common gossip will not retail the things in which you go right but rather those in which you go wrong. The bad are better known to blame than are the

fueron conocidos muchos hasta que delinquieron: ni bastan todos
los aciertos juntos a desmentir un solo y mínimo desdoro: y
desengáñese todo hombre, que le serán notadas todas las malas,
pero ninguna buena, de la malevolencia.

170

Usar del retén en todas las cosas.   Es asegurar la importancia.
No todo el caudal se ha de emplear ni se han de sacar todas las
fuerzas cada vez.   Aun en el saber ha de haber resguardo, que es
un doblar las perfecciones: siempre ha de haber a que apelar en un
aprieto de salir mal; más obra el socorro que el acometimiento,
porque es de valor y de crédito.   El proceder de la cordura
siempre fué al seguro; y aun en este sentido es verdadera aquella
paradoja picante: 'Más es la mitad que el todo.'

171

No gastar el favor.   Los amigos grandes son para las grandes
ocasiones: no se ha de emplear la confianza mucha en cosas pocas,
que sería desperdicio de la gracia: la sagrada áncora se reserva
siempre para el último riesgo.   Si en lo poco se abusa de lo
mucho, ¿qué quedará para después?   No hay cosa que más
valga que los valedores, ni más preciosa hoy que el favor: hace
y deshace en el mundo, hasta dar ingenio o quitarlo.   A los
sabios, lo que les favorecieron naturaleza y fama les envidió la
fortuna.   Más es saber conservar las personas, y tenerlas, que los
haberes.

172

No empeñarse con quien no tiene que perder.   Es reñir con
desigualdad.   Entra el otro con desembarazo porque trae hasta
la vergüenza perdida; remató con todo, no tiene más que perder,
y así se arroja a toda impertinencia.   Nunca se ha de exponer a

good to praise; many, indeed, have remained in obscurity until they did something wrong: neither does the sum total of our successes suffice to conceal one single trifling defect: and let no one deceive himself, for malice will keep a tally of all a man's vices and none of his virtues.

170

In all matters, keep something in reserve. This makes your position secure. Do not use up all your capital nor put out all your strength on every occasion. You should even keep some of your knowledge in reserve: for that is to double the number of your endowments. In a tight corner, when defeat looms ahead, you must be able to fall back upon something; a relieving force is always more effective than an attacking one because it has the name of being courageous. Wisdom always walks on the safe side, and even in this sense that shrewd paradox: 'The half is greater than the whole' is true.

171

Do not waste influence. Powerful friends are for great occasions: in trifling matters, one should not try to make use of a close friend, for this would be to waste a favour: the sheet-anchor is always kept in reserve for the last extremity. If powerful influence is misused for insignificant ends, what will be left of it for a future occasion? There is nothing more precious than a patron, nothing in these days, more valuable than favour: it makes and unmakes [men] in this world, even to the point of imparting genius, or taking it away. Fortune is envious of those gifts bestowed upon the wise by Nature and by Fame. It is more [important] to know how to keep and hold people than possessions.

172

Never contend with a man who has nothing to lose. To do so is to enter into an unequal conflict. The other fellow enters [the lists] unencumbered, because he has forfeited everything, even shame; he is completely finished, has no more to lose, and so rushes headlong into every kind of folly. You should never

tan cruel riesgo la inestimable reputación. Costó muchos años de ganar, y viene a perderse en un punto de un puntillo. Hiela[1] un desaire mucho lucido sudor. Al hombre de obligaciones hácele reparar el tener mucho que perder, mirando por su crédito: mira por el contrario, y como se empeña con atención, procede con tal detención, que da tiempo a la prudencia para retirarse con tiempo, y poner en cobro el crédito. Ni con el vencimiento se llegará a ganar lo que se perdió ya con el exponerse a perder.

173

No ser de vidrio en el trato y menos en la amistad. Quiebran algunos con gran facilidad, descubriendo la poca consistencia; llénanse a sí mismos de ofensión, a los demás de enfado. Muestran tener la condición más niña que las de los ojos, pues no permite ser tocada ni de burlas, ni de veras; oféndenla las motas, que no son menester ya notas. Han de ir con gran tiento los que las tratan, atendiendo siempre a sus delicadezas: guárdanles los aires, porque el más leve desaire los desazona. Son éstos ordinariamente muy suyos, esclavos de su gusto, que por él atropellarán con todo, idólatras de su honrilla. La condición del amante tiene la mitad de diamante en el durar y en el resistir.

174

No vivir aprisa. El saber repartir las cosas es saberlas gozar. A muchos les sobra la vida y se les acaba la felicidad; malogran los contentos, que no los gozan, y querrían después volver atrás cuando se hallan tan adelante. Postillones del vivir, que a más del común correr del tiempo, añaden ellos su atropellamiento genial. Querrían devorar en un día lo que apenas podrán

[1] *Vide* Appendix, p. 306.

expose your priceless reputation to such a cruel risk. It cost
you many years to earn it and it is lost in a second, impaled
upon the point of a punctilio. Much honourable toil may be
rendered useless by one false step. A man in a responsible
position reflects that he has a lot to lose and looks to his reputation: he sums up the situation of his adversary and, as he
enters the fight with caution, pursues it with such care that he
gives prudence a chance to withdraw in time, and so safeguard
his good name. Not even by [final] victory will one succeed in
winning what one lost merely by laying oneself open to defeat.

173

*Do not be too sensitive in social intercourse, and still less so in
friendship.* Some people are excessively brittle and so reveal
their lack of stability; they fill themselves with grievances and
other people with vexation. They seem to be more sensitive
than the pupils of their eyes, for they will not allow themselves
to be touched, either in jest or in earnest: motes offend them,
so that there is no need for beams. Those who frequent
their company must be exceedingly careful and always have an
eye to their sensitive spots: they must be protected from the very
air itself, for the slightest draught upsets them. Such people
are usually extremely selfish, slaves to their desires, for the
gratification of which they will ride rough-shod over everybody
and everything. They are worshippers of punctilio. The
nature of a lover has a half diamond-like quality about it,
enduring and unbreakable.

174

Do not force the pace of life. To know how to apportion
things is to know how to enjoy them. Many people are satiated
with life, and happiness is at an end for them; they waste rather
than enjoy opportunities for pleasure and, later, when they discover they are so far ahead, would like to retrace their steps.
[Such men are] life's postillions, imposing the haste of their
temperament upon the normal pace of the years. They would
like to devour in one day what they would scarcely be able to

digerir en toda la vida. Viven adelantados en las felicidades, cómense los años por venir, y como van con tanta priesa, acaban presto con todo. Aun en el querer saber ha de haber modo para no saber las cosas mal sabidas. Son más los días que las dichas. En el gozar, a espacio; en el obrar, aprisa. Las hazañas, bien están hechas; los contentos, mal, acabados.

<h2 style="text-align:center">175</h2>

Hombre sustancial,—y el que lo es no se paga de los que no lo son. Infeliz es la eminencia que no se funda en la sustancia. No todos los que lo parecen son hombres: hay los de embuste, que conciben de quimera y paren embelecos; y hay otros sus semejantes, que los apoyan y gustan más de lo incierto que promete un embuste, por ser mucho, que de lo cierto que asegura una verdad, por ser poco. Al cabo sus caprichos salen mal, porque no tienen fundamento de entereza. Sola la verdad puede dar reputación verdadera, y la sustancia entra en provecho. Un embeleco ha menester otros muchos, y así toda la fábrica es quimera; y como se funda en el aire, es preciso venir a tierra. Nunca llega a viejo un desconcierto: el ver lo mucho que promete, basta hacerlo sospechoso, así como lo que prueba demasiado es imposible.

<h2 style="text-align:center">176</h2>

Saber o escuchar a quien sabe. Sin entendimiento no se puede vivir, o propio o prestado; pero hay muchos que ignoran que no saben, y otros que piensan que saben, no sabiendo. Achaques de necedad son irremediables, que como los ignorantes no se conocen, tampoco buscan lo que les falta. Serían sabios algunos, si no creyesen que lo son. Con esto, aunque son raros los oráculos de cordura, viven ociosos, porque nadie los consulta.

digest in an entire lifetime.   They live on overdrafts upon the
bank of pleasures, eat up the years in advance, and, as they go
[through life] at such a pace, soon get through everything.
Moderation should be exercised even in the desire for knowledge,
lest our learning be ill digested.   We have more days to live
through than pleasures.   Take your time over your play; but
be expeditious in your work.   There is satisfaction in great
deeds performed, but sorrow in pleasures that are no more.

175

A man of solid worth.   And such a man finds no satisfaction
in those who are not [as he].   Unhappy he whose high office is
not founded upon solid worth.   Not all are men who appear to be
men : some people are frauds, for they become pregnant by fancy
and bring forth delusions; and there are others like them, who
abet them, and take more delight in falsehood, because it promises
much, than in the certainty which truth ensures, because it performs little.   In the long run, their fancies come to a bad end
because they have no firm foundation.   Truth alone can provide
genuine fame, and solid worth true benefit.   One illusion
requires many others [to support it], so that the whole edifice
of fancy is unreal; and, as it is built upon air, so it must, of
necessity, fall to the ground.   An ill-conceived project never
reaches maturity: one glance at its swollen promises is enough
to lay it open to suspicion, just as a scheme which attempts too
much is impossible of fulfilment.

176

Be wise yourself, or listen to someone who is.   It is impossible
to live without intelligence, either one's own, or borrowed; there
are many, nevertheless, who do not know that they are ignorant
and others, who think they are wise when they are not.   The
failings of folly are incurable, for the ignorant not only lack
knowledge themselves but do not even go in search of what they
lack.   Some people would be wise if they did not believe themselves to be so.   Thus it happens that, although reliable oracles
are rare, they lead idle lives because nobody consults them.   To

G

No disminuye la grandeza ni contradice la capacidad el aconsejarse; antes el aconsejarse bien, la acredita. Debata en la razón, para que no le combata la desdicha.

177

Excusar llanezas en el trato. Ni se han de usar ni se han de permitir. El que se allana pierde luego la superioridad que le daba su entereza, y tras ella la estimación. Los astros, no rozándose con nosotros, se conservan en su esplendor; la divinidad solicita decoro. Toda humanidad facilita el desprecio. Las cosas humanas, cuanto se tienen más, se tienen en menos; porque con la comunicación se comunican las imperfecciones que se encubrían con el recato. Con nadie es conveniente el allanarse: no con los mayores, por el peligro, ni con los inferiores por la indecencia. Menos con la villanía que es atrevida por lo necio; y no reconociendo el favor que se le hace, presume obligación. La facilidad es ramo de vulgaridad.

178

Creer al corazón, y más cuando es de prueba. Nunca le desmienta, que suele ser pronóstico de lo que más importa: oráculo casero. Perecieron muchos de lo que se temían; mas ¿de qué sirvió el temerlo sin el remediarlo? Tienen algunos muy leal el corazón: ventaja del superior natural, que siempre los previene y toca a infelicidad para el remedio. No es cordura salir a recibir los males, pero sí el salirles al encuentro para vencerlos.

179

La retentiva es el sello de la capacidad: pecho sin secreto, es carta abierta: donde hay fondo, están los secretos profundos; que hay grandes espacios y ensenadas donde se hunden las cosas de monta. Procede de un gran señorío de sí, y el vencerse en esto es el verdadero triunfar. A tantos pagan pecho, a cuantos

ask advice does not diminish your importance nor imply lack of ability; on the contrary, it is a mark of distinction to seek good guidance. Take counsel with reason, so that you will not be attacked by misfortune.

177

Avoid familiarities in social intercourse. They should be neither practised nor permitted. The man who makes himself familiar immediately sacrifices the dignity which his reserve bestowed upon him; and in the train of dignity departs respect. The stars preserve their splendour because they have no dealings with us; the Divine demands decorum.[1] Every human weakness breeds contempt. In human affairs, the more familiar things are, the less men value them; for easy intercourse lays bare failings which reserve concealed. It never does to be familiar with any one; not with superiors, because of the risk [involved], nor with subordinates, because in their case familiarity is unseemly: least of all with the low-born, whose insolence proceeds from stupidity: and as they do not regard a favour done to them as such, they treat it, rather, as their due. Familiarity is an off-shoot of vulgarity.

178

Trust your heart, especially when it is put to the test. Never let it down, for it usually foresees what is most significant: [it is] a domestic oracle. Many have met with disaster owing to self-distrust, but what is the good of such fear if no remedy is found for it? For some men, their heart is their most loyal friend: the endowment of their superior nature, which always forewarns them of disaster so that they may seek out a remedy in time. It is unwise to meet troubles half-way, but wise, indeed, to march boldly forth to conquer them.

179

Reticence is the hall-mark of ability: a heart without a secret is an open letter: profound secrets lie in deep water; there are vast stretches and bays where matters of moment lie submerged. [Reticence] springs from a high degree of self-control and, in this matter, self-conquest is the true victory. We pay tribute to all

[1] (J).

se descubre. En la templanza interior consiste la salud de la prudencia. Los riesgos de la retentiva son la ajena tentativa: el contradecir para torcer; el tirar varillas para hacer. Saldrá aquí el atento más cerrado. Las cosas que se han de hacer no se han de decir, y las que se han de decir no se han de hacer.

180

Nunca regirse por lo que el enemigo había de hacer. El necio nunca hará lo que el cuerdo juzga, porque no alcanza lo que conviene. Si es discreto, tampoco,[1] porque querrá desmentirle el intento penetrado, y aun prevenido. Hanse de discurrir las materias por entrambas partes, y resolverse por el uno y otro lado, disponiéndolas a dos vertientes. Son varios los dictámenes: esté atenta la indiferencia, no tanto para lo que será, cuanto para lo que puede ser.

181

Sin mentir, no decir todas las verdades. No hay cosa que requiera más tiento que la verdad: que es un sangrarse del corazón. Tanto es menester para saberla decir como para saberla callar. Piérdese con sola una mentira todo el crédito de la entereza: es tenido el engaño por falto y el engañador por falso, que es peor. No todas las verdades se pueden decir: unas porque me importan a mí, otras porque al otro.

182

Un grano de audacia con todo, es importante cordura. Hase de moderar el concepto de los otros, para no concebir tan altamente de ellos que les tema; nunca rinda la imaginación al corazón. Parecen mucho algunos, hasta que se tratan; pero el comunicarlos, más sirvió de desengaño que de estimación. Ninguno

[1] *Vide* Appendix, p. 307.

those to whom we disclose ourselves.   Prudence finds security
in a steady breast.   The dangers which reticence encounters are
[to be seen in] the curiosity of others : [in their use] of contradiction for the purpose of distorting [the truth] ; in their employment
of petty provocations in order to inflame us.   The prudent man
will be the more reticent in such circumstances.   Things which
have to be done should not be spoken of, and those which have
to be spoken of should not be done.

180

*Do not be influenced by the course of action which your enemy
had to adopt.*   A fool will never do what a wise man judges [to
be appropriate] because he does not grasp the meaning of
expediency.   Neither will a prudent man adopt a plan designed
by another, because he will wish to conceal a purpose which has
been fathomed and even forestalled.   Matters must be looked at
from more than one angle, resolved with reference to both sides,
decided from two distinct points of view.   Judgments vary:
an undecided person should be on the look-out not so much for
what will happen as for what can happen.

181

Without lying, do not tell the whole truth.   Nothing requires
greater tact than [telling the] truth : for to do so is to draw away
the heart's blood.   As much [skill] is needed to know when to
tell it as to know how to keep quiet about it.   A reputation for
honesty may be completely ruined by a single lie: deceit is
regarded as bad coin and, what is worse, the deceiver as a coiner.
Not all truths can be told: some must be concealed in my own
interest, others in that of my fellows.

182

*It is a large part of wisdom to behave with a grain of audacity in
all one's affairs.*   Be moderate in the ideas you form of others
in order not to think so highly of them that you come to fear
them; imagination should never yield to the heart.   A great
many people appear to be important until you have dealings with
them; but closer acquaintance provides grounds for disillusion

excede los cortos límites de hombre; todos tienen su *si no*, unos en el ingenio, otros en el genio. La dignidad da autoridad aparente, pocas veces le acompaña la personal, que suele vengar la suerte la superioridad del cargo en la inferioridad de los méritos. La imaginación se adelanta siempre y pinta las cosas mucho más de lo que son. No sólo concibe lo que hay, sino lo que pudiera haber. Corrija la razón tan desengañada a experiencias; pero ni la necedad ha de ser atrevida, ni la virtud temerosa. Y si a la simplicidad la valió la confianza ¿cuánto más al valer y al saber?

183

No aprehender fuertemente. Todo necio es persuadido, y todo persuadido necio, y cuanto más erróneo su dictamen es mayor su tenacidad. Aun en caso de evidencia es ingenuidad el ceder; que no se ignora la razón que tuvo, y se conoce la galantería que tiene. Más se pierde con el arrimamiento que se puede ganar con el vencimiento. No es defender la verdad, sino la grosería. Hay cabezas de hierro, dificultosas de convencer, con extremo irremediable; cuando se junta lo caprichoso con lo persuadido, cásanse indisolublemente con la necedad. El tesón ha de estar en la voluntad, no en el juicio. Aunque hay casos de excepción para no dejarse perder y ser vencido dos veces: una en el dictamen, otra en la ejecución.

184

No ser ceremonial. Que aun en un rey la afectación en esto fué solemnizada por singularidad. Es enfadoso el puntuoso, y hay naciones tocadas de esta delicadeza. El vestido de la necedad se cose de estos puntos. Idólatras de su honra, y que muestran que se funda sobre poco, pues se temen que todo la pueda ofender. Bueno es mirar por el respeto, pero no sea tenido por gran maestro de cumplimientos. Bien es verdad que

rather than esteem.   No one transcends the restricted bounds of humanity, all have their limitations, some of the mind, others of character.   Rank confers an apparent authority [but] it is rarely accompanied by personal worth, for fortune usually counter-balances the loftiness of the position with an inferiority of merits in its holder.   Imagination always leaps ahead and paints things far brighter than they are.   It conceives not only that which is, but also that which might be.   Reason, so often disillusioned by experience, should correct this tendency; but folly ought not to be rash, nor virtue fearful.   And if confidence helps the simple, how much more the worthy and the wise!

183

Do not be opinionated.   Every fool is opinionated, and every opinionated person is a fool; and the more mistaken his judgment the greater his pertinacity.   Even when matters are self-evident it is gracious to give way, for the reason you had [on your side] does not go unrecognized and the courtesy which you show is acknowledged.   More is lost by obstinacy than can be gained by victory.   Obstinacy does not champion truth but rather boorishness.   There are blockheads whom it is difficult to con-vince on account of their extreme and incurable obstinacy; and when inconsistency is combined with stubbornness these two are indissolubly wedded to folly.   Tenacity should be a quality of the will, not of the judgment.   There are, nevertheless, exceptional cases in which you must not give way and thereby suffer a twofold defeat: in the one case of your ideas, in the other of their execution.

184

Do not stand on ceremony.   For even in a monarch, affectation of this kind is held to be eccentric.   The punctilious fellow is a bore, and there are nations infected with this formality.   The garment of folly is woven out of such niceties.   [Punctilious folk] are idolaters of their dignity and show that it rests upon but a slight foundation, since they fear that everything may detract from it.   It is right to take dignity into account, but do not be regarded as a great master of forms and ceremonies.   It is

el hombre sin ceremonias necesita de excelentes virtudes. Ni se
ha de afectar, ni se ha de despreciar la cortesía: no muestra ser
grande el que repara en puntillos.

185

Nunca exponer el crédito a prueba de sola una vez, que si no sale
bien aquélla, es irreparable el daño. Es muy contingente errar
una y más la primera: no siempre está uno de ocasión, que por
eso se dijo 'estar de día.' Afiance, pues, la segunda a la primera;
si se errare y si se acertare, será la primera desempeño de la
segunda. Siempre ha de haber recurso a la mejoría, y apelación a
más: dependen las cosas de contingencias, y de muchas; y así es
rara la felicidad del salir bien.

186

Conocer los defectos por más autorizados que estén. No
desconozca la entereza el vicio, aunque se revista de brocado:
corónase tal vez de oro, pero no por eso se puede disimular el
yerro. No pierde la esclavitud de su vileza, aunque se desmienta
con la nobleza del sujeto. Bien pueden estar los vicios realzados,
pero no son realces. Ven algunos que aquél héroe tuvo aquel
accidente, pero no ven que no fué héroe por aquello. Es tan
retórico el ejemplo superior, que aun las fealdades persuade;
hasta las del rostro afectó tal vez la lisonja, no advirtiendo que,
si en la grandeza se disimulan, en la bajeza se abominan.

187

Todo lo favorable, obrarlo por sí; todo lo odioso, por terceros.
Con lo uno se concilia la afición, con lo otro se declina la malevolencia. Mayor gusto es hacer bien que recibirlo, para grandes
hombres, que es felicidad de su generosidad. Pocas veces se da
disgusto a otro sin tomarlo, o por compasión o por repasión.

certainly true that the unceremonious man needs outstanding virtues.   Courtesy should be neither affected nor despised: a man who bothers about punctilios shows no mark of greatness.

185

Never expose your reputation to the test of a single throw.   For if that miscarries the damage is irreparable.   A man may very easily fail once, and more especially at the first attempt: one is not always up to the mark, hence the saying: 'To have one's lucky day.'   So clinch your first shot with a second; whether you miss or hit your first shot will justify a second.   You should always have recourse to better means, and draw upon ampler resources; things depend upon chance, and chance is manifold; hence the joy of success is infrequent.

186

Recognize faults, however high the places in which they may be [found].   Honest men will not fail to recognize vice, although it may be clad in brocade: it may, possibly, wear a golden crown, but that will not enable it to hide its guilt.   The nobility of a slave does not wipe out the disgrace of servitude.   Vices may well be adorned but they are not adornments.   Some people observe that a certain great man had such and such a weakness, but they fail to see that he was not great on that account.   The example of great men is so powerful an advocate that it even induces us to admire the hideous; personal ugliness, too, is sometimes the object of flattery and the flatterers do not realize that what they overlook in the mighty they detest in the humble.

187

Do everything pleasant yourself; everything unpleasant through intermediaries.   By adopting the first course you win favour, by taking the second you diminish ill will.   The great derive more satisfaction from conferring a benefit than from receiving one: it is a privilege of their generous hearts.   You can rarely cause pain to another without suffering it yourself, out of either compassion or remorse.   Important cases cannot be dealt with except

* G

Las causas superiores no obran sin el premio o el apremio. Influya inmediatamente el bien y mediatamente el mal. Tenga donde den los golpes del descontento, que son el odio y la murmuración. Suele ser la rabia vulgar, como la canina, que desconociendo la causa de su daño, revuelve contra el instrumento; y aunque éste no tenga la culpa principal, padece la pena de inmediato.

188

Traer que alabar es crédito del gusto, que indica tenerlo hecho a lo muy bueno y que se le debe la estimación de lo de acá. Quien supo conocer antes la perfección, sabrá estimarla después. Da materia a la conversación y a la imitación, adelantando las plausibles noticias. Es un político modo de vender la cortesía a las perfecciones presentes; otros al contrario, traen siempre que vituperar, haciendo lisonja a lo presente, con el desprecio de lo ausente. Sáleles bien con los superficiales, que no advierten la treta del decir mucho mal de unos con otros. Hacen política algunos de estimar más las medianías de hoy que los extremos de ayer. Conozca el atento estas sutilezas del llegar, y no le cause desmayo la exageración del uno ni engreimiento la lisonja del otro; y entienda que del mismo modo proceden en las unas partes que en las otras: truecan los sentidos, y ajústanse siempre al lugar en que se hallan.

189

Valerse de la privación ajena, que si llega a deseo es el más eficaz torcedor. Dijeron ser nada los filósofos, y ser el todo los políticos. Estos la conocieron mejor. Hacen grada unos para alcanzar sus fines del deseo de los otros. Válense de la ocasión, y en la dificultad de la consecución, irrítanle el apetito. Prométense más del conato de la pasión que de la tibieza de la posesión;

by having recourse to reward or constraint.   Let the good come from you and the evil from others.   Provide yourself with a target for the shafts of discontent, which take the form of hatred and slander.   The fury of the mob, like that of a dog, being unaware of the cause of its injury, usually turns upon the instrument [of punishment,] and although the instrument is not chiefly to blame, it suffers as though it were.

188

Introduce praiseworthy topics.   To do so does credit to your taste and shows that the latter is very well developed and that you are deserving of esteem in the company you keep.   The man who has once learned how to recognize perfection will know how to value it on future occasions.   Make some complimentary remark; you will start the ball of conversation rolling and others will follow you.   It is a polite way of selling courtesy to your accomplished audience; there are others, on the contrary, who always have something to abuse: flattering present company by decrying the absent.   They are successful with the superficial, who fail to see through this trick of saying extremely nasty things about certain people to certain other people.   Some adopt the technique of praising the mediocrities of to-day more highly than the great geniuses of the past.   The cautious man must beware of both types of careerist and he must not be dismayed by the exaggeration of the one, nor unduly elated by the flattery of the other; he must realize that both types adopt the same methods; they equivocate and always adapt themselves to the situation in which they find themselves.

189

Take advantage of another's need, for if the latter develops into craving, it is the most effective of thumbscrews.   Philosophers have said that poverty is nothing, politicians that it is everything. The latter were better acquainted with its nature.   Some make the craving of others a ladder for the attainment of their own ends.   They profit by their opportunities and. titillate desire by [pointing out] the difficulties in the way of its fulfilment.   They believe that they will profit more from the pricking of desire than from the lukewarm joy of possession; and desire is

y al paso que crece la repugnancia, se apasiona más el deseo. Gran sutileza del conseguir el intento, conservar las dependencias.

190

Hallar el consuelo en todo. Hasta de inútiles lo es el ser eternos. No hay afán sin conorte : los necios lo tienen en ser venturosos, y también se dijo 'ventura de fea.' Para vivir mucho es arbitrio valer poco. La vasija quebrantada es la que nunca se acaba de romper, que enfada con su durar. Parece que tiene envidia la fortuna a las personas más importantes, pues iguala la duración con la inutilidad de las unas, la importancia con la brevedad de las otras. Faltarán cuantos importaren, y permanecerá eterno el que es de ningún provecho, ya porque lo parece, ya porque realmente es así. Al desdichado parece que se conciertan en olvidarle la suerte y la muerte.

191

No pagarse de la mucha cortesía, que es especie de engaño. No necesitan algunos para hechizar de las hierbas de Tesalia, que con sólo el buen aire de una gorra encantan necios, digo desvanecidos. Hacen precio de la honra, y pagan con el viento de unas buenas palabras. Quien lo promete todo, promete nada, y el prometer es desliz para necios. La cortesía verdadera es deuda, la afectada engaño, y más la desusada ; no es decencia, sino dependencia. No hacen la reverencia a la persona, sino a la fortuna ; y la lisonja no a las prendas que reconoce, sino a las utilidades que espera.

192

Hombre de gran paz, hombre de mucha vida. Para vivir, dejar vivir. No sólo viven los pacíficos, sino que reinan. Hase de oír y ver, pero callar. El día sin pleito hace la noche soñolienta. Vivir mucho y vivir con gusto es vivir por dos, y fruto de la paz.

proportionately intensified with every obstacle that is put in its way. To keep people dependent upon you is a great and subtle device to gain your ends.

190

Find consolation in everything. It is the consolation even of the futile that they are immortal. Every trouble has its compensation: in the case of fools it is their luck, and the 'luck of the ugly' is also proverbial. In order to live long it is expedient to be worth little. It is the cracked vessel which never gets completely broken that annoys you by its durability. It would seem that Fortune envies persons of great distinction, for she evens things up by giving a long life to the useless and a short one to the worthy. All those who might matter will die off: and the worthless will live on for ever, either because they appear to do so, or because they do so in fact. To the unlucky man it seems that both good fortune and death conspire to forget him.

191

Do not be pleased by extreme politeness, for it is a kind of swindle. Some people do not need the herbs of Thessaly in order to cast a spell, for they can bewitch fools, presumptuous asses I would call them, with nothing more than a courteous raising of the cap. They set a price upon esteem and pay for it in the windy coinage of a few fine words. He who promises everything promises nothing, and promises are stumbling-blocks for fools. True courtesy is a duty, affected politeness a swindle, especially when it is overdone; it is not civility but dependence. Respect is being paid not to the man himself but to his wealth; and flattery is accorded not to merits which it recognizes but to advantages which it anticipates.

192

The man who loves peace greatly has a long life. Live and let live. The peaceable not only live, but rule. You should listen and observe, but keep your mouth shut. A day without a quarrel means a good night's sleep. To live long and enjoy one's life is to live twice over, and [that is] the reward of peaceableness. The man who does not bother himself about what

Todo lo tiene a quien no se le da nada de lo que no le importa. No hay mayor despropósito que tomarlo todo de propósito. Igual necedad que le pase el corazón a quien no le toca, y que no le entre de los dientes adentro a quien le importa.

193

Atención al que entra con la ajena por salir con la suya. No hay reparo para la astucia como la advertencia. Al entendido, un buen entendedor. Hacen algunos ajeno el negocio propio, y sin la contracifra de intenciones se halla a cada paso empeñado uno en sacar del fuego el provecho ajeno, con daño de su mano.

194

Concebir de sí y de sus cosas cuerdamente, y más al comenzar a vivir. Conciben todos altamente de sí, y más los que menos son. Suéñase cada uno su fortuna, y se imagina un prodigio. Empéñase desatinadamente la esperanza, y después nada cumple la experiencia. Sirve de tormento a su imaginación vana el desengaño de la realidad verdadera. Corrija la cordura semejantes desaciertos, y aunque puede desear lo mejor, siempre ha de esperar lo peor para tomar con ecuanimidad lo que viniere. Es destreza asestar algo más alto para ajustar el tiro, pero no tanto que sea desatino.[1] Al comenzar los empleos, es precisa esta reformación de concepto, que suele desatinar la presunción sin la experiencia. No hay medicina más universal para todas necedades que el seso. Conozca cada uno la esfera de su actividad y estado, y podrá regular con la realidad el concepto.

195

Saber estimar. Ninguno hay que no pueda ser maestro de otro en algo; ni hay quien no exceda al que excede. Saber

[1] *Vide* Appendix, p. 307.

does not concern him possesses everything. There is no greater foolishness than to take everything seriously. It is as stupid to give your heart away to one who does not concern you as not to be greatly concerned about someone who is of importance to you.

193

Be careful of the man who starts to work in the interests of another in order to get his own way in the end. There is no defence against cunning like vigilance. Set a thief to catch a thief. Some look after their own affairs while appearing to look after those of others, and if you do not possess the key to their motives you will be obliged, at every turn, to snatch their chestnuts out of the fire at the cost of burning your own fingers.

194

Take a sensible view of yourself and your concerns, and more especially when you are making a start in life. All think highly of themselves, and more especially those who have least grounds for doing so. Every one dreams about his good fortune and imagines himself to be a prodigy. Hope dashes recklessly into the fray and, later, experience accomplishes nothing. The disillusionment which hard facts bring in their train puts vain imaginings on the rack. The sensible man should correct such errors and although he may hope for the best let him always expect the worst, so that he may take whatever may come with equanimity. It is a good plan to aim a little higher than your target so as to make your shot sure, but not so high that you overshoot the mark. At the beginning of your career, this adjustment of ideas is necessary because assumption of responsibility without experience to back it usually 'gangs agley.' There is no greater panacea for every kind of folly than common sense. Each man should know his proper sphere of activity and his station in life. He will then be able to reconcile his dreams with realities.

195

Know how to appraise aright. There is no one who cannot be somebody's master in something; and there is no one so

desfrutar a cada uno es útil saber: el sabio estima a todos, porque reconoce lo bueno en cada uno, y sabe lo que cuestan las cosas, de hacerse bien.   El necio desprecia a todos, por ignorancia de lo bueno y por elección de lo peor.

196

Conocer su estrella.   Ninguno tan desvalido que no la tenga, y si es desdichado es por no conocerla.   Tienen unos cabida con príncipes y poderosos sin saber cómo ni por qué, sino que su misma suerte les facilitó el favor; sólo queda para la industria el ayudarla.   Otros se hallan con la gracia de los sabios: fué alguno más acepto en una nación que en otra, y más bien visto en esta ciudad que en aquélla.   Experiméntase también más dicha en un empleo y estado que en los otros, y todo esto en igualdad y aun identidad de méritos.   Baraja como y cuando quiere la suerte: conozca la suya cada uno, así como su Minerva, que va el perderse o el ganarse.   Sépala seguir y ayudar; no las trueque, que sería errar el norte a que le llama la vecina bocina.

197

Nunca embarazarse con necios.   Eslo el que no los conoce, y más el que, conocidos, no los descarta.   Son peligrosos para el trato superficial, y perniciosos para la confidencia.   Y aunque algún tiempo los contenga su recelo propio y el cuidado ajeno, al cabo hacen la necedad, o la dicen, y si tardaron, fué para hacerla más solemne.   Mal puede ayudar al crédito ajeno quien no le tiene propio; son infelicísimos, que es el sobrehueso de la necedad, y se pagan una y otra.   Sola una cosa tienen menos mala, y es que, ya que a ellos los cuerdos no les son de algún provecho, ellos sí de mucho a los sabios, o por noticia o por escarmiento.

excellent that he cannot be excelled. It is useful to know how to get something out of everybody: the sensible man respects everybody because he recognizes the good there is in every one and knows what it costs to do things well. The fool despises everybody because he does not recognize the good, and chooses the worst.

196

Know your [lucky] star. Nobody is so helpless as not to have one, and if he is unfortunate it is because he does not know which one it is. Some are in the good graces of princes and potentates without knowing why or wherefore, except that their good luck itself brought them into favour; it only remains for them to foster it by their own exertions. Others find themselves in favour with the wise; one man is better received in one country than in another, or is more in favour in this city than in that. It also happens that a man gets on better in a certain position or station in life than in another for which he has equal, and even identical, qualifications. Fortune shuffles the cards how and when she will: let each man know his luck as well as his capacities, for success or failure is at stake here. You should know how to follow your lucky star and help it on its way; do not abandon it for another, and so wander from the course set by the navigator, Destiny.

197

Never be bothered by fools. The man who does not recognize fools when he sees them is himself a fool; and he is a bigger fool who, having recognized them, does not avoid them. Fools are dangerous in everyday intercourse and disastrous as intimates. And even though their own timidity and the caution of others may keep them within bounds for a time, in the long run they do or say something silly; and if they bide their time it is only to make their idiocy more solemn. One who himself has no reputation can scarcely enhance that of another; fools are very unlucky: that is their trouble, for bad luck and folly are insepar- able. Fools have only one extenuating feature: to wit, although the wise are of no use to them they are of great use to the wise, either as a warning or as a punishment.

198

Saberse trasplantar. Hay naciones que para valer se han de remudar, y más en puestos grandes. Son las patrias madrastras de las mismas eminencias: reina en ellas la envidia como en tierra connatural, y más se acuerdan de las imperfecciones con que uno comenzó, que de la grandeza a que ha llegado: un alfiler pudo conseguir estimación, pasando de un mundo a otro, y un vidrio puso en desprecio al diamante porque se trasladó. Todo lo extraño es estimado, ya porque vino de lejos, ya porque se logra hecho y en su perfección. Sujetos vimos que ya fueron el desprecio de su rincón, y hoy son la honra del mundo, siendo estimados de los propios y extraños; de los unos porque los miran de lejos, de los otros porque lejos. Nunca bien venerará la estatua en el ara el que la conoció tronco en el huerto.

199

Saberse hacer lugar a lo cuerdo, no a lo entremetido. El verdadero camino para la estimación es el de los méritos, y si la industria se funda en el valor, es atajo para el alcanzar. Sola la entereza no basta, sola la solicitud es indigna, que llegan tan enlodadas las cosas, que son asco de la reputación. Consiste en un medio de merecer y de saberse introducir.

200

Tener que desear. Para no ser felizmente desdichado, respira el cuerpo y anhela el espíritu. Si todo fuere posesión, todo sería desengaño y descontento; aun en el entendimiento siempre ha de quedar que saber en que se cebe la curiosidad. La esperanza alienta; los hartazgos de felicidad son mortales. En el premiar es destreza nunca satisfacer: si nada hay que desear, todo es de

198

Know how to transplant yourself.   There are some countries
which a man must leave if he is to get on in life, especially if he
aspires to high office.   A motherland is often a stepmother even
to her distinguished sons: envy reigns in her as on its native soil
and she remembers rather one's early failings than the distinction
one has achieved later: a pin has been highly prized when it has
been brought from the New World to the Old, and a piece of
glass, because it was transported, has outshone a diamond.
Everything foreign is esteemed, either because it comes from a
distance, or because it is acquired in a finished and perfect state.
We have met people who were once the laughing-stock of their
village and who are, to-day, honoured by the great world,
respected both by their fellow countrymen and foreigners, by
the former because they are seen at a distance, and by the
latter because they come from afar.   The image on the altar will
never be properly revered by the man who knew it when it was a
tree trunk in the garden.

199

*Know how to get on in the world by the exercise of good sense,
not by pushfulness.*   The true way to win esteem is by the path
of merit, and if diligence has its roots in worth it provides a
short cut to attainment [of success].   Integrity alone is not
sufficient and mere importunity is degrading, for things are so
besmirched when you attain them that your reputation is thereby
rendered unsavoury.   The right road to success lies half-way
between that of merit and that of pushfulness.

200

Leave something to be desired.   So that we may not be unhappy
in our happiness the body respires and the soul aspires.   If one
possessed everything, there would be nothing but disillusion and
discontent; even in the field of knowledge something should
always remain to be learned, something upon which curiosity
may feed.   Hope gives encouragement; surfeits of happiness are
fatal.   When giving a reward it is good policy not to satisfy
[entirely]: if there is nothing left to desire, there is everything to

temer: dicha desdichada. Donde acaba el deseo comienza el temor.

201

Son tontos todos los que lo parecen y la mitad de los que no lo parecen. Alzóse con el mundo la necedad, y si hay algo de sabiduría, es estulticia con la del cielo; pero el mayor necio es el que no se lo piensa y a todos los otros difine. Para ser sabio, no basta parecerlo, menos parecérselo: aquél sabe que piensa que no sabe; y aquél no ve que los otros ven. Con estar todo el mundo lleno de necios, ninguno hay que lo piense, ni aun lo recele.

202

Dichos y hechos hacen un varón consumado. Hase de hablar lo muy bueno y obrar lo muy honroso; la una es perfección de la cabeza, la otra del corazón, y entrambas nacen de la superioridad del ánimo. Las palabras son sombra de los hechos: son aquéllas las hembras, éstos los varones. Más importa ser celebrado que ser celebrador. Es fácil el decir y difícil el obrar. Las hazañas son la sustancia del vivir, y las sentencias el ornato: la eminencia en los hechos dura, en los dichos pasa. Las acciones son el fruto de las atenciones: los unos sabios, los otros hazañosos.

203

Conocer las eminencias de su siglo. No son muchas: un fénix en todo un mundo, un gran capitán, un perfecto orador, un sabio en todo un siglo, un eminente rey en muchos. Las medianías son ordinarias en número y aprecio, las eminencias raras en todo, porque piden complemento de perfección, y cuanto más sublime la categoría, más dificultoso el extremo. Muchos los tomaron los renombres de magnos a César y Alejandro, pero en vacío, que sin los hechos no es más la voz que un poco de aire: pocos Sénecas ha habido, y un solo Apeles celebró la fama.

fear: [and that is] a wretched kind of felicity.   Where desire
ends, fear begins.

201

*All those who appear to be fools are such, and so are half those who
do not.*   Folly has run away with the world, and if there is any
wisdom [on earth] it is but stupidity as compared with that of
heaven; the biggest fool, moreover, is the man who, while calling
everybody else one, thinks that he is no fool himself.   In order
to be wise it is not enough to appear so, least of all to appear so to
oneself: the man who thinks he does not know, knows; and he
does not see through whom others see.   Though the world is
full of fools, no one thinks, or even suspects, that he himself is
one of them.

202

Words and deeds make a perfect man.   You should speak very
well [of every one] and act most honourably; the one shows
excellence of mind, the other of heart, and both arise from loftiness of soul.   Words are the shadows of deeds: the former are
female, the latter male.   It is more important to be the object
than the giver of praise.   Talking is easy and action is difficult.
Deeds are the very stuff of life, and words are its embroidery:
great deeds endure, fine words pass away.   Deeds are the fruit
of careful thoughts: if the latter are wise the former will be
gallant.

203

Know the great men of your time.   There are not many of
them: [there is only] one paragon in the whole world, only one
great captain, one perfect orator, one wise man, in an entire
century, one great monarch in the course of many.   Mediocrities are common, both in number and esteem; outstanding
personalities are rare in every way, for they strive after complete
perfection, and the loftier the category the more difficult it is to
attain the highest rank in it.   Many have usurped the reputation
of Caesar and Alexander for greatness, but in vain, for without
deeds words are no more than a puff of wind: there have been
few Senecas, and fame has sung the praises of but one Apelles.

204

Lo fácil se ha de emprender como dificultoso y lo dificultoso como fácil. Allí porque la confianza no descuide, aquí porque la desconfianza no desmaye: no es menester más para que no se haga la cosa que darla por hecha. Y al contrario, la diligencia allana la imposibilidad. Los grandes empeños aun no se han de pensar: basta ofrecerse, porque la dificultad advertida no ocasione el reparo.

205

Saber jugar del desprecio. Es treta para alcanzar las cosas despreciarlas. No se hallan comúnmente cuando se buscan, y después al descuido se vienen a la mano. Como todas las de acá son sombras de las eternas, participan de la sombra aquella propiedad: huyen de quien las sigue y persiguen a quien las huye. Es también el desprecio la más política venganza. Única máxima de sabios, nunca defenderse con la pluma, que deja rastro, y viene a ser más gloria de la emulación que castigo del atrevimiento. Astucia de indignos oponerse a grandes hombres para ser celebrado por indirecta, cuando no lo merecían de derecho. Que no conociéramos a muchos si no hubieran hecho caso de ellos los excelentes contrarios. No hay venganza como el olvido, que es sepultarlos en el polvo de su nada. Presumen, temerarios, hacerse eternos, pegando fuego a las maravillas del mundo y de los siglos. Arte de reformar la murmuración, no hacer caso: impugnarla causa perjuicio, y si crédito, descrédito. A la emulación, complacencia; que aun aquella sombra de desdoro deslustra, ya que no escurece del todo la mayor perfección.

204

Set about easy tasks as though they were difficult and about difficult tasks as though they were easy. In the one case, so that confidence may not be careless and, in the other, so that self-distrust may not give rise to dismay: for a thing to remain undone it is only necessary to regard it as done. Diligence, on the other hand, overcomes impossibilities. Great enterprises should not even be pondered: it is sufficient to go straight ahead, so that realization of the difficulties to come may not arouse misgiving.

205

Know how to play the card of contempt. A shrewd way of getting the things you want is to despise them. They are not usually to be found when you are looking for them, and, later, when you have ceased to care about them, they fall into your hands. As all things here below are but shadows of things eternal, they share this property of a shadow: they flee from him who follows them and pursue him who runs away from them. Contempt is also the most politic kind of revenge. A unique maxim of the wise is : ' Never defend yourself with the pen,' which leaves traces, and eventually turns out to be an advantage to a rival rather than a punishment for his insolence. It is a cunning device of the unworthy to attack great men so as to win notoriety in a roundabout way when they do not deserve it of their own right. For there are many of whom we should have known nothing if their distinguished opponents had taken no notice of them. There is no revenge like oblivion, for it is the entombment of the unworthy in the dust of their own nothingness. These rash fools think they secure immortality for themselves by setting fire to the wonders of the world and of the ages. The art of circumventing calumny is to take no notice of it : to combat it is prejudicial to our interests, and if it is taken seriously, it redounds to our discredit. It provides a source of satisfaction for our rivals : for even that shadow of a blemish dulls the lustre of our reputation, although it cannot altogether tarnish the highest of all qualities.

206

Sépase que hay vulgo en todas partes, en la misma Corinto, en la familia más selecta.   De las puertas adentro de su casa lo experimenta cada uno.   Pero hay vulgo y revulgo, que es peor.   Tiene el especial las mismas propiedades que el común, como los pedazos del quebrado espejo, y aún más perjudicial.   Habla a lo necio y censura a lo impertinente; gran discípulo de la ignorancia, padrino de la necedad y aliado de la hablilla.   No se ha de atender a lo que dice y menos a lo que siente.   Importa conocerlo para librarse de él, o como parte o como objeto; que cualquiera necedad es vulgaridad, y el vulgo se compone de necios.

207

Usar del reporte.   Hase de estar más sobre el caso en los acasos.   Son los ímpetus de las pasiones deslizaderos de la cordura, y allí es el riesgo de perderse.   Adelántase uno más en un instante de furor o contento que en muchas horas de indiferencia. Corre tal vez en breve rato, para correrse después toda la vida. Traza la ajena astuta intención estas tentaciones de prudencia para descubrir tierra o ánimo; válese de semejantes torcedores de secretos, que suelen apurar el mayor caudal.   Sea contra ardid el reporte, y más en las prontitudes; mucha reflexión es menester para que no se desboque una pasión, y gran cuerdo el que a caballo lo es.   Va con tiento el que concibe el peligro.   Lo que parece ligera la palabra al que la arroja, le parece pesada al que la recibe y la pondera.

208

No morir de achaque de necio.   Comúnmente, los sabios mueren faltos de cordura.   Al contrario, los necios hartos de consejo.   Morir de necio es morir de discurrir sobrado.   Unos

206

Realize that the vulgar are to be found everywhere, even in Corinth itself, in the most select of families.   Every one can put this statement to the test within the gates of his own house. There is, moreover, vulgarity and super-vulgarity, which is worse.   This special blend of vulgarity has the same qualities as the ordinary kind, just as fragments of a broken mirror have the properties of the whole glass, and [it also has a quality] even more pernicious.   It talks foolishly and passes impudent censure; it is an outstanding disciple of ignorance, a patron of stupidity, and an ally of gossip.   One should pay no heed to what it says, still less to what it thinks.   It is important to recognize vulgarity in order to rid oneself of it, either as a part [of one's make-up] or as an object [of one's experience]; for any kind of folly is vulgarity, and the rabble is made up of fools.

207

Exercise restraint.   We must be all the more alert in unexpected situations.   Passionate impulses cause prudence to slip, and on such occasions there is the risk of disaster.   A moment of anger or pleasure carries you farther than many hours of apathy.   It happens sometimes that a brief moment may later give rise to lifelong shame.   The subtle cunning of others contrives these temptations for your prudence in order to discover the lie of the land, or your state of mind; it makes use of thumbscrews of this kind in order to extort secrets, for such instruments usually undermine the strongest character.   Self-control should provide a means for resisting such devices, and especially in emergencies; much reflection is needed to prevent passion taking the bit between its teeth, and he is a wise man indeed who is so when on horseback.   He who scents danger proceeds with caution.   Light as a word appears to the one who utters it, it may seem weighty to him who hears and ponders it.

208

Do not die of the fool's disease.   The wise usually die lacking in wisdom.   Fools, on the contrary, die overflowing with advice.   To die the death of a fool is to die from talking too

mueren porque sienten, y otros viven porque no sienten. Y así, unos son necios porque no mueren de sentimiento, y otros lo son porque mueren de él. Necio es el que muere de sobrado entendido: de suerte que unos mueren de entendedores y otros viven de no entendidos; pero con morir muchos de necios, pocos necios mueren.

209

Librarse de las necedades comunes es cordura bien especial. Están muy validas por lo introducido, y algunos, que no se rindieron a la ignorancia particular, no supieron escaparse de la común. Vulgaridad es no estar contento ninguno con su suerte, aun la mayor, ni descontento de su ingenio, aunque el peor. Todos codician, con descontento de la propia, la felicidad ajena. También alaban los de hoy las cosas de ayer, y los de acá las de allende. Todo lo pasado parece mejor, y todo lo distante es más estimado. Tan necio es el que se ríe de todo como el que se pudre de todo.

210

Saber jugar de la verdad. Es peligrosa, pero el hombre de bien no puede dejar de decirla. Ahí es menester el artificio. Los diestros médicos del ánimo intentaron el modo de endulzarla; que cuando toca en el desengaño es la quinta esencia de lo amargo. El buen modo se vale aquí de su destreza. Con una misma verdad lisonjea uno y aporrea a otro. Hase de hablar a los presentes en los pasados. Con el buen entendedor basta brujulear; y cuando nada bastare, entra el caso de enmudecer. Los príncipes no se han de curar con cosas amargas: para eso es el arte de dorar los desengaños.

much. Some die because they feel, and others live because they do not; thus, some are fools because they do not die of grief, and others because they do. The man who dies of a surfeit of knowledge is a fool: thus some people die because they know and others go on living because they do not. Nevertheless, although many die of folly, few fools [ever] die.

209

To rid oneself of vulgar follies is a very special [*kind of*] *wisdom.* Such follies are very powerful because they are commonly accepted, and some who are not led astray by the ignorance of an individual cannot escape [the effects of] general ignorance. It is generally admitted that nobody is contented with his lot, not even with the greatest good fortune, nor dissatisfied with his intelligence, however mean it may be. All, while discontented with their own lot, covet that of others. The men of to-day praise, moreover, the achievements of bygone ages, and the people who inhabit this part of the world, those of distant lands. Everything in the past seems better, and everything remote is more highly esteemed. The man who laughs at everything is as foolish as the man who is disgruntled with everything.

210

Know how to play the card of truth. Truth is dangerous, but an honest man cannot fail to tell it. Here skill is necessary. Expert physicians of the mind endeavour to find a means of sweetening the pill of truth; for when it involves disillusion it is the quintessence of bitterness. Here, a pleasant manner has an opportunity for the display of its skill. With one and the same truth, you can flatter one person and belabour another. You should speak to those present in terms of those who are gone. For the man who is quick to understand, hints are enough; and if these are insufficient it is a case for silence. Rulers must not be cured with bitter potions: here the art of gilding the pill of disillusionment comes in.

211

En el cielo todo es contento; en el infierno todo es pesar.   En el mundo, como en medio, uno y otro.   Estamos entre dos extremos, y así se participa de entrambos.   Altérnanse las suertes: ni todo ha de ser felicidad, ni todo adversidad.   Este mundo es un cero: a solas, vale nada, juntándolo con el cielo, mucho.   La indiferencia a su variedad es cordura, ni es de sabios la novedad.   Vase empeñando nuestra vida como en comedia: al fin viene a desenredarse: la atención, pues, al acabar bien.

212

Reservarse siempre las últimas tretas del arte.   Es de grandes maestros, que se valen de su sutileza en el mismo enseñarla. Siempre ha de quedar superior y siempre maestro.   Hase de ir con arte en comunicar el arte; nunca se ha de agotar la fuente del enseñar, así como ni la del dar.   Con eso se conserva la reputación y la dependencia.   En el agradar y en el enseñar se ha de observar aquella gran lición de ir siempre cebando la admiración y adelantando la perfección.   El retén en todas las materias fué gran regla de vivir, de vencer, y más en los empleos más sublimes.

213

Saber contradecir.   Es gran treta del tentar, no para empeñarse, sino para empeñar.   Es el único torcedor el que hace saltar los afectos; es un vomitivo para los secretos la tibieza en el creer, llave del más cerrado pecho.   Hácese con grande sutileza la tentativa doble de la voluntad y del juicio.   Un desprecio sagaz de la misteriosa palabra del otro da caza a los secretos más profundos, y válos con suavidad bocadeando, hasta traerlos a la lengua, y a que den en las redes del artificioso engaño.   La detención en el atento hace arrojarse a la del otro en el recato, y descubre el ajeno sentir, que de otro modo era el corazón inescrutable.   Una duda afectada es la más sutil ganzúa de la

211

In heaven all is bliss: in hell all is misery. On earth, as it lies between the two, there is a mixture of both. We are between two extremes, and thus have a share in both of them. Destinies vary: every one cannot be happy, nor can every one be miserable. This world is a cipher: in itself it is worth nothing, but if joined to heaven, a great deal. It is wise to be indifferent to its mutability, and nothing comes as a surprise to wise men. Our life grows involved, as in a play: at the finish the plot is unravelled: take care, then, to have a good end.

212

Always keep the ultimate tricks of your trade to yourself. This is [a device] of great masters, who make use of craft in the very act of teaching their own. You should always be on top, always the master. You must proceed craftily in the teaching of your craft; the source of teaching, like that of giving, must never be exhausted. Thus the respect [of others] and their dependence upon you is preserved. In entertaining and teaching you should follow the great maxim that one must always go on providing food for admiration and continue progressing towards perfection. [To keep something in] reserve in all your concerns is a great rule for living and for success, more especially in the highest positions.

213

Know how to contradict. This is an excellent device for feeling your way, thereby involving others without involving yourself. It is the thumbscrew which can make the passions jump, unique in its kind; lukewarm belief is an emetic of secrets, a key to the most closely locked heart. It probes both the judgment and the will in the most subtle fashion. A shrewd depreciation of the mysterious remarks of another worms out the most profound secrets and, with some tasty bait, gently coaxes them to the tip of the tongue so that they are caught in the nets of specious deceit. Reserve on the part of a cautious man leads his opponents to take a chance with theirs and so lays bare thoughts which would otherwise be inscrutably locked away in his breast. An affected

curiosidad para saber cuanto quisiere; y aun para el aprender es treta del discípulo contradecir al maestro, que se empeña con más conato en la declaración y fundamento de la verdad; de suerte que la impugnación moderada da ocasión a la enseñanza cumplida.

214

No hacer de una necedad dos.   Es muy ordinario para remendar una cometer otras cuatro: excusar una impertinencia con otra mayor es de casta de mentira, o ésta lo es de necedad; que para sustentarse una necesita de muchas.   Siempre del mal pleito fué peor el patrocinio; más mal que el mismo mal no saberlo desmentir.   Es pensión de las imperfecciones dar a censo otras muchas; en un descuido puede caer el mayor sabio, pero en dos no, y de paso, que no de asiento.

215

Atención al que llega de segunda intención.   Es ardid del hombre negociante descuidar la voluntad para acometerla, que es vencida en siendo convencida.   Disimulan el intento para conseguirlo, y pónese segundo para que en la ejecución sea primero; asegúrase el tiro en lo inadvertido.   Pero no duerma la atención cuando tan desvelada la intención.   Y si ésta se hace segunda para el disimulo, aquélla primera para [1] el conocimiento. Advierta la cautela el artificio con que llega, y nótele las puntas que va echando para venir a parar al punto de su pretensión. Propone uno y pretende otro, y revuelven con sutileza a dar en el blanco de su intención; sepa, pues, lo que le concede, y tal vez convendrá dar a entender que ha entendido.

[1] 1659 omits 'para.'

doubt is curiosity's most subtle picklock, enabling it to find out all that it wants to know: and, even for the purpose of learning, it is a subtle device of a pupil to contradict his master, who then puts forth a greater effort to expound and establish truth; so that a moderate amount of contradiction gives rise to thorough teaching.

214

Do not turn one blunder into two. It very often happens that four additional blunders are committed in order to remedy one: to make amends for one piece of stupidity with another, greater one is akin to lying, or, rather, lies are akin to foolish acts for, in both cases, many are needed to support one. The defence of a bad cause is always worse than the cause itself; and inability to conceal evil is worse than evil itself. It is the disagreeable duty of failings to contribute to the support of many others of their kin; the wisest man may trip up once, but not twice, and when walking, not when sitting down.

215

Beware of the man with an ulterior motive. It is a device of the business man to put your will off its guard in order to attack it for, in the process of being convinced, it is conquered. Such men conceal their purpose in order to attain it and give it second place so that, in execution, it may have the first; they make sure of their shot through the heedlessness of their opponent. Attention, however, should not be asleep when intention is so wide awake; and, if the latter plays second fiddle for the purpose of dissimulation, heed should play the first, in order to be aware of what is going on. Caution notes the ruses which such a man employs and the tricks he makes use of in order to attain his end. He sets out to do one thing while pretending to do another and his aims craftily change and change about in order to hit the target of his design; understand, then, what you are conceding him, and it will sometimes be advisable to give him to understand that you have understood.

216

Tener la declarativa es no sólo desembarazo, pero despejo en e concepto. Algunos conciben bien y paren mal, que sin la claridad no salen a luz los hijos del alma, los conceptos y decretos. Tienen algunos la capacidad de aquellas vasijas que perciben mucho y comunican poco; al contrario, otros dicen aún más de lo que sienten. Lo que es la resolución en la voluntad, es la explicación en el entendimiento: dos grandes eminencias: los ingenios claros son plausibles, los confusos fueron venerados por no entendidos, y tal vez conviene la oscuridad para no ser vulgar. Pero, ¿cómo harán concepto los demás de los que les oyen, si no les corresponde concepto mental a ellos de lo que dicen?

217

No se ha de querer ni aborrecer para siempre. Confiar de los amigos hoy como enemigos mañana, y los peores; y pues pasa en la realidad, pase en la prevención. No se han de dar armas a los tránsfugas de la amistad, que hacen con ellas la mayor guerra; al contrario con los enemigos, siempre puerta abierta a la reconciliación, y sea la de la galantería: es la más segura. Atormentó alguna vez después la venganza de antes, y sirve de pesar el contento de la mala obra que se le hizo.

218

Nunca obrar por tema, sino por atención. Todo tema es postema, gran hija de la pasión, la que nunca obró cosa a derechas. Hay algunos que todo lo reducen a guerrilla; bandoleros del trato, cuanto ejecutan querrían que fuese vencimiento: no saben proceder pacíficamente. Estos, para mandar y regir, son perniciosos, porque hacen bando del gobierno, y enemigos de los que habían de hacer hijos: todo lo quieren disponer con traza y

216

To possess the gift of exposition reveals not only lack of embarrassment but liveliness of wit. Some conceive easily and give birth with difficulty, for without clarity, the children of the mind, ideas and decisions, cannot see the light of day. Some have the capacity of those vessels which hold a great deal and let out very little; on the other hand, some people say even more than they think. Resolution is to the will what explanation is to the understanding: [these are] two great gifts: clear minds are admirable; muddled ones are esteemed because they are not understood, and obscurity is, indeed, to be recommended at times so that you may avoid the commonplace. Yet how can others form an opinion concerning those who listen to them if the latter have no idea what these others are saying?

217

One should neither love nor hate for ever. Trust the friends of to-day as though they were the enemies of to-morrow, and your worst enemies, and since this is actually the case, your foresight should behave as though it were. Do not provide renegade friends with weapons, for they use them to wage the most bitter warfare; with enemies, on the contrary, always keep open the door for reconciliation, and see that it is also the door of magnanimity: it is the safest one. The revenge of yesterday has sometimes given torment later on and the satisfaction once provided by the harm done to you is turned into remorse.

218

Never act out of obstinacy, but with circumspection. All stubbornness is a tumour [on the mind], the monstrous daughter of passion, which has never done anything properly. There are some people who reduce everything to guerrilla warfare; the bandits of social intercourse, they would like everything they do to be a victory: they are incapable of peaceable behaviour. Such men make very bad rulers and governors because they turn the government into a guerrilla faction and make enemies of those whom they ought to have treated as their children: they try to bring strategy into everything and achieve everything as the

H

conseguir como fruto de su artificio; pero en descubriéndoles el paradojo humor los demás, luego se apunta con ellos. Procúranles estorbar sus quimeras, y así nada consiguen. Llévanse muchos hartazgos de enfados, y todos les ayudan al disgusto. Estos tienen el dictamen leso y tal vez dañado el corazón; el modo de portarse con semejantes monstruos es huir a los antípodas, que mejor se llevará la barbaridad de aquéllos que la fiereza de éstos.

219

No ser tenido por hombre de artificio, aunque no se pueda ya vivir sin él. Antes prudente que astuto. Es agradable a todos la lisura en el trato, pero no a todos por su casa. La sinceridad no dé en el extremo de simplicidad, ni la sagacidad de astucia. Sea antes venerado por sabio, que temido reflexo. Los sinceros son amados, pero engañados. El mayor artificio sea encubrir lo que se tiene por engaño. Floreció en el siglo de oro la llaneza; en este de hierro, la malicia. El crédito de hombre que sabe lo que ha de hacer, es honroso y causa confianza; pero el de artificioso, es sofístico y engendra recelo.

220

Cuando no puede uno vestirse de piel de león, vístase la de la vulpeja. Saber ceder al tiempo es exceder: el que sale con su intento nunca pierde reputación; a falta de fuerza, destreza; por un camino o por otro, o por el real del valor o por el atajo del artificio. Más cosas ha obrado la maña que la fuerza, y más veces vencieron los sabios a los valientes, que al contrario. Cuando no se puede alcanzar la cosa, entra el desprecio.

221

No ser ocasionado ni para empeñarse ni para empeñar. Hay tropiezos del decoro, tanto propio como ajeno, siempre a punto

fruits of their cunning; but when others have discovered their
perverse disposition, they turn sour on them at once. Others try
to upset their fantastic schemes, and in consequence they attain
nothing. Such people are overburdened with vexations and all
these help to mortify them. The judgment of these people is
defective and, as likely as not, their hearts are in the wrong place;
the way to deal with monsters like these is to fly to the Antipodes,
the barbarity of which will be easier to put up with than the
savagery of such men as these.

219

Do not be regarded as a crafty person, although it may be no
longer possible to live without craft. [Be] prudent rather than
astute. Frankness in your dealings is pleasing to every one,
but not all find it agreeable in their domestic circle. Do not
let sincerity go to the extreme of ingenuousness nor sagacity to
that of cunning. Rather be respected as a wise man than feared
as a sly one. Sincere people are loved, but deceived. Let your
greatest skill reside in concealing what is regarded as deceit.
Candour flourished in the Age of Gold; in this Age of Iron,
cunning is supreme. A reputation for being a man who knows
what he ought to do is an honourable one and inspires confidence; but a reputation for slyness is regarded as a mark of
sophistry and engenders suspicion.

220

*When you cannot clothe yourself in a lion's skin, don that of a
fox.* To know how to yield to the times is to surpass them: the
man who gets his own way never loses his reputation; when you
lack power, use cunning; [get on] somehow or other, either by
the highway of merit or by the byway of artifice. Craft has
achieved more than power and the wise have overcome the
brave more often than the brave the wise. When you cannot
get the thing [you want], people come to despise you.

221

Do not be provocative by compromising either yourself or others.
Some people are stumbling-blocks in the way of good manners,

de necedad. Encuéntranse con gran facilidad y rompen con infelicidad; no lo hacen al día con cien enfados; tienen el humor al repelo, y así contradicen a cuantos hay. Calzáronse el juicio al revés, y así todo lo reprueban. Pero los mayores tentadores de la cordura son los que nada hacen bien y de todo dicen mal. Que hay muchos monstruos en el extendido país de la impertinencia.

222

Hombre detenido, evidencia de prudente. Es fiera la lengua, que si una vez se suelta, es muy dificultoso de poderse volver a encadenar: es el pulso del alma, por donde conocen los sabios su disposición. Aquí pulsan los atentos el movimiento del corazón: el mal es que el que había de serlo más, es menos reportado. Excúsase el sabio enfados y empeños, y muestra cuán señor es de sí. Procede circunspecto, Jano en la equivalencia, Argos en la verificación. Mejor Momo hubiera echado menos los ojos en las manos que la ventanilla en el pecho.

223

No ser muy individuado, o por afectar o por no advertir. Tienen algunos notable individuación con acciones de manía, que son más defectos que diferencias; y así como algunos son bien conocidos por alguna singular fealdad en el rostro, así éstos por algún exceso en el porte. No sirve el individuarse sino de nota, con una impertinente especialidad, que conmueve alternativamente en unos la risa, en otros el enfado.

224

Saber tomar las cosas, nunca al repelo, aunque vengan. Todas tienen haz y envés: la mejor y más favorable si se toma por el

their own as well as their neighbours': they are always on the point of doing something stupid. One encounters them with great ease, and parts from them full of uneasiness; a hundred vexations a day are nothing to them; they are cross-grained, and so contradict everybody. They put on their judge's robes inside out, and so disapprove of everything. But the people who try one's patience most are those who do nothing well themselves and speak ill of everything. For there are many monsters in the wide realm of folly.

222

A reserved man shows himself to be a prudent one. The tongue is a wild beast, and if once it gets loose it is very difficult to chain it up again: it is the pulse by which wise men judge the state of the soul. By this pulse careful observers feel the movement of the heart. The trouble is that he who ought to be the most discreet is, in fact, the least so. The wise man avoids vexations and embarrassments and shows to what extent he is master of himself. He behaves with circumspection, a Janus of adaptability, an Argus of discernment. Momus would have missed the eyes in the hands less than the little window in the breast.

223

Do not be eccentric, either out of affectation or through carelessness. Some people have extraordinary personal idiosyncrasies, together with crazy mannerisms which are defects rather than differentiations; and just as some people are easily recognizable by some peculiar facial deformity, so eccentrics may be recognized by a certain extravagance of bearing. To be different from others merely serves to brand oneself with a special mark of folly which excites, in turn, derision in some people and annoyance in others.

224

Learn never to take things amiss, even though they may come so. Everything has its right side and its wrong side: the best and most effective [weapon] will injure you if you take hold of it by the

corte, lastima; al contrario, la más repugnante defiende, si por la empuñadura. Muchas fueron de pena que, si se consideraran las conveniencias, fueran de contento. En todo hay convenientes y inconvenientes: la destreza está en saber topar con la comodidad. Hace muy diferentes visos una misma cosa, si se mira a diferentes luces: mírese por la de la felicidad. No se han de trocar los frenos al bien y al mal: de aquí procede que algunos en todo hallan el contento y otros el pesar. Gran reparo contra los reveses de la fortuna, ya gran regla del vivir para todo tiempo y para todo empleo.

225

Conocer su defecto rey. Ninguno vive sin el contrapeso de la prenda relevante, y si le favorece la inclinación, apodérase a lo tirano. Comience a hacerle la guerra publicando el cuidado contra él; y el primer paso sea el manifiesto, que en siendo conocido será vencido; y más si el interesado hace el concepto de él como los que notan. Para ser señor de sí es menester ir sobre sí; rendido este cabo de imperfecciones, acabarán todas.

226

Atención a obligar. Los más no hablan ni obran como quien son, sino como les obligan. Para persuadir lo malo cualquiera sobra, porque lo malo es muy creído, aunque tal vez increíble. Lo más y lo mejor que tenemos depende de respeto ajeno. Conténtanse algunos con tener la razón de su parte, pero no basta, que es menester ayudarla con la diligencia. Cuesta a veces muy poco el obligar, y vale mucho. Con palabras se compran obras: no hay alhaja tan vil en esta gran casa del universo que una vez al año no sea menester, y aunque valga poco, hará gran falta: cada uno habla del objeto según su afecto.

blade; on the other hand, the most unsatisfactory one will serve to defend you if [you grasp it] by the hilt. Pain may be caused by many things which, if their advantageous aspect had been considered, might have given rise to satisfaction. There is a favourable and an unfavourable side to everything: the skill consists in knowing how to hit upon the favourable one. One and the same thing has very different aspects if it is examined in different lights: look at things on the bright side. The reins of good and evil should not be interchanged; it is thus that some find satisfaction, and others vexation, in everything. [This advice is] a strong shield against reverses of fortune and an admirable rule of life at all times, and in all occupations.

225

Know your chief failing. There is no person alive who does not have some counterpoise to his outstanding good quality and, if inclination favours it, it wields tyrannical power. Start to make war upon it by issuing a public warning against it; and let this manifesto be your first step, for once your failing is known it will be overcome; and more especially if you, the interested party, see it in the same light as do the onlookers. To attain self-mastery, one must lay siege to oneself; if the chief failing surrenders, all the others will be overcome.

226

Take care to be obliging. Most people neither talk nor act according to their true nature but, rather, as they are obliged to do. Anything is more than enough to persuade people of evil, for although it is sometimes unbelievable, evil is very readily believed. All that is greatest and best in us depends upon the regard in which we are held by others. Some are satisfied if they have right on their side, but that is not enough, for it must be reinforced by diligence. It often costs very little to oblige people, and to do so is worth a lot. Deeds are bought with words: in this mansion of the universe there is no utensil so humble that it may not be needed on one occasion during the year, and although it may be of little value, it will be sorely missed. Every one speaks of a thing according to his inclination.

227

No ser de primera impresión. Cásanse algunos con la primera información, de suerte que las demás son concubinas; y como se adelanta siempre la mentira, no queda lugar después para la verdad: ni la voluntad con el primer objeto, ni el entendimiento con la primera proposición se han de llenar, que es cortedad de fondo. Tienen algunos la capacidad de vasija nueva, que el primer olor le ocupa, tanto del mal licor como del bueno. Cuando esta cortedad llega a conocida, es perniciosa, que da pie a la maliciosa industria: previénense los mal intencionados a teñir de su color la credulidad: quede siempre lugar a la revista. Guarde Alejandro la otra oreja para la otra parte, quede lugar para la segunda y tercera información: arguye incapacidad el impresionarse, y está cerca del apasionarse.

228

No tener voz de mala voz. Mucho menos tener tal opinión, que es tener fama de contrafamas. No sea ingenioso a costa ajena, que es más odioso que dificultoso: vénganse todos de él diciendo mal todos de él; y como es solo y ellos muchos, más presto será él vencido que convencidos ellos. Lo malo nunca ha de contentar, pero ni comentarse. Es el murmurador siempre aborrecido, y aunque a veces personajes grandes atraviesen con él, será más por gusto de su fisga que por estimación de su cordura: y el que dice mal, siempre oye peor.

229

Saber repartir su vida a lo discreto, no como se vienen las ocasiones, sino por providencia y delecto. Es penosa sin descansos, como jornada larga sin mesones; hácela dichosa la

227

Do not be influenced by first impressions.   Some people espouse the first account they hear, so that all other versions of a story are concubines; and, as falsehood always elbows its way forward, there is, later, no room for the truth: you should neither satisfy your desire with the first object that meets your eyes nor your judgment with the first proposition that is offered, for that is [a sign of] limited ability.   Some people have the capacity of new flasks which preserve the bouquet of the first liquor they hold, be it bad or good.   When this limited capacity of theirs comes to be known, it is disastrous for them, since it provides a foothold for the activities of the malicious: men of ill will are ready to colour the minds of the credulous according to their way of thinking: room should always be left for second thoughts. Let Alexander keep the other ear for the other side, let there be room for the second and third version of a story: to be [easily] impressed argues lack of ability, and is very close to being swayed by one's emotions.

228

Do not have the tongue of a scandalmonger, much less the name of being one, for that is to be notorious as a destroyer of good repute.   Do not be witty at the expense of another, for to be so is more odious than difficult: all men revenge themselves upon a slanderer by all speaking ill of him; and, as he is but one and they are many, he will be more speedily conquered than they will be convinced.   Evil should never be a source of satisfaction, nor even a subject of comment.   The scandalmonger is always detested and, although eminent people may sometimes consort with him, it will be rather because they enjoy his backbiting than because they value his wisdom: and the man who speaks ill always hears worse.

229

Know how to divide up your life in a sensible way, not as opportunities present themselves, but with foresight and discrimination.   Life is tedious without restful interludes, like a long journey [on a road] without any inns; a variety of learned

* H

variedad erudita.   Gástase la primera estancia del bello vivir en hablar con los muertos; nacemos para saber y sabernos, y los libros con fidelidad nos hacen personas.   La segunda jornada se emplea con los vivos: ver y registrar todo lo bueno del mundo. No todas las cosas se hallan en una tierra; repartió los dotes el Padre universal, y a veces enriqueció más la fea.   La tercera jornada sea toda para sí: última felicidad el filosofar.

230

Abrir los ojos con tiempo.   No todos los que ven han abierto los ojos, ni todos los que miran ven.   Dar en la cuenta tarde, no sirve de remedio sino de pesar; comienzan a ver algunos cuando no hay, que deshicieron sus casas y sus cosas antes de hacerse ellos.   Es dificultoso dar entendimiento a quien no tiene voluntad, y más dar voluntad a quien no tiene entendimiento: juegan con ellos los que les van al rededor, como con ciegos, con risa de los demás; y porque son sordos para oir, no abren los ojos para ver.   Pero no falta quien fomenta esta insensibilidad, que consiste su ser en que ellos no sean.   Infeliz caballo cuyo amo no tiene ojos: mal engordará.

231

Nunca permitir a medio hacer las cosas: gócense en su perfección.   Todos los principios son informes, y queda después la imaginación de aquella deformidad; la memoria de haberlo visto imperfecto no lo deja lograr acabado.   Gozar de un golpe el objeto grande, aunque embaraza el juicio de las partes, de por sí adecua el gusto: antes de ser todo es nada, y en el comenzar a ser se está aún muy dentro de su nada.   El ver guisar el manjar más regalado sirve antes de asco que de apetito; recátese, pues, todo

pursuits makes it pleasant.   The first stage of this splendid life is spent in conversing with the dead; we are born to acquire knowledge and to know ourselves, and books make us truly men. The second stage is spent with the living: in observing and taking note of everything that is good in the world.   Everything is not found in any one country; the Father of All has shared out His gifts and has sometimes granted the richest of these to the ugly.   The third stage should be devoted entirely to oneself: to the ultimate delight, philosophizing.

230

Open your eyes in time.   Not all those who see have opened their eyes, nor do all those who look, see.   To realize things too late is not a help but a cause of regret; some people begin to see when there is nothing [to be seen], for they pull down their houses and wreck their fortunes before they have built up their own personalities.   It is difficult to bestow understanding upon those who lack will, and more difficult to bestow will upon those who lack understanding: the people around them play at blind-man's-buff with such folk and make them a laughing-stock in the eyes of others; and, as they are hard of hearing, such men do not open their eyes in order to see [what is going on].   There is, however, no lack of persons to foment this insensibility because their own existence depends upon the non-existence of the others.   Unhappy the horse whose owner has no eyes: it will certainly not grow fat.

231

Never allow yourself to do things by halves, let them be enjoyed in their perfection.   All beginnings are formless and a mental picture of this lack of form remains afterwards; the memory of having seen something in an imperfect state does not allow us to enjoy it when it is completed.   Although it may hamper our appreciation of its parts, a full view of some great work, all at once, is itself enough to satisfy our taste: before it is complete it is nothing and while it is at its beginnings there is still a great deal of nothingness about it.   To see the tastiest of morsels while it is being cooked serves to provoke nausea rather than

gran maestro de que le vean sus obras en embrión: aprenda de la naturaleza a no exponerlas hasta que puedan parecer.

232

Tener un punto de negociante. No todo sea especulación: haya también acción. Los muy sabios son fáciles de engañar, porque aunque saben lo extraordinario, ignoran lo ordinario del vivir, que es más preciso. La contemplación de las cosas sublimes no les da lugar para las manuales, y como ignoran lo primero que habían de saber y en que todos parten un cabello, o son admirados, o son tenidos por ignorantes del vulgo superficial. Procure, pues, el varón sabio tener algo de negociante, lo que baste para no ser engañado y aun reído: sea hombre de lo agible, que aunque no es lo superior, es lo más precioso del vivir. ¿De qué sirve el saber si no es plático? Y el saber vivir es hoy el verdadero saber.

233

No errarle el golpe al gusto, que es hacer un pesar por un placer. Con lo que piensan obligar algunos, enfadan por no comprender los genios. Obras hay que para unos son lisonja y para otros ofensa; y el que se creyó servicio fué agravio. Costó a veces más el dar disgusto, que hubiera costado el hacer placer: pierden el agradecimiento y el don porque perdieron el norte del agradar. Si no se sabe el genio ajeno, mal se le podrá satisfacer; de aquí es que algunos pensaron decir un elogio y dijeron un vituperio, que fué bien merecido castigo. Piensan otros entretener con su elocuencia, y aporrean el alma con su locuacidad.

appetite; so let every great master take care that his works shall not be seen in embryo: he should learn from nature not to put them on view until they are fit to be seen.

232

Be a bit of a business man. Speculation should not be all in all: there should be action as well. Very learned people are easy to deceive because, although they are versed in abstruse matters, they lack the more necessary knowledge of everyday affairs. The contemplation of higher things leaves them with no room for mundane matters, and as they do not know the first things they ought to know, and of which everybody shares some knowledge, they are either admired or feared by the ignorant members of the superficial mob. The wise man should, then, try to have something of the trader about him, enough to prevent him from being swindled and even ridiculed: he should be a practical person for, if practical matters are not the highest, they are the most [materially] valuable things in life. What is the good of knowledge if it serves no useful purpose? And in these days, true knowledge consists in knowing how to live.

233

Do not miscalculate where taste is concerned, for to do so is to turn a source of pleasure into one of irritation. Because they do not understand the temperaments of others, some people provoke annoyance by doing the very thing which they intend to be obliging. Certain actions are agreeable to some people and an offence to others; and he who thinks he has done a service may well have given offence. It often costs more to vex a man than it would have cost to please him; both the gift and the thanks for it are lost because your guide to tastes has been mislaid. If you do not know another's temperament it is quite impossible to please him; hence some people think they are paying a compliment when they are proffering an insult, which leads to a well-deserved reproach. Others think they are entertaining you with their eloquence when they are boring you to death with their loquaciousness.

234

Nunca fiar reputación sin prendas de honra ajena.   Hase de ir a la parte del provecho en el silencio, del daño en la facilidad.   En intereses de honra siempre ha de ser el trato de compañía, de suerte que la propia reputación ha de cuidar de la ajena.   Nunca se ha de fiar; pero si alguna vez, sea con tal arte que pueda ceder la prudencia a la cautela.   Sea el riesgo común y recíproca la causa, para que no se le convierta en testigo el que se reconoce partícipe.

235

Saber pedir.   No hay cosa más dificultosa para algunos, ni más fácil para otros.   Hay unos que no saben negar: con éstos no es menester ganzúa.   Hay otros que el 'no' es su primer palabra a todas horas.   Con éstos es menester la industria, y con todos la sazón: un coger los espíritus alegres, o por el pasto antecedente del cuerpo o por el del ánimo, si a la atención del reflexo que atiende no previene la sutileza en el que intenta.   Los días del gozo son los del favor, que redunda del interior a lo exterior.   No se ha de llegar cuando se ve negar a otro; que está perdido el miedo al no.   Sobre tristeza no hay buen lance.   El obligar de antemano es cambio donde no corresponde la villanía.

236

Hacer obligación antes de lo que habría de ser premio después: es destreza de grandes políticos; favores antes de méritos, son prueba de hombres de obligación.   El favor así anticipado tiene dos eminencias, que con lo pronto del que da, obliga más al que recibe.   Un mismo don, si después es deuda, antes es empeño.

234

Never trust your reputation to another unless you have his honour in pawn. You should so contrive it that silence may be mutually advantageous and a ready tongue a danger to both. Where honour is at stake the bargain must always be mutual, so that each party watches over the other's reputation for the sake of his own. Never be a surety; but if, on some occasion, [you are obliged to be such], you should so devise it that prudence may be able to give way to caution. The risk should be common to both parties and the undertaking mutual, so that the self-confessed accomplice may not turn king's evidence.

235

Know how to ask. There is nothing more difficult for some people nor, for others, easier. There are some people who cannot refuse: in their case you do not require a picklock. There are others whose first word is 'no' on any and every occasion. With these, persistence is needed and, with all types of people, the auspicious moment: they should be got at when they are in a cheerful frame of mind or when they have just feasted their bodies or their souls, provided that the reflective heed of the hearer does not forestall the subtlety of the applicant. Days of rejoicing are of good omen for those who seek favours, for joy overflows from within outwards. Do not turn up at a time when you see that someone else is being refused; for then the fear of saying 'no' has already been overcome. A mood of melancholy does not provide a favourable occasion. To put a person under an obligation to oneself beforehand is a safe bill of exchange when one is not dealing with a cad.

236

Grant beforehand as a favour what you would later have to give as a reward: it is a clever device of great politicians; to anticipate deserts by favours is the touchstone of men of honour. A favour accorded thus in advance possesses two outstanding advantages, for the readiness of the giver puts the receiver under a greater obligation. The very gift which would later be a debt, owing, constitutes an obligation if it is granted beforehand.

Sutil modo de transformar obligaciones, que la que había de estar en el superior para premiar recae en el obligado para satisfacer. Esto se entiende con gente de obligaciones, que para hombres viles más sería poner freno que espuela, anticipando la paga del honor.

237

Nunca partir secretos con mayores. Pensará partir peras y partirá piedras; perecieron muchos de confidentes. Son éstos como cuchar de pan, que corre el mismo riesgo después. No es favor del príncipe, sino pecho, el comunicarlo. Quiebran muchos el espejo porque les acuerda la fealdad: no puede ver al que le pudo ver, ni es bien visto el que vió mal. A ninguno se ha de tener muy obligado, y al poderoso menos. Sea antes con beneficios hechos que con favores recibidos; sobre todo, son peligrosas confianzas de amistad. El que comunicó sus secretos a otro hízose esclavo de él; y en soberanos es violencia que no puede durar. Desean volver a redimir la libertad perdida, y para esto atropellarán con todo, hasta la razón. Los secretos, pues, ni oirlos ni decirlos.

238

Conocer la pieza que le falta. Fueran muchos muy personas si no les faltara un algo, sin el cual nunca llegan al colmo del perfecto ser. Nótase en algunos que pudieran ser mucho si repararan en bien poco. Háceles falta la seriedad, con que deslucen grandes prendas; a otros la suavidad de la condición, que es falta que los familiares echan presto menos, y más en personas de puesto. En algunos se desea lo ejecutivo y en otros lo reportado; todos estos desaires, si se advirtiesen, se podrían suplir con

This is a subtle way of transposing duties, for the obligation which would have compelled the superior to reward now falls upon the recipient of the favour and compels him to satisfy it. This applies to men of honour for, in the case of low fellows, the payment in advance would act rather as a bit than a spur.

237

Never share secrets with superiors. You will think you are sharing pears and will share [only] stones: many have come to grief through being confidants. These men are like a piece of bread used as a scoop, and run the same risk [of being devoured] later. It is no favour on the part of a ruler to disclose a secret, but rather a levy [which he imposes upon you]. Many people break their mirrors because these remind them of their ugliness: we do not like seeing those who have been able to see through us, nor do we look favourably upon one to whom we have shown ourselves in a bad light. You should not be greatly beholden to anybody, least of all to the powerful. With them it should be a case of benefits conferred rather than favours received; friendly confidences are, above all, dangerous. The person who has disclosed his secrets to another has made himself that man's slave; and, in the case of monarchs, it is an unnatural situation which cannot last. They wish to recover their lost freedom and, in order to do so, they will ride rough-shod over everything, even reason itself. So do not listen to secrets, and do not tell them.

238

Know the quality in which you are lacking. Many men would have been great individuals if they had not lacked something without which they can never rise to the completeness of perfect being. In the case of some men, it is to be observed that they would be capable of great things if only they would pay attention to very little things. They lack seriousness of purpose and this deficiency dulls the lustre of their great gifts; other people lack gentleness of disposition, a deficiency which associates are quick to observe, and more especially in persons who occupy important posts. Some lack executive ability and others self-control; all

facilidad, que el cuidado puede hacer de la costumbre segunda naturaleza.

239

No ser reagudo; más importa prudencial.   Saber más de lo que conviene es despuntar, porque las sutilezas comúnmente quiebran.   Más segura es la verdad asentada.   Bueno es tener entendimiento, pero no bachillería.   El mucho discurrir ramo es de cuestión.   Mejor es un buen juicio sustancial, que no discurre más de lo que importa.

240

Saber usar de la necedad.   El mayor sabio juega tal vez de esta pieza, y hay tales ocasiones que el mejor saber consiste en mostrar no saber; no se ha de ignorar, pero sí afectar que se ignora.   Con los necios poco importa ser sabio, y con los locos, cuerdo.   Hásele de hablar a cada uno en su lenguaje: no es necio el que afecta la necedad, sino el que la padece.   La sencilla lo es, que no la doble, que hasta eso llega el artificio.   Para ser bienquisto el único medio es vestirse la piel del más simple de los brutos.

241

Las burlas, sufrirlas, pero no usarlas.   Aquello es especie de galantería, esto de empeño.   El que en la fiesta se desazona, mucho tiene de bestia y muestra más.   Es gustosa la burla sobrada; saberla sufrir es argumento de capacidad.   Da pie al que se pica a que le repique.   A lo mejor se han de dejar, y lo más seguro es no levantarlas.[1]   Las mayores veras nacieron siempre de las burlas.   No hay cosa que pida más atención y destreza.   Antes de comenzar se ha de saber hasta qué punto de sufrir llegará el genio del sujeto.

[1] *Vide* Appendix, p. 307.

these wants could, if noted, easily be supplied, for care can make habit a second nature.

239

Do not be too clever by half; it is more important [to be] discreet. To know more than is desirable blunts your weapons, for fine points usually break. Established truth is safer. It is good to have understanding, but not to babble. Lengthy argument is a kind of contentiousness. Good, sound judgment is better, for it does not [prompt you to] talk more than is necessary.

240

Know how to play the daft laddie. The wisest man plays this card at times and there are occasions upon which the highest wisdom consists in appearing not to know; you must not be ignorant but actually pretend you are. It is not much good being wise among fools, and sane among lunatics. You must speak to every one in his own language: he who poses as one is not a fool but rather he who is the victim of folly. Simple folly is stupid, not so that of duplicity, for cunning reaches that pitch. The only way to be well liked is to clothe yourself in the skin of the silliest of the animals.

241

Put up with banter, but do not indulge in it. To tolerate it is a kind of courtesy, to indulge in it is embarrassing. The man who is disagreeable at a party has a good deal of the brute in him and displays even more. Banter is very delightful; to know how to put up with it is a mark of capability. The man who is nettled by it invites people to sting him again. One should drop it at the right moment and it is safer not to embark upon it. The greatest truths have always been spoken in jest. Nothing demands more care and skill than banter. Before you begin you must know to what extent the temper of the other fellow will put up with it.

242

Seguir los alcances. Todo se les va a algunos en comenzar, y nunca acaban; inventan, pero no prosiguen. Instabilidad de genio: nunca consiguen alabanza, porque nada prosiguen: todo pára en parar; si bien nace en otros en impaciencia de ánimo; tacha de españoles, así como la paciencia es la ventaja de los belgas. Estos acaban las cosas, aquéllos acaban con ellas: [1] hasta vencer la dificultad sudan, y conténtanse con el vencer. No saben llevar al cabo la victoria: prueban que pueden, mas no quieren. Pero siempre es defecto de imposibilidad o liviandad. Si la obra es buena, ¿por qué no se acaba? Y si es mala, ¿por qué se comenzó? Mate, pues, el sagaz la caza: no se le vaya todo en levantarla.

243

No ser todo columbino. Altérnense la calidez de la serpiente con la candidez de la paloma. No hay cosa más fácil que engañar a un hombre de bien. Cree mucho el que nunca miente, y confía mucho el que nunca engaña. No siempre procede de necio el ser engañado, que tal vez de bueno. Dos géneros de personas previenen mucho los daños: los escarmentados, que es muy a su costa, y los aturdidos, que es muy a la ajena. Muéstrese tan extremada la sagacidad para el recelo como la astucia para el enredo, y no quiera uno ser tan hombre de bien que ocasione al otro serlo de mal; sea uno mixto de paloma y de serpiente; no monstruo, sino prodigio.

244

Saber obligar. Transforman algunos el favor propio en ajeno, y parece, o dan a entender, que hacen merced cuando la reciben.

[1] *Vide* Appendix, p. 307.

242

Follow up your advantages. All the virtue goes out of some people at the start and they never finish [anything]: they invent, but never get any further. [This is due to] instability of character: they never win praise because they do not follow anything up: they always finish by stopping short: in others, this failing arises out of impatience, the besetting sin of the Spaniards, just as patience is the virtue of the Belgians. The latter carry affairs through to a conclusion, while the former are carried to a conclusion by affairs; they sweat away until a difficulty is overcome and are satisfied when they have surmounted it. They do not know how to push their victory home: they show that they have the ability, but not the determination, to do so. This defect, moreover, always arises out of either incapacity or instability. If the undertaking is sound, why not see it through? And if it is unsound, why was it begun? The wise man, then, should kill his quarry: let him not exhaust himself completely in the starting of it.

243

Do not be completely dovelike. Alternate the cunning of the serpent with the candour of the dove. There is nothing easier than to deceive an honourable man. The person who never tells lies is extremely credulous and the man who never deceives is very trusting. To be taken in is not always the result of stupidity but sometimes of virtue. There are two types of men who ward off injuries with ease: those who have suffered them, very much to their own cost, and those morally insensible people who have learned their lesson at very great cost to their fellows. The wise should show themselves as ready to suspect as are the cunning to ensnare, and no one should want to be so good a man as to cause another to be bad: one should be a mixture of dove and serpent; not a monster, but a prodigy.

244

Know how to put others under an obligation. Some turn a favour received into a favour bestowed, and it appears, or they give it to be understood, that they are doing a favour when they

Hay hombres tan advertidos, que honran pidiendo y truecan el provecho suyo en honra del otro; de tal suerte trazan las cosas que parezca que a los otros les hacen servicio cuando les dan, trastrocando con extravagante política el orden de obligar.   Por lo menos, ponen en duda quién hace favor a quién: compran a precio de alabanzas lo mejor, y del mostrar gusto de una cosa hacen honra y lisonja: empeñan la cortesía, haciendo deuda de lo que había de ser su agradecimiento.   De esta suerte truecan la obligación de pasiva en activa: mejores políticos que gramáticos. Gran sutileza ésta, pero mayor lo sería el entendérsela, destrocando la necedad, volviéndoles su honra, y cobrando cada uno su provecho.

245

Discurrir tal vez a lo singular y fuera de lo común, arguye superioridad de caudal: no ha de estimar al que nunca se le opone, que no es señal de amor que le tenga, sino del que él se tiene; no se deje engañar de la lisonja pagándola, sino condenándola.   También tenga por crédito el ser murmurado de algunos, y más de aquéllos que de todos los buenos dicen mal.   Pésele de que sus cosas agraden a todos, que es señal de no ser buenas: que es de pocos lo perfecto.

246

Nunca dar satisfacción a quien no la pedía, y aunque se pida, es especie de delito si es sobrada.   El excusarse antes de ocasión es culparse: y el sangrarse en salud es hacer del ojo al mal y a la malicia.   La excusa anticipada despierta al recelo que dormía. Ni se ha de dar el cuerdo por entendido de la sospecha ajena, que

are receiving one. Some men are so astute that they confer a favour by demanding one and turn their own advantage into an honour done to another; they so contrive matters that they appear to be doing others a service when the latter are granting one to them, thereby transposing the order of the obligations with extraordinary speciousness. At least, they excite doubt as to who is obliging whom: they buy the best of everything at the price of praise and convert their manifestation of pleasure in a thing into a flattering honour: they put courtesy in pawn and thus turn what should have been their gratitude into a debt owing to them by others. They thus change the obligation from a passive into an active form, thereby proving themselves to be better politicians than they are grammarians. This is a very clever trick, but it would be even more astute to see through it and to return the goods offered in this fool's bargain by repaying the favours of the bargainer in the same coin, so that each party may come into his own.

245

To talk from time to time in a striking and unusual way is a mark of superior ability: you should not think a great deal of a person who never contradicts you, for this is not a sign that he is fond of you, but rather that he is in love with himself; do not allow yourself to be taken in by flattery and pay for it in its own coin, but rather condemn it. Regard it, also, as an honour to be censured by some people, and more especially by those who speak ill of all good men. It should worry you if your actions please everybody, for it is a sign that they are no good: perfection is for the few.

246

Never offer an apology to a person who did not ask for it, and, even if one is demanded, it is a kind of offence if it is exaggerated. To excuse yourself prematurely is to accuse yourself; and to have yourself bled when in good health is to court misfortune and malevolence. An excuse in advance arouses suspicion from its slumbers. Nor ought a sensible man to reveal that he is aware of another's suspicions, for that is to go in search of insults; you

es salir a buscar el agravio; entonces le ha de procurar desmentir
con la entereza de su proceder.

247

Saber un poco más y vivir un poco menos.   Otros discurren al
contrario: más vale el buen ocio que el negocio.   No tenemos
cosa nuestra sino el tiempo, donde vive quien no tiene lugar.
Igual infelicidad es gastar la preciosa vida en tareas mecánicas
que en demasía de las sublimes; ni se ha de cargar de ocupaciones
ni de envidia: es atropellar el vivir y ahogar el ánimo.   Algunos
lo extienden al saber, pero no se vive si no se sabe.

248

No se le lleve el último.   Hay hombres de última información,
que va por extremos la impertinencia.   Tienen el sentir y el
querer de cera: el último sella y borra los demás; éstos nunca
están ganados, porque con la misma facilidad se pierden: cada
uno los tiñe de su color.   Son malos para confidentes, niños de
toda la vida, y así, con variedad en los juicios y afectos, andan
fluctuando, siempre cojos de voluntad y de juicio, inclinándose a
una y otra parte.

249

No comenzar a vivir por donde se ha de acabar.   Algunos toman
el descanso al principio y dejan la fatiga para el fin: primero ha de
ser lo esencial, y después, si quedare lugar, lo accesorio.   Quieren
otros triunfar antes de pelear.   Algunos comienzan a saber por
lo que menos importa, y los estudios de crédito y utilidad dejan
para cuando se les acaba el vivir.   No ha comenzado a hacer
fortuna el otro, cuando ya se desvanece.   Es esencial el método
para saber y poder vivir.

should, then, try to disarm suspicion by the integrity of your
conduct.

247

Know a little more and live a little less. Others say the
opposite: leisure well spent is more valuable than business. We
have nothing of our own except time, the abode [even] of the
homeless. Whether you waste precious life in performing
menial tasks or in too much toil over lofty ones, you will be
equally unhappy; you should burden yourself with neither work
nor envy: that is to ride roughshod over life and stifle the spirit.
Some extend this principle to the sphere of knowledge, but if
you do not have knowledge you are not alive at all.

248

Do not be carried away by the last comer. There are people
who go by the latest news, for folly goes to extremes. Their
feelings and their will are of wax: 'the latest' sets its seal upon
them and blots out everything else; such people are never won
over because they are lost as easily as they are won: every one
dyes them with his own tint. They are no good as intimate
friends, [remain] children all their days and so, because of this
instability of judgment and feeling, they stagger along the path
of life, permanent cripples in will and judgment, tottering from
one side [of the road] to the other.

249

Do not begin life at the point where it should finish. Some take
their ease at the start and leave toil till the end: essentials should
come first and accessories later, if there is room for them.
Others want victory before they have fought. Some start by
learning what is of least importance and leave reputable and
useful studies till the time when their life is drawing to a close.
Another has not yet started to make a career when he disappears
from the scene. Method is essential both in acquiring knowledge and in the art of living.

250

—*¿Cuándo se ha de discurrir al revés?*—Cuando nos hablan a la malicia.   Con algunos todo ha de ir al encontrado: el sí es no y el no es sí; el decir mal de una cosa se tiene por estimación de ella, que el que la quiere para sí la desacredita para los otros.   No todo alabar es decir bien, que algunos, por no alabar los buenos, alaban también los malos; y para quien ninguno es malo, ninguno será bueno.

251

Hanse de procurar los medios humanos como si no hubiese divinos, y los divinos como si no hubiese humanos: regla de gran maestro, no hay que añadir comento.

252

Ni todo suyo ni todo ajeno.   Es una vulgar tiranía.   Del quererse todo para sí, se sigue luego querer todas las cosas para sí: no saben éstos ceder a la más mínima ni perder un punto de su comodidad.   Obligan poco, fíanse de su fortuna, y suele falsearles el arrimo.   Conviene tal vez ser de otros para que los otros sean de él, y quien tiene empleo común ha de ser esclavo común, o 'renuncie al cargo con la carga,' dirá la vieja a Adriano. Al contrario otros, todos son ajenos, que la necedad siempre va por demasías; y aquí, infeliz, no tiene día ni aun hora suya, con tal exceso de ajenos que alguno fué llamado 'el de todos.'   Aun en el entendimiento, que para todos saben y para sí ignoran. Entienda el atento que nadie la busca a él, sino su interés en él y por él.

250

When must we talk at cross purposes? When others are trying to dissimulate. With some people, you must take everything in the opposite sense: their 'yes' means 'no' and their 'no' means 'yes'; [in their case], to speak ill of a thing is to express their esteem for it, for what they want for themselves they run down to others. To praise something is not always to speak highly of it, for some people, by failing to praise the good, also praise the bad; and nobody is good to him in whose eyes nobody is bad.

251

Human means must be sought as though there were no divine ones, and divine means as though there were no human ones: the precept of a great master, no comment need be added.

252

Do not live altogether for yourself, nor altogether for others. Both ways of behaving are a vulgar form of tyranny. If you are entirely self-centred it soon follows that you want everything for yourself: people like that will not yield a jot nor sacrifice a tittle of their comfort. They are rarely obliging, they trust to their good luck, and the staff upon which they lean usually lets them down. It is convenient at times to belong to others so that they may belong to you, and the man who holds a public position is bound to be the slave of the public or, as the old woman said to Hadrian: 'Let him give up his berth with his burden.' On the other hand, some men devote themselves entirely to others, for folly always goes to extremes; in this case the poor wretch hasn't a day or even an hour to himself and is so completely at the service of others that he is called 'everybody's man.' This can apply even to knowledge, for such men can know everything in the interests of other people and nothing in their own. The shrewd person knows that no men want him for himself but, rather, for the advantages they may derive, directly and indirectly, through him.

253

No allanarse sobrado en el concepto. Los más no estiman lo que entienden, y lo que no perciben lo veneran. Las cosas, para que se estimen, han de costar: será celebrado cuando no fuese entendido. Siempre se ha de mostrar uno más sabio y prudente de lo que requiere aquél con quien trata para el concepto, pero con proporción más que exceso, y si bien con los entendidos vale mucho el seso en todo, para los más es necesario el remonte: no se les ha de dar lugar a la censura, ocupándolos en el entender. Alaban muchos lo que preguntados no saben dar razón. Porque todo lo recóndito veneran por misterio, y lo celebran porque oyen celebrarlo.

254

No despreciar el mal por poco, que nunca viene uno solo: andan encadenados, así como las felicidades. Van la dicha y la desdicha, de ordinario, adonde más hay, y es que todos huyen del desdichado y se arriman al venturoso. Hasta las palomas, con toda su sencillez, acuden al homenaje más blanco. Todo le viene a faltar a un desdichado: él mismo a sí mismo, el discurso y el conorte. No se ha de despertar la desdicha cuando duerma: poco es un deslizar, pero síguese aquel fatal despeño sin saber dónde se vendrá a parar. Que así como ningún bien fué del todo cumplido, así ningún mal del todo acabado. Para el que viene del cielo es la paciencia; para el que del suelo, la prudencia.

255

Saber hacer el bien, poco, y muchas veces. Nunca ha de exceder el empeño a la posibilidad: quien da mucho no da, sino que vende. No se ha de apurar el agradecimiento, que en viéndose imposibilitado quebrará la correspondencia. No es menester

253

Do not make your thoughts too clear. Most men have a poor opinion of what they understand and revere what they do not. In order to be prized, things must be expensive: when anything is not understood it will be extolled. If you are dealing with someone whose good opinion you desire you must always appear wiser and more discreet than he esteems you to be, but there should be moderation rather than excess in this matter, and although good sense in all things is worth a great deal when dealing with sensible people, exaggeration is necessary in the case of the majority: you must not give them a chance to disapprove, but keep them busy trying to understand you. Many people praise a thing without being able, if they are asked, to say why they do so. [This is] because they revere everything recondite as a mystery and praise it because they hear it praised.

254

Never make light of a misfortune, however insignificant it may be, for troubles never come singly: they are linked together just like strokes of good luck. Fortune and misfortune usually frequent places where their fellows are most numerous, and it is a fact that everybody avoids the unlucky and seeks the company of the fortunate. Even doves, with all their simplicity, resort to the fairest turret. Everything eventually fails an unlucky man: he himself, his utterances, and his courage. You must not awaken misfortune when she slumbers: a slip is a trifling matter, but some fatal disaster follows in its train and you cannot know where it will eventually end. For just as no happiness is perfect, so no misfortune is complete. Patience is the virtue of the angels; for us, here on earth, prudence will do.

255

Know how to do good a little at a time, and often. You should never enter into an obligation which it is impossible to fulfil: the man who gives a lot does not give, but rather makes a sale. You should not exhaust gratitude, for when the recipient of a favour sees that no return is possible he will break off relations with you. It is the case with many people that you need do no

más para perder a muchos que obligarlos con demasía; por no pagar se retiran, y dan en enemigos, de obligados. El ídolo nunca querría ver delante al escultor que lo labró, ni el empeñado su bienhechor al ojo. Gran sutileza del dar, que cueste poco y se desee mucho para que se estime más.

256

Ir siempre prevenido contra los descorteses, porfiados, presumidos y todo género de necios. Encuéntranse muchos, y la cordura está en no encontrarse con ellos. Ármese cada día de propósitos al espejo de su atención, y así vencerá los lances de la necedad. Vaya sobre el caso, y no expondrá a vulgares contingencias su reputación: varón prevenido de cordura no será combatido de impertinencia. Es dificultoso el rumbo del humano trato por estar lleno de escollos del descrédito. El desviarse es lo seguro, consultando a Ulises de astucia. Vale aquí mucho el artificioso desliz. Sobre todo, éche por la galantería, que es el único atajo de los empeños.

257

Nunca llegar a rompimiento, que siempre sale de él descalabrada la reputación. Cualquiera vale para enemigo, no así para amigo. Pocos pueden hacer bien, y casi todos mal. No anida segura el águila en el mismo seno de Júpiter el día que rompe con un escarabajo; con la zarpa del declarado irritan los disimulados el fuego, que estaban a la espera de la ocasión: de los amigos maleados salen los peores enemigos. Cargan con defectos ajenos, el propio en su afición; de los que miran, cada uno habla como siente, y siente como desea: condenando a todos, o en los principios de falta de providencia, o en los fines de espera, y siempre de

more than heap excessive favours upon them in order to lose
their friendship; as they cannot repay you, they retire into the
background and, from being your debtors, become your enemies.
The idol would never want to see before it the sculptor who
fashioned it, nor does the recipient of a favour like to have his
benefactor always within sight.   The great art of giving consists in this: the gift should cost very little and yet be greatly
coveted, so that it may be the more highly appreciated.

256

*Always be forearmed against rude, obstinate, presumptuous
persons, and every species of fool.*   One comes across many of
these, and wisdom consists in avoiding them.   Arm yourself
every day, with a firm purpose, before the mirror of your caution,
and you will thus overcome the onslaughts of folly.   Be ready
for the occasion and you will not expose your reputation to
vulgar risks: a man forearmed with good sense will not be
attacked by the presumptuous.   The voyage of human intercourse is a difficult one because it abounds in shoals which en-
danger our good name.   The surest way is to get off the main
route, taking counsel from the wily Ulysses.   In such matters, a
feigned false step is most valuable.   Above all else, practise
courtesy, which provides the only short way out of bad bargains.

257

Never let things reach breaking point, for, if they do, your reputation always emerges injured.   Any one at all can matter as an
enemy, but not as a friend.   Few people can do [you] good and
nearly everybody can do [you] harm.   Even in the bosom of
Jove himself, the eagle does not rest securely on the day that he
has fallen out with a beetle; hidden enemies use the paw of a
declared foe to stir up the fires of wrath, for they were lying in
wait for the opportunity: the worst enemies come from among
disaffected friends.   They make the shortcomings of their
fellows take the blame for their own pet failing; among the
onlookers each man speaks as he thinks, and thinks as he wants
to think: condemning everybody, either from the start, for lack
of foresight, or at the finish, for lack of patience, and always for

cordura. Si fuere inevitable el desvío, sea excusable antes con tibieza de favor que con violencia de furor; y aquí viene bien aquello de una bella retirada.

258

Buscar quien le ayude a llevar las infelicidades. Nunca será solo, y menos en los riesgos, que sería cargarse con todo el odio. Piensan algunos alzarse con toda la superintendencia, y álzanse con toda la murmuración. De esta suerte tendrá quien le excuse o quien le ayude a llevar el mal. No se atreven tan fácilmente a dos, ni la fortuna ni la vulgaridad, y aun por eso el médico sagaz, ya que erró la cura, no yerra en buscar quien, a título de consulta, le ayude a llevar el ataúd: repártese el peso y el pesar, que la desdicha a solas se redobla para intolerable.

259

Prevenir las injurias y hacer de ellas favores. Más sagacidad es evitarlas que vengarlas. Es gran destreza hacer confidente del que había de ser émulo; convertir en reparos de su reputación los que la amenazaban tiros. Mucho vale el saber obligar: quita el tiempo para el agravio el que le ocupó con el agradecimiento, y es saber vivir convertir en placeres los que habían de ser pesares: hágase confidencia de la misma malevolencia.

260

Ni será ni tendrá ninguno todo por suyo; no son bastantes la sangre, ni la amistad, ni la obligación más apretante, que va gran diferencia de entregar el pecho o la voluntad. La mayor unión admite excepción; ni por eso se ofenden las leyes de la fineza. Siempre se reserva algún secreto para sí el amigo, y se recata en algo el mismo hijo de su padre; de unas cosas se celan con unos

[want of] wisdom. If a break should be unavoidable, let it be excusable: let it come rather as a cooling of regard than as the result of a violent outburst of rage. In this case the maxim concerning a good retreat is to the point.

258

Find someone who will help you to bear your misfortunes. Never be alone, and least of all in dangerous situations, for that would be to bear the whole burden of hatred yourself. Some people want to take everything upon their shoulders and they get all the blame. So you should have someone to help you to avoid, or bear, troubles. Neither fortune nor the mob is so bold against two, and it is precisely for this reason that the clever doctor who has failed to cure [his patient] does not go wrong when he looks round for somebody who, under the guise of a consultation, will help him to carry out the coffin: share the weight and the woe, for misfortune endured alone is twofold wretchedness, and becomes unbearable.

259

Forestall injuries and turn them into favours. It is wiser to avoid than to avenge insults. It is a skilful device to make an intimate of a potential rival; to make those who threatened to open fire on it defenders of your reputation. It helps a great deal to know how to oblige: for he has no time left for insults who occupies it with gratitude, and to turn potential sources of pain into pleasures is to know how to live: take even malice itself into your confidence.

260

Let no one be entirely in your confidence, nor you in his: blood relationship, friendship, the most pressing obligation, are not sufficient [to justify such intimacy], for there is a big difference between giving your affection and surrendering your will. The closest intimacy allows for exceptions; and the laws of good breeding are not thereby offended. A friend always keeps some secret to himself, and even a son hides something from his father; certain things which you conceal from one you reveal to

I

que comunican a otros, y al contrario; con que se viene uno a conceder todo y negar todo, distinguiendo los de la correspondencia.

261

No proseguir la necedad. Hacen algunos empeño del desacierto,[1] y porque comenzaron a errar les parece que es constancia el proseguir. Acusan en el foro interno su yerro, y en el externo lo excusan; conque, si cuando comenzaron la necedad fueron notados de inadvertidos, al proseguirla son confirmados en necios. Ni la promesa inconsiderada, ni la resolución errada inducen obligación. De esta suerte continúan algunos su primera grosería, y llevan adelante su cortedad; quieren ser constantes impertinentes.

262

Saber olvidar más es dicha que arte. Las cosas que son más para olvidadas son las más acordadas: no sólo es villana la memoria para faltar cuando más fué menester, pero necia para acudir cuando no convendría: en lo que ha de dar pena es prolija, y en lo que había de dar gusto es descuidada. Consiste a veces el remedio del mal en olvidarlo, y olvídase el remedio; conviene, pues, hacerla a tan cómodas costumbres, porque basta a dar felicidad o infierno. Exceptúanse los satisfechos, que en el estado de su inocencia gozan de su simple felicidad.

263

Muchas cosas de gusto no se han de poseer en propiedad. Más se goza de ellas ajenas que propias: el primer día es lo bueno para su dueño, los demás para los extraños. Gózanse las cosas ajenas con doblada fruición; esto es, sin el riesgo del daño, y con el gusto de la novedad sabe todo mejor a privación. Hasta el agua ajena se miente néctar. El tener las cosas, a más de que

----
[1] 1659 has 'desacierte.'

another, and vice versa; hence you eventually disclose every-thing and withhold everything by making a distinction between individual members of your circle.

261

Do not persist in folly. Some people turn a blunder into an obligation and because they started out on the wrong path think that it is a sign of consistency to continue in it. While they excuse it outwardly, they acknowledge their fault before the interior tribunal of their minds; and so, if they were censured as rash when they started upon their stupid course of action, their folly is confirmed when they persist in it. Neither an ill-con-sidered promise nor a mistaken decision gives rise to an obliga-tion. Yet some people persist in their first clumsy course and carry their stupidity further; they want to be consistent asses.

262

To know how to forget is more a matter of luck than of skill. The things which are better forgotten are those we remember best: memory is not merely a rogue in failing us when it is most needed, but a fool in turning up at inconvenient times: in matters which will prove troublesome, it is long, and in those which ought to be a source of pleasure it is heedless. Some-times the cure for a misfortune consists in forgetting it, and the remedy is forgotten; it is advisable, therefore, to train the memory to good habits, for it can turn life into a heaven or a hell. Contented people form an exception to the rule, for in their state of innocence they enjoy their simple happiness.

263

Many pleasant things ought not to be our own exclusive property. We enjoy them more if they belong to others rather than to our-selves alone: the owner has the good of them on the first day, on the remaining days they are enjoyed by strangers. A twofold pleasure is to be derived from what belongs to others: for there is no risk of loss and, owing to the relish provided by novelty, everything tastes better if you have been deprived of it. Even water from another's well is regarded as nectar.

disminuye la frución, aumenta el enfado, tanto de prestarlas como de no prestarlas.   No sirve sino de mantenerlas para otros, y son más los enemigos que se cobran que los agradecidos.

264

No tenga días de descuido.   Gusta la suerte de pegar una burla, y atropellará todas las contingencias para coger desapercibido. Siempre han de estar a prueba el ingenio, la cordura y el valor, hasta la belleza, porque el día de su confianza será el de su descrédito.   Cuando más fué menester el cuidado faltó siempre, que el no pensar es la zancadilla del perecer.   También suele ser estratagema de la ajena intención coger al descuido las perfecciones para el riguroso examen del apreciar.   Sábense ya los días de la ostentación, y perdónales la astucia; pero el día que menos se esperaba, ése escoge para la tentativa del valer.

265

Saber empeñar los dependientes.   Un empeño en su ocasión hizo personas a muchos, así como un ahogo saca nadadores: de esta suerte descubrieron muchos el valor, ya el saber quedaría sepultado en su encogimiento si no se hubiera ofrecido la ocasión. Son los aprietos lances de reputación, y puesto el noble en contingencias de honra, obra por mil.   Supo con eminencia esta lición de empeñar la católica reina Isabela, así como todas las demás; y a este político favor debió el Gran Capitán su renombre, y otros muchos su eterna fama; hizo grandes hombres con esta sutileza.

266

No ser malo de puro bueno.   Eslo el que nunca se enoja; tienen poco de personas los insensibles.   No nace siempre de indolencia,

Besides diminishing your enjoyment of things, owning them increases your troubles, whether you lend your possessions or not. It merely involves looking after them for others, and the enemies you acquire outnumber the grateful.

264

Have no heedless days. Fate is fond of playing a trick and will ride roughshod over every probability in order to catch you unawares. Your wit, wisdom, courage, even your good looks, must always be ready for the test, for their day of [careless] confidence will be that of their undoing. Caution always fails you when it is most needed, for thoughtlessness is the stumbling-block which brings about your downfall. Catching your good qualities off their guard and putting them to the rigorous test of appraisal is, moreover, a stratagem devised by the malice of others. Parade days are known beforehand and the shrewd allow them to pass by unheeded; but the day that was least expected, that is the one they choose for a test of your worth.

265

Give your underlings difficult tasks to perform. A hard task at an opportune moment has been the making of many a man, just as drowning makes swimmers: in this way, many have discovered courage, and even knowledge would remain buried beneath its own diffidence if an opportunity were not afforded for its display. Emergencies provide occasions to win fame and if a man of worth finds himself in a situation where his honour is at stake he does the work of a thousand. The Catholic Queen, Isabella, had learned supremely well, together with all other lessons, this technique of setting her subjects difficult tasks; and the Great Captain owed his renown, as did many others their undying fame, to this shrewd favour at her hands; by this skilful device she made great men.

266

Do not go wrong by dint of sheer good nature. He does so who never loses his temper; insensitive people have little individuality. This fault does not invariably arise out of

sino de incapacidad. Un sentimiento en su ocasión es acto personal; búrlanse luego las aves de las apariencias de bultos. Alternar lo agrio con lo dulce es prueba de buen gusto: sola la dulzura es para niños y necios. Gran mal es perderse de puro bueno en este sentido de insensibilidad.

267

Palabras de seda con suavidad de condición. Atraviesan el cuerpo las jaras, pero las malas palabras el alma. Una buena pasta hace que huela bien la boca. Gran sutileza del vivir saber vender el aire. Lo más se paga con palabras, y bastan ellas a desempeñar una imposibilidad; negóciase en el aire con el aire, y alienta mucho el aliento soberano. Siempre se ha de llevar la boca llena de azúcar para confitar palabras, que saben bien a los mismos enemigos: es el único medio para ser amable el ser apacible.

268

Haga al principio el cuerdo lo que el necio al fin. Lo mismo obra el uno que el otro; sólo se diferencia en los tiempos, aquél en su sazón y éste sin ella. El que se calzó al principio el entendimiento al revés, en todo lo demás prosigue de ese modo: lleva entre pies lo que había de poner sobre su cabeza; hace siniestra de la diestra, y así es tan zurdo en todo su proceder: sólo hay un buen caer en la cuenta. Hacen por fuerza lo que pudieran de grado; pero el discreto luego ve lo que ha de hacer tarde o temprano, y ejecútalo con gusto y con reputación.

269

Válgase de su novedad, que mientras fuere nuevo será estimado. Aplace la novedad por la variedad universalmente; refréscase el gusto y estímase más una medianía flamante que un extremo acostumbrado. Rózanse las eminencias y viénense a envejecer; y advierta que durará poco esta gloria de novedad: a cuatro días

indolence, but, rather, from incapacity. To show resentment when the occasion demands is an action which reveals personality; birds soon mock at scarecrows. It is a mark of good taste to alternate the bitter with the sweet: sweetness alone is for children and fools. It is a great misfortune to lapse into this state of insensitiveness out of sheer good nature.

267

Silken words and an even temper. Arrows pierce the body but harsh words pierce the soul. A good biscuit makes the mouth smell sweet. It is a great art in life to know how to sell air. Most things are paid for in the coin of words and they are sufficient to perform ostensibly impossible feats; thus, in an airy fashion, we deal in air and a powerful breath of it is very stimulating. You should always have your mouth full of sugar to sweeten your words, so that they taste nice even to your enemies: the only way to be amiable is to be peaceable.

268

The wise man should do at the start what the fool does in the end. Both behave in the same way; the only difference is in the time at which they do it, the former, in season, the latter, out of it. The man who has donned his wits the wrong way round from the start does the same in every other concern: he carries between his feet what he should have put upon his head; he turns right into left and is thus equally clumsy in everything he does: there is only one right way of behaving. [Fools] do by compulsion what they might have done voluntarily; but the sensible man immediately sees what he will have to do, sooner or later, and he does it willingly, and in a way which redounds to his credit.

269

Exploit your position as a newcomer, for you will be appreciated so long as you are new. Novelty pleases everybody because it provides a change: the taste is refreshed and a brand-new mediocrity is more highly thought of than a great genius to whom we are accustomed. Talents wear out and eventually grow stale; note, too, that this lustre of novelty will endure for but a

le perderán el respeto. Sepa, pues, valerse de esas primicias de la estimación, y saque en la fuga del agradar todo lo que pudiera pretender, porque si se pasa el calor de lo reciente resfriaráse la pasión, y trocarse ha el agrado de nuevo en enfado de acostumbrado, y crea que todo tuvo también su vez, y que pasó.

270

No condenar sólo lo que a muchos agrada. Algo hay bueno, pues satisface a tantos, y aunque no se explica, se goza. La singularidad siempre es odiosa, y cuando errónea, ridícula. Antes desacreditará su mal concepto que el objeto; quedarse ha solo con su mal gusto. Si no sabe topar con lo bueno, disimule su cortedad y no condene a bulto: que el mal gusto ordinariamente nace de la ignorancia. Lo que todos dicen, o es, o quiere ser.

271

El que supiere poco, téngase siempre a lo más seguro en toda profesión, que aunque no le tengan por sutil, le tendrán por fundamental. El que sabe puede empeñarse y obrar de fantasía, pero saber poco y arriesgarse es voluntario precipicio: téngase siempre a la mano derecha, que no puede faltar lo asentado. A poco saber, camino real; y a toda ley, tanto del saber como del ignorar, es más cuerda la seguridad que la singularidad.

272

Vender las cosas a precio de cortesía, que es obligar más. Nunca llegará el pedir del interesado al dar del generoso obligado. La cortesía no da, sino que empeña, y es la galantería la mayor obligación. No hay cosa más cara para el hombre de bien que la

brief period: regard for it is lost in a matter of four days.   Know,
then, how to exploit those first-fruits of esteem and snatch from
your transient popularity everything to which you can lay claim,
for, if the heat of novelty cools, enthusiasm will cool and the
pleasure taken in what is new will once again become boredom
with the commonplace.   And realize that everything else has
also had its day, and that its day was transitory.

270

*Do not be alone in your condemnation of something which pleases
a great many people.*   There is something good in it because
it satisfies so many, and even though there is no explanation as
to why it should be so, it is a source of enjoyment.   Peculiarity
is always odious, and ridiculous when misguided.   It will bring
your own bad judgment rather than the object of your censure
into disrepute; and you will be left alone with your bad taste.
If you cannot find the good [in a thing], conceal your limitations,
and do not condemn it wholesale: for bad taste usually arises
out of ignorance.   What everybody says either is so, or will
be so.

271

*In every profession, if a man knows very little he should stick to
what he knows best,* for if you may not be regarded as acute, you
will be considered sound.   An expert can enter into obligations
and act as his fancy prompts him, but to know little and run
risks is to bring about, voluntarily, your own downfall: always
keep on the safe side, for what is securely established cannot
fail you.   A man who knows little should stick to the beaten
track; and, according to the rules of both knowledge and
ignorance, security is wiser than singularity.

272

Sell things at the price which courtesy sets upon them, for you
oblige people the more in that way.   The bid of a calculating
buyer will never be as good as a gift made in return by the
generous recipient of a favour.   Courtesy does not give [pre-
sents] but rather puts people under an obligation, and politeness

* I

que se le da : es venderla dos veces y a dos precios : del valor y de
la cortesía.   Verdad es que para el ruin es algarabía la galantería,
porque no entiende los términos del buen término.

273

Comprensión de los genios con quien trata.   Para conocer los
intentos.   Conocida bien la causa, se conoce el efecto, antes en
ella y después en su motivo.   El melancólico siempre agüera
infelicidades, y el maldiciente, culpas; todo lo peor se les ofrece,
y no percibiendo el bien presente, anuncian el posible mal.   El
apasionado siempre habla con otro lenguaje diferente de lo que
las cosas son : habla en él la pasión, no la razón, y cada uno según
su afecto o su humor; y todos muy lejos de la verdad.   Sepa
descifrar un semblante y deletrear el alma en los señales; conozca
al que siempre ríe por falto, y al que nunca, por falso; recátese
del preguntador, o por fácil o por notante; espere poco bueno del
de mal gesto, que suelen vengarse de la naturaleza éstos, y así
como ella los honró poco a ellos, la honran poco a ella.   Tanta
suele ser la necedad, cuanta fuere la hermosura.

274

Tener la atractiva, que es un hechizo políticamente cortés.   Sirva
el garabato galante más par atraer voluntades que utilidades, o
para todo; no bastan méritos, si no se valen del agrado, que es el
que da la plausibilidad, el más plático instrumento de la soberanía.   Un caer en picadura, es suerte, pero socórrese del artificio,
que donde hay gran natural asienta mejor lo artificial : de aquí se
origina la pía afición, hasta conseguir la gracia universal.

is the highest of favours. For an honourable man, there is
nothing more costly than that which he receives as a gift: you
sell it to him twice over and he pays twofold: once for its value,
and again for your courtesy. It is true that, to a rascal,
generosity is mere nonsense, for he does not understand the
language of good manners.

273

Understand the temperaments of the people with whom you deal,
so that you may be aware of their intentions. If the cause is
properly understood, so is the effect, first in the cause itself, and
afterwards in the motive. The gloomy person is always antici-
pating disasters, and the scandalmonger faults; the worst side of
everything occurs to them and, while they take no account of
present good, they foresee possible ills. A man who is passion's
slave always speaks of things as otherwise than they really are:
emotion speaks through him, not reason, and every one speaks
as he is prompted to do by his inclinations or his mood; and all
are very far from speaking the truth. Learn how to read a face
and spell out the soul in the features; realize that a man who is
always laughing is lacking [in good sense] and that one who
never laughs is false; beware of the inquisitive man, he is either
a chatterbox or a fault-finder; expect little good from the ugly,
for these generally revenge themselves upon Nature and do
her little honour because she has done little to them. Good
looks and stupidity are usually combined in equal proportions.

274

Have charm, for it is a profitable and polite kind of wizardry.
Let the magnet of your pleasing qualities serve to attract goodwill
rather than material advantages, but make use of it in everything;
talents are not enough unless they have recourse to charm, which
wins general praise, and provides the most effective means of con-
trolling others. To get home a thrust with the goad is a matter
of luck, but it is helped by skill, for art takes root more easily
in a soil well endowed by nature: goodwill originates there and
eventually wins general favour.

275

Corriente, pero no indecente.   No esté siempre de figura y de enfado; es ramo de galantería: hase de ceder en algo al decoro para ganar la afición común; alguna vez puede pasar por donde los más, pero sin indecencia.   Que quien es tenido por necio en público no será tenido por cuerdo en secreto.   Más se pierde en un día genial que se ganó en toda la seriedad; pero no se ha de estar siempre de excepción.   El ser singular es condenar a los otros; menos afectar melindres: déjense para su sexo; aun los espirituales son ridículos.   Lo mejor de un hombre es parecerlo, que la mujer puede afectar con perfección lo varonil, y no al contrario.

276

Saber renovar el genio con la naturaleza y con el arte.   De siete en siete años dicen que se muda la condición; sea para mejorar y realzar el gusto.   A los primeros siete entra la razón; entra después a cada lustro una nueva perfección.   Observe esta variedad natural para ayudarla, y esperar también de los otros la mejoría.   De aquí es que muchos mudaron de porte, o con el estado o con el empleo; y a veces no se advierte hasta que se ve el exceso de la mudanza.   A los veinte años será pavón, a los treinta león, a los cuarenta camello, a los cincuenta serpiente, a los sesenta perro, a los setenta mona y a los ochenta nada.

277

Hombre de ostentación.   Es el lucimiento de las prendas.   Hay vez para cada una: lógrese, que no será cada día el de su triunfo. Hay sujetos bizarros, en quienes lo poco luce mucho, y lo mucho hasta admirar.   Cuando la ostentativa se junta con la eminencia pasa por prodigio.   Hay naciones ostentosas, y la española lo es

275

Conform, but not beyond the bounds of decorum.   Do not always be showing off and [thus become] a bore; this injunction is a branch of good manners; up to a point you must yield a touch of dignity in order to gain general goodwill; you may sometimes go with the majority, but not beyond the bounds of propriety. For the man who is regarded as a fool in his public life will not be considered wise in his private affairs.   More may be lost on a holiday than may be won in all your serious moods; but you must not always be the exception.   To be exceptional is to condemn others; it is still less [advisable] to play the prude; leave that to the appropriate sex; even spiritual prudery is ridiculous. The best thing about a man is his manly appearance; a woman may perfectly well put on a manly air, but a man must not be effeminate.

276

Know how to renew your genius with [the help of] nature and art. It is said that a man's make-up changes every seven years; let it be a change for the improvement and embellishment of your taste.   In the first seven years of life reason comes to a man; and thereafter a new gift comes with each lustrum.   Observe this change in your nature in order to foster it, and hope also for improvement in the following periods.   It is due to this altera-tion that many people change their behaviour when they change their status or occupation; and sometimes the transformation is not noticed until its extreme character becomes apparent.   At twenty a man will be a peacock, at thirty a lion, at forty a camel, at fifty a serpent, at sixty a dog, at seventy a monkey, and at eighty, nothing at all.

277

Put yourself on view.   This brings your talents to light. Each has its own appropriate occasion [for display]: it should profit by it, for it will not enjoy a triumph every day.   There are some dashing persons who make a great show with very little and excite amazement with a great deal.   When outstanding talent is combined with the ability to display it, it is regarded as

con superioridad. Fué la luz pronto lucimiento de todo lo criado. Llena mucho el ostentar, suple mucho, y da un segundo ser a todo, y más cuando la realidad se afianza. El cielo, que da la perfección, previene la ostentación, que cualquiera a solas fuera violenta: es menester arte en el ostentar. Aun lo muy excelente depende de circunstancias y no tiene siempre vez. Salió mal la ostentativa cuando le faltó su sazón: ningún realce pide ser menos afectado y perece siempre de este desaire, porque está muy al canto de la vanidad y ésta del desprecio. Ha de ser muy templada, porque no dé en vulgar, y con los cuerdos está algo desacreditada su demasía. Consiste a veces más en una elocuencia muda, en un mostrar la perfección al descuido: que el sabio disimulo es el más plausible alarde, porque aquella misma privación pica en lo más vivo a la curiosidad. Gran destreza suya no descubrir toda la perfección de una vez, sino por brújula irla pintando, y siempre adelantando. Que un realce sea empeño de otro mayor, y el aplauso del primero mueva expectación de los demás.

278

Huir la nota en todo; que, siendo notados, serán defectos los mismos realces. Nace esto de singularidad, que siempre fué censurada; quédase solo el singular. Aun lo lindo, si sobresale, es descrédito; en haciendo reparar ofende, y mucho más singularidades desautorizadas. Pero en los mismos vicios quieren algunos ser conocidos, buscando novedad en la ruindad para conseguir tan infame fama. Hasta en lo entendido, lo sobrado degenera en bachillería.

prodigious.   There are ostentatious nations, and among these the Spanish is in the highest rank.   It was light which first caused all creation to shine forth.   Display fills up many blanks, supplies many deficiencies, and gives everything a second life, especially when it is backed by genuine merit.   Heaven, which bestows gifts, provides the means for their display, for one without the other would be abortive: skill is needed in ostentation. Even the highest quality is dependent upon circumstances and [its display] is not always opportune.   It is out of place when it is out of season: more than any other accomplishment, it needs to be free from affectation, and it is always through this failing that display comes to naught, for it borders very nearly upon vanity, and vanity is very close to contempt.   In order not to be vulgar, display must be very limited; an excess of it is in somewhat bad repute among the wise.   It consists, at times, rather in a dumb eloquence, a careless disclosure of merit: for when it is tactfully hidden its worth is often most effectively revealed, for that very reticence pricks curiosity to the quick.   It will, moreover, be very wise of you not to reveal an accomplishment in its entirety but rather to display it bit by bit, as in a peep-show, always disclosing a little more as time goes on.   Let every accomplishment be the guarantor of another and a greater one, for the applause excited by the first should stir up expectation of others [yet to be revealed].

278

Avoid notoriety in all things: for even good qualities will become defects if they are the object of comment.   Notoriety is born of eccentricity, always an object of censure; the eccentric person is left alone.   Even beauty is discreditable if it forces itself upon one's attention; it gives offence by the notice it attracts, and disreputable peculiarities are even more repugnant. Nevertheless, some people like to be notorious even for their vices, seeking out new kinds of misbehaviour in order to attain so infamous a kind of fame.   Even where wit is concerned, an excess of it degenerates into idle chatter.

279

No decir al contradecir. Es menester diferenciar cuándo
procede de astucia o vulgaridad. No siempre es porfía, que tal
vez es artificio. Atención, pues, a no empeñarse en la una, ni
despeñarse en la otra. No hay cuidado más logrado que en
espías,[1] y contra la ganzúa de los ánimos no hay mejor contratreta
que el dejar por dentro la llave del recato.

280

Hombre de ley. Está acabado el buen proceder: andan desmentidas las obligaciones; hay pocas correspondencias buenas, al
mejor servicio el peor galardón: a uso ya de todo el mundo.[2]
Hay naciones enteras proclives al mal trato: de unas se teme
siempre la traición, de otras la inconstancia y de otras el engaño.
Sirva, pues, la mala correspondencia ajena, no para la imitación,
sino para la cautela. Es el riesgo de desquiciar la entereza a vista
de ruin proceder. Pero el varón de ley nunca se olvida de quién
es por lo que los otros son.

281

Gracia de los entendidos. Más se estima el tibio sí de un varón
singular, que todo un aplauso común; porque regüeldos de
aristas no alientan.[3] Los sabios hablan con el entendimiento, y
así su alabanza causa una mortal satisfacción. Redujo el juicioso
Antígono todo el teatro de su fama a sólo Cenón, y llamaba
Platón toda su escuela a Aristóteles. Atienden algunos a sólo
llenar el estómago, aunque sea de broza vulgar. Hasta los
soberanos han menester a los que escriben, y temen más sus
plumas que las feas a los pinceles.

282

Usar de la ausencia, o para el respeto o para la estimación. Si
la presencia disminuye la fama, la ausencia la aumenta. El que

<hr/>

[1] *Vide* Appendix, p. 307.   [2] *Vide* Appendix, p. 307.
                    [3] *Vide* Appendix, p. 307.

279

Do not gainsay contradiction. It is necessary to differentiate when this arises out of cunning or vulgarity. It is not always obstinacy but sometimes artifice. Take care, then, neither to be embarrassed by the one nor taken in by the other. Care is never more fittingly employed than in spying, and there is no better way to circumvent a picklock of the mind than to leave the key of caution on the inside of the door.

280

The trustworthy man. Honourable dealing is no more: obligations are repudiated; there are few good relationships; the greater the service the more wretched the reward: that is the way of the whole world nowadays. There are entire nations given up to double dealing: from some, treachery is always to be feared, from others, unreliability, and from yet others, deceit. So let the bad behaviour of others serve not as a model but as a warning. The danger is that the sight of villainous conduct may undermine your own integrity. Nevertheless, a man of honour never forgets what he is because of what others are.

281

The favour of the wise. The lukewarm approval of an eminent man is worth more than all the applause of the mob; for re-gurgitations of chaff are not stimulating. Wise men speak with their understanding, and so their praise gives rise to over-whelming satisfaction. Antigonus attributed all the fame he had won to Zeno alone, and Plato called Aristotle his entire school. Some people are concerned only with filling their bellies, albeit with vulgar trash. Even monarchs have need of writers, and they fear the pen more than ugly women fear the painter's brush.

282

Make use of absence, in order to win respect or esteem. If presence diminishes fame, absence augments it. A man who

ausente fué tenido por león, presente fué ridículo parto de los montes. Deslústranse las prendas si se rozan, porque se ve antes la corteza del exterior que la mucha sustancia del ánimo. Adelántase más la imaginación que la vista, y el engaño que entra de ordinario por el oído, viene a salir por los ojos; el que se conserva en el centro de su opinión conserva la reputación; que aun la fénix se vale del retiro para el decoro y del deseo para el aprecio.

283

Hombre de inventiva a lo cuerdo. Arguye exceso de ingenio, pero, ¿cuál será sin el grano de demencia? La inventiva es de ingeniosos: la buena elección, de prudentes. Es también de gracia, y más rara, porque el elegir bien lo consiguieron muchos; el inventar bien, pocos, y los primeros en excelencia y en tiempo. Es lisonjera la novedad, y si feliz, da dos realces a lo bueno. En los asuntos del juicio es peligrosa por lo paradojo; en los del ingenio, loable; y si acertadas, una y otra plausibles.

284

No sea entremetido y no será desairado. Estímese si quisiere que le estimen. Sea antes avaro que pródigo de sí. Llegue deseado y será bien recebido. Nunca venga sino llamado, ni vaya sino enviado. El que se empeña por sí, si sale mal, se carga todo el odio sobre sí, y si sale bien, no consigue el agradecimiento. Es el entremetido terrero de desprecios, y por lo mismo que se introduce con desvergüenza, es tripulado en confusión.

when absent is regarded as a lion, becomes when present the ridiculous offspring of the mountains. Talents lose their lustre if we become too familiar with them, for the outer shell of the mind is more readily seen than its rich inner kernel. Imagination reaches farther than sight, and deception, which usually comes in through the ear, eventually goes out through the eyes; the man who keeps himself to himself preserves his good name, for even the outstanding genius makes use of retirement so that men may honour him and so that the yearning aroused by his absence may cause him to be esteemed.

283

The discreetly inventive man. Inventiveness implies the highest degree of genius, but what would genius be without a grain of madness? Geniuses possess the gift of inventiveness; prudent men, the ability to make a sound choice. [Inventiveness] is also the portion of a ready wit, and is rarer [than the ability to choose well]; for many succeed in making a right choice; few in making good inventions; and the latter have priority in both merit and time. Novelty is pleasing and, if felicitous, gives a twofold lustre to what is excellent. In matters of judgment, novelty is dangerous because it is given to paradox; in matters of wit, it is commendable; and if [inventiveness and judgment] hit the mark, they are both praiseworthy.

284

Do not be a busybody and you will not be rebuffed. Respect yourself if you want to be respected. Be sparing rather than lavish with your presence. Turn up when you are wanted and you will be well received. Never come unless you are called, nor go unless you are sent. The man who undertakes anything on his own incurs all the odium if he is not successful and gets no thanks if he is. The busybody is a target for contempt and, for the very reason that he pushes himself forward shamelessly, is laden with confusion.

285

No perecer de desdicha ajena. Conozca el que está en el lodo, y note que le reclamará para hacer consuelo del recíproco mal. Buscan quien les ayude a llevar la desdicha, y los que en la prosperidad le daban espaldas, ahora la mano. Es menester gran tiento con los que se ahogan, para acudir al remedio sin peligro.

286

No dejarse obligar del todo, ni de todos, que sería ser esclavo y común. Nacieron unos más dichosos que otros: aquéllos para hacer bien y éstos para recibirle. Más preciosa es la libertad que la dádiva, por que se pierde. Guste mas que dependan de él muchos que no depender él de uno. No tiene otra comodidad el mando sino el poder hacer más bien. Sobre todo, no tenga por favor la obligación en que se mete, y las más veces la diligenciará la astucia ajena para prevenirle.

287

Nunca obrar apasionado: todo lo errará. No obre por sí quien no está en sí, y la pasión siempre destierra la razón. Substituya entonces un tercero prudente, que lo será si desapasionado. Siempre ven más los que miran que los que juegan, porque no se apasionan. En conociéndose alterado, toque a retirar la cordura: porque no acabe de encendérsele la sangre, que todo lo ejecutará sangriento, y en poco rato dará materia para muchos días de confusión suya y murmuración ajena.

285

Never come to grief through the misfortune of another.   Recognize the man who is stuck in the mud and note that he will appeal to you to console him by sharing his wretchedness.   Such people are on the look-out for someone to help them bear their misfortune, and those who gave them the cold shoulder when they were prosperous now lend them a hand.   Great care is needed when dealing with the drowning in order to go to their rescue without danger [to oneself.]

286

Do not commit yourself entirely, nor be obliged to everybody, for that is to be a slave, and a slave of every man.   Some are born more fortunate than others: the former to do good, the latter to receive it.   Freedom is more precious than the gift in exchange for which it is lost.   You should prefer many people to depend upon you rather than that you should depend upon one person. Authority has no advantage other than the power it gives to do more good.   Above all, do not look upon an obligation into which you enter as though it were a favour conferred upon you, for, in most cases, it will be the cunning device of another to get you into his power.

287

Never do anything when you are in a temper: [for] you will do everything wrong.   A man who has lost control of himself should not do anything on his own, and passion always banishes reason.   In such circumstances, let a discreet intermediary act in your stead, and he will be that if he is dispassionate.   The onlookers see more of the game than the players because they do not get excited.   When you realize that you are put out, let prudence summon you to retire: for no sooner is the blood up than it will do everything in a bloody fashion and, in a few moments, occasion may be given for many days of humiliation for yourself and for backbiting on the part of others.

288

Vivir a la ocasión. El gobernar, el discurrir, todo ha de ser al caso. Querer cuando se puede, que la sazón y el tiempo a nadie aguardan. No vaya por generalidades en el vivir, si ya no fuere en favor de la virtud, ni intime leyes precisas al querer, que habrá de beber mañana del agua que desprecia hoy. Hay algunos tan paradojamente impertinentes que pretenden que todas las circunstancias del acierto se ajusten a su manía, y no al contrario. Mas el sabio sabe que el norte de la prudencia consiste en portarse a la ocasión.

289

El mayor desdoro de un hombre es dar muestras de que es hombre; déjanle de tener por divino el día que le ven muy humano. La liviandad es el mayor contraste de la reputación. Así como el varón recatado es tenido por más hombre, así el liviano por menos que hombre. No hay vicio que más desautorice: porque la liviandad se opone frente a frente a la gravedad. Hombre liviano no puede ser de sustancia, y más si fuere anciano, donde le obliga a la cordura. Y con ser este desdoro tan de muchos, no le quita el estar singularmente desautorizado.

290

Es felicidad juntar el aprecio con el afecto; no ser muy amado para conservar el respeto. Más atrevido es el amor que el odio; afición y veneración no se juntan bien. Y aunque no ha de ser uno muy temido ni muy querido, el amor introduce la llaneza, y al paso que éste entra, sale la estimación. Sea amado antes apreciativamente, que afectivamente, que es amor muy de personas.

291

Saber hacer la tentativa. Compita la atención del juicioso con la detención del recatado. Gran juicio se requiere para medir

288

Live as the occasion demands. The direction of affairs, discourse, everything, must be appropriate to the occasion. Resolve while you can, for time and tide wait for no man. Do not run your life on general principles, except in so far as they favour virtue, nor lay down precise rules for [the attainment of] your desires, for to-morrow you will have to drink from the stream you despise to-day. Some people are so absurdly paradoxical that they expect all the circumstances making for success to conform to their own whim, and not vice versa. The wise man, however, knows that the first rule of prudence demands that he should behave as the occasion demands.

289

The greatest discredit into which a man can fall is incurred when he shows himself to be a [mere] man; on the day that he is seen to be extremely human, he will cease to be regarded as divine. Levity is the weightiest counterpoise to our reputation. Just as the reserved man is regarded as more of a man, so the frivolous one is regarded as less than a man. There is no failing which so undermines respect; for levity is diametrically opposed to gravity. A frivolous person cannot have much in him, especially if he is old, for old age demands prudence. And although this defect is characteristic of a great many people, that does not prevent it from being especially discreditable.

290

It is a piece of good fortune to combine esteem with affection: in order to preserve the respect of your fellows do not be greatly loved. Love is bolder than hate; affection and veneration do not go well together. You should be neither greatly feared nor greatly loved. Affection induces familiarity, and when the latter enters esteem departs. Be loved with respect rather than with tenderness, for respectful love is sought by the great.

291

Know how to weigh people up. Let the vigilance of the wise vie with the reticence of the cautious. A sound judgment is needed

el ajeno.   Más importa conocer los genios y las propiedades de
las personas, que de las hierbas y piedras.   Acción es ésta de las
más sutiles de la vida ; por el sonido se conocen los metales, y por
el habla las personas.   Las palabras muestran la entereza, pero
mucho más las obras.   Aquí es menester el extravagante reparo :
la observación profunda, la sutil nota y la juiciosa crisi.

292

Venza el natural las obligaciones del empleo, y no al contrario.
Por grande que sea el puesto, ha de mostrar que es mayor la
persona.   Un caudal con ensanche vase dilatando y ostentando
más con los empleos.   Fácilmente le cogerán el corazón al que
le tiene estrecho, y al cabo viene a quebrar con obligación y
reputación.   Preciábase el grande Augusto de ser mayor hombre
que príncipe : aquí vale la alteza de ánimo, y aun aprovecha la
confianza cuerda de sí.

293

De la madurez.   Resplandece en el exterior, pero más en las
costumbres.   La gravedad material hace precioso al oro, y la
moral a la persona ; es el decoro de las prendas, causando veneración.   La compostura del hombre es la fachada del alma.   No es
necedad con poco meneo, como quiere la ligereza, sino una
autoridad muy sosegada ; habla por sentencias, obra con aciertos.
Supone un hombre muy hecho, porque tanto tiene de persona
cuanto de madurez ; en dejando de ser niño comienza a ser grave
y autorizado.

294

Moderarse en el sentir.   Cada uno hace concepto según su
conveniencia, y abunda de razones en su aprehensión.   Cede en
los más el dictamen al afecto.   Acontece el encontrarse dos

to assess that of another. It is more important to be acquainted with the temperaments and qualities of people than with the properties of plants and stones. To be so is to possess one of the most subtle accomplishments in life; you can recognize metals by their ring and people by their speech. Words reveal integrity, but deeds do so to a much greater extent. Here exceedingly careful observation is required: very close attention, keen discernment, and sound judgment.

292

Your natural endowments should be superior to the demands of your office, and not the other way round. However high the position, the person [who holds it] should show that he is superior to it. Great ability develops and reveals itself increasingly with every fresh post. A mean-spirited man will easily lose heart and, in the end, his responsibilities and reputation will come to grief. The great Augustus prided himself on being a greater man than he was a ruler: here magnanimity, and even a discreet confidence in oneself, are of service.

293

Concerning maturity. This shines forth in externals, but more so in morals. It is material weight that gives its value to gold and moral weight which gives value to a man; it enhances his talents and inspires respect. A man's poise is the façade of his soul. It is not dullness and lack of animation, as the superficial like to believe, but, rather, a very quiet air of authority; a man with such poise talks judiciously and his labours are crowned with success. [Maturity] implies the full attainment of manhood, for a man is only a person in so far as he has reached it; upon ceasing to be a child, he begins to be serious and responsible.

294

Be moderate in your views. Every man holds the opinions which suit his own interests and he can discover any number of reasons for holding them. In most people, judgment yields to inclination. Two men holding mutually contradictory views

contradictoriamente y cada uno presume de su parte la razón. Mas ella, fiel, nunca supo hacer dos cosas. Proceda el sabio con reflexa en tan delicado punto, y así el recelo propio reformará la calificación del proceder ajeno. Póngase tal vez de la otra parte; examínele al contrario los motivos; con eso, ni le condenará a él, ni se justificará a sí tan a lo desalumbrado.

295

No hazañero, sino hazañoso. Hacen muy de los hacendados los que menos tienen para qué. Todo lo hacen misterio, con mayor frialdad. Camaleones del aplauso, dando a todos hartazgos de risa. Siempre fué enfadosa la vanidad: aquí reída. Andan mendigando hazañas las hormiguillas del honor. Afecte menos sus mayores eminencias. Conténtese con hacer, y deje para otros el decir. Dé las hazañas, no las venda. Ni se han de alquilar plumas de oro para que escriban lodo, con asco de la cordura. Aspire antes a ser heroico que a sólo parecerlo.

296

Varón de prendas, y majestuosas. Las primeras hacen los hombres; equivale una sola a toda una mediana pluralidad. Gustaba aquél que todas sus cosas fuesen grandes; hasta las usuales alhajas: cuanto mejor el varón grande debe procurar que las prendas de su ánimo lo sean. En Dios todo es infinito, todo inmenso: así, en un héroe todo ha de ser grande y majestuoso, de suerte que todas sus acciones y aun razones vayan revestidas de una trascendente grandiosa majestad.

297

Obrar siempre como a vista. Aquél es varón remirado que mira que le miran o que le mirarán. Sabe que las paredes oyen,

may meet and each of them assumes that he has reason on his side. Reason, however, is loyal, and never a double-dealer. Let the wise man proceed cautiously in so delicate a matter, and thus misgivings as to his own conduct will cause him to revise his judgment with regard to that of others. He should sometimes put himself in the other fellow's place; examine his adversary's motives; if he does this he will not condemn him, nor will he defend his own point of view in so unenlightened a fashion.

295

Be busy, but not a busybody. Many people who affect to be very busy have the least to do. They make a mystery of everything in the most ludicrous fashion. Chameleons of applause, they give everybody plenty to laugh at. Vanity is always irritating; in this case it is ridiculous. These petty pismires of honour go about begging for the glory of great deeds. Make the least ado about your greatest gifts. Be content with action, and leave the talking to others. Give your achievements away, do not offer them for sale. And do not offend against decency by hiring venal pens to write filth. Aspire to be a great man rather than merely to appear to be one.

296

The man of high and noble qualities. High qualities make a man; a single one of them is worth a host of mediocre gifts. The man of distinction likes all his surroundings to be first-rate; even his everyday utensils. How much more should a great man strive to see that the qualities of his spirit are great. In God, everything is infinite, everything immense; thus, in a great man, everything should be great and glorious, so that all he does, and even all he says, should be invested with an all-pervading and surpassing majesty.

297

Always behave as though you were being watched. He is a prudent man who realizes that he is being observed, or will be observed. He knows that walls have ears and that evil deeds

y que lo mal hecho revienta por salir. Aun cuando solo, obra como a vista de todo el mundo, porque sabe que todo se sabrá: ya mira como a testigos ahora a los que por la noticia lo serán después. No se recataba de que le podían registrar en su casa desde las ajenas, el que deseaba que todo el mundo le viese.

298

Tres cosas hacen un prodigio y son el don máximo de la suma liberalidad: ingenio fecundo, juicio profundo y gusto relevántemente jocundo. Gran ventaja concebir bien, pero mayor discurrir bien. Entendimiento del bueno. El ingenio no ha de estar en el espinazo, que sería más laborioso que agudo. Pensar bien es el fruto de la racionalidad. A los veinte años reina la voluntad, a los treinta el ingenio, a los cuarenta el juicio. Hay entendimientos que arrojan de sí luz, como los ojos del lince, y en la mayor oscuridad discurren más. Hay los de ocasión, que siempre topan con lo más a propósito: ofréceseles mucho y bien; felicísima fecundidad. Pero un buen gusto sazona toda la vida.

299

Dejar con hambre. Hase de dejar en los labios aun con el néctar. Es el deseo [1] medida de la estimación. Hasta la material sed es treta de buen gusto picarla, pero no acabarla; lo bueno, si poco, dos veces bueno. Es grande la baja de la segunda vez: hartazgos de agrado son peligrosos, que ocasionan desprecio a la más eterna eminencia. Única regla de agradar: coger el apetito picado con el hambre con que se quedó. Si se ha de irritar, sea antes por impaciencia del deseo que por enfado de la fruición: gústase al doble de la felicidad penada.

[1] 1659 has 'desea.'

are bursting to come out into the light of day. Even when he is alone he behaves as though the eyes of the whole world were upon him, for he realizes that everything will eventually come to light: he regards people who will later hear of his deeds as already witnesses of them. The man who would like the whole world to see inside his home will not be a prey to misgivings just because others can observe him from theirs.

298

Three things [go to] make a genius, and they are the choicest gifts of the divine bounty: a fertile brain, sound judgment, and an outstandingly cheerful disposition. It is a great advantage to have a good understanding but a greater one to think aright. A good man knows this. Wit should not be in the backbone, where it would be more slow than sharp. Right thinking is the fruit of reasonableness. At twenty, the will is in command, at thirty the intellect, at forty the judgment. There are minds which, like the eyes of the lynx, emit light [in the dark], and the more obscure matters are, the more clearly will they reason. Other minds function best on the spur of the moment and always hit upon what is most to the point: they are always well and fully stocked, a most happy fecundity. Good taste, moreover, gives savour to everything in life.

299

Leave off while you are still hungry. Traces, even of nectar, must be left upon the lips. Desire is the measure of esteem. Even in the case of physical thirst, it is a mark of sound judgment to diminish rather than completely quench it; a good thing is doubly good when there is not much of it. A second dose is far less satisfying: surfeits of pleasure are dangerous and bring the most enduring qualities into disrepute. The only way to enjoy things is to stimulate the appetite with the hunger which is left over [after the meal]. If appetite must be titillated, let it be rather with the eagerness of desire than the satiety of repletion; happiness hardly won is doubly enjoyable.

300

En una palabra, santo: que es decirlo todo de una vez.   Es la
virtud cadena de todas las perfecciones, centro de las felicidades.
Ella hace un sujeto prudente, atento, sagaz, cuerdo, sabio,
valeroso, reportado, entero, feliz, plausible, verdadero y universal héroe.   Tres *eses* hacen dichoso: santo, sano y sabio; la
virtud es sol del mundo menor y tiene por hemisferio la buena
conciencia.   Es tan hermosa, que se lleva la gracia de Dios y de
las gentes.   No hay cosa amable sino la virtud, ni aborrecible
sino el vicio.   La virtud es cosa de veras: todo lo demás, de
burlas.   La capacidad y grandeza se ha de medir por la virtud,
no por la fortuna.   Ella sola se basta a sí misma: vivo el hombre,
le hace amable; y muerto, memorable.

300

In a word, be a saint: that is the sum total of all my advice. Virtue links all high qualities together, it is the focus of [all] felicities.   It makes a person prudent, heedful, sagacious, virtuous, wise, courageous, restrained, trustworthy, happy, honoured, a truly great man, universally acclaimed.   Three S's make a man happy: Saintly, Sound, and Sensible: virtue is the sun of Man the Microcosm, and it has a clear conscience for its hemisphere. Virtue is so lovely that it finds favour with both God and Man. Nothing is desirable but virtue, nothing detestable but vice. Virtue is real: everything else is but a mockery.   Ability and greatness are to be measured by virtue, not by wealth.   Virtue alone is self-sufficing: it makes a man lovable during his lifetime, and memorable after his death.

NOTES

(A) refers to Amelot de la Houssaie's rendering; (S) to Schopenhauer's; (J) to that of Jacobs. lit. = literally; mod. = modern. The French of (A) has not been modernized.

Title-page. *Oráculo Manual y Arte de Prudencia:* lit. 'Manual Oracle and Art of Discretion.' 'Manual' is here used adjectivally in the Spanish. No exact rendering into good English is possible.

1. *en su punto: i.e.* the highest point they are able to reach. (J) 'acme.'
siete: The reference is, of course, to the Seven Sages.

2. *Genio y ingenio:* (S) 'Herz und Kopf'; (A) 'L'Esprit et le Génie.' The distinction here is between genius and wit, the latter in the sense of intelligence, talent, or mere cleverness. Both (A) and (S) appear to have gone astray here. (J) 'Character and intellect' is just possible but the antithesis between genius and mere intelligence seems to be indicated by the context.
Los dos ejes: lit. 'The two axes' (or 'axles').
genial: The word has a variety of meanings but the sense here is quite clear from the context.
llevar: lit. 'bear,' 'carry.'

3. ... *es estimación de los aciertos:* (A) 'est ce qui fait estimer les succès'; (S) 'ist schon eine Wertschätzung seines Gelingens'; (J) goes astray with 'heightens the value of your achievements.'
el jugar a juego descubierto: lit. 'to play a disclosed game.'
amaga: lit. 'conceals.' The verb *amagar* no longer has this meaning.
nunca fué estimada: lit. 'was never esteemed.'

4. *alternan:* lit. 'alternate.'
oscuras: the modern form. 1653 and 1659 have *escuras.*
Consejo y fuerzas: (A) 'La prudence et la force;' (S) 'Einsicht und Kraft.' *Consejo* = 'wisdom' in the sense of 'good judgment.' The context indicates *fuerzas* = 'courage' rather than 'strength.' *fuerza* can have both meanings.

5. *dora:* lit. 'gilds.'
cae del oro al lodo: lit. 'falls from the gold into the mud.'
correspondencia : (A) 'correspondance'; (S) 'Hochachtung'; (J) goes astray with 'good behaviour.' The sense is 'agreement' or 'harmony.'
coronado : lit. 'crowned.'

6. *punto:* Here, again, the idea is the 'peak' of a man's powers, his 'full stature'; (A) 'L'homme au comble de sa perfection'; (S) 'seine Vollendung'; (J) 'Man at his highest point.'
lo defecado: lit. 'the purified, or clarified, state of our will.'

7. *de la misma superioridad :* lit. 'by superiority itself.'

8. *ocupare la personal:* (A) 's'empare de l'esprit'; (S) 'den Person bemächtigen'; (J) 'rules the character.'

y aun de atajar para la reputación: (A) misses the point with 'et de se mettre en haute réputation'; (S) gets the sense of *atajar* with 'ja sogar auf dem kürzesten Wege zu Ansehen zu gelangen.'

(J) goes astray with ''tis the shortest way back to good repute.'

9. *que cupo . . . cenit:* (A) 'pour y avoir rencontré une plus favorable étoile'; (S) 'indem ein günstigerer Himmel sie umfieng'; (J) 'because there is a more favourable sky in the zenith' (hardly English). The literal meaning of *cenit* is 'zenith' but here the reference is obviously astrological rather than astronomical. 'Their star' or 'their stars' is the idea.

lo que menos se esperaba, se estimó más. One of many instances in which Gracián's past tenses are best rendered by the present tense in English.

10. *se diligencia:* lit. 'is furthered by.'

11. *penetrando:* lit. 'permeating.'

13. *milicia . . . contra la malicia.* An example of Gracián's fondness for playing with words. lit. 'a militia against malice'; (A) 'un combat contre la malice de l'homme même'; (S) 'ein Krieg . . . gegen die Bosheit des Menschen'; (J) 'a warfare against the malice of men.' *Milicia =* 'manœuvre' retains both the alliteration and the sense.

la sagacidad: lit. 'sagacity.' Here, as in many other cases, the abstract noun in the Spanish original is better rendered by a concrete noun in English.

sí. Used here for emphasis : 'yes'; 'indeed.'

amaga al aire: lit. 'it threatens the air.'

la émula atención: lit. 'rival attention.'

la observación: lit. 'watchfulness.'

las tinieblas revestidas de la luz: lit. 'the darkness clothed in light.'

14. *La realidad y el modo:* (A) 'La chose et la manière'; (S) 'Die Sache und die Art.' The context indicates that Gracián had here in mind the distinction which the scholastic philosophers made between 'substance' and 'accidents,' the underlying reality and its particular modes of manifestation. He returns to this antithesis with 'substancia' and 'circunstancia.' (J) has 'The thing itself and the way it is done.' An apt English rendering is difficult to find.

(S) is nearest to '*No basta la substancia . . . circunstancia*' with 'Das Wesentliche in den Dingen ist nicht ausreichend, auch die begleitenden Umstände sind erfordert.' (A) is weak with 'Ce n'est pas assez que la substance, il y faut aussi la circonstance.'

el cómo: lit. 'the how.'

15. *de todo ignorante aprieto:* lit. 'from every ignorant tight corner.'

Hacen . . . elección de la lición: lit. 'They make choice of the lesson (or reading).' (A) 'Attendu que ces sages lui dressent sa leçon . . .'; (S) 'Suchen zuvörderst die Lection zusammen.'

17. *para deslumbrar la atención:* lit. 'to leave the attention (of others) in uncertainty.'   (A) 'pour frustrer la curiosité . . .'; (S) 'damit man die Aufmerksamkeit zumal die der Widersacher verwirre'; (J) 'to distract attention.'   The latter rendering misses the mark.

18. *Minerva:* lit. 'Minerva' (the goddess of wisdom).   (A) 'le génie'; (S) 'Talent.'
exceso: The English 'excess' is inadequate here.
se deseó: lit. 'was to be desired.'

19. *No entrar con sobrada expectación:* lit. 'Do not enter with excessive expectation.'
exceso: Here, again, the English 'excess' is inadequate.
empeñar el objeto: (A) 'et non à en engager l'objet'; (S) 'ohne dem Gegenstand derselben Verplichtungen aufzulegen'; (J) 'without pledging one to the final object.'   The last is hardly good English.
misma: the modern form.   1653 and 1659 have *mesma*.
con aplauso: here, 'happily' in the sense of 'in a praiseworthy way.' (A) 'avec plus d'applaudissement' misses the point; (S) paraphrases with 'so sieht man solche gern widerlegt'; (J) 'they are defeated amid general applause,' is a complete mistranslation.

20. This was one of Schopenhauer's favourite maxims and it is written on his own copy of *Die Welt als Wille und Vorstellung.*   (J).
en su siglo: lit. 'in his age.'

21. *arbitrio.*   (J) confuses this word with *árbitro* and renders 'there is no other umpire . . .'   The sense here is 'means,' 'expedient,' 'way'; cf. (S) 'giebt es keinen anderen Weg.'

22. *Hombre de plausibles noticias:* difficult to render well in English. (A) paraphrases with 'l'homme de mise' and (S) renders by 'Ein Mann von vollkommenden Kenntnissen,' which gives the idea.   (J) 'A man of knowledge to the point,' is hardly English.
más a lo noticioso, menos a lo vulgar: (A) 'plus il a de tout cela, moins il tient du vulgaire,' is inaccurate; (S) has the idea with 'jedoch mehr auf eine gelehrte als auf eine gemeine Weise.'

23. *Lastímase la ajena cordura:* lit. 'The wisdom (or prudence) of others is injured.'   (J) renders thus: 'The keenness of others often regrets . . .' which is wide of the mark.
laurear el natural desaire: lit. 'to laureate his natural defect' (his baldness).

24. *Templar:* lit. 'To moderate.'
la necedad: lit. 'folly.'
verdugo casero de necios: 'the domestic executioner of fools' is exact. (J) renders this by 'the mortifying lash of these fools.'

25. *entendedor:* lit. 'one who understands.'

26. *torcedor:* anything which causes displeasure, pain, or grief.
Hásele . . . el verbo.   A crux.   (A) renders by 'Il faut premièrement connoître le vrai caractère de la personne et puis lui tâter le pouls'; (S) has

'Jetzst muss man zuvörderst sein Gemüth bearbeiten, dann ihn durch ein Wort den Anstoss geben . . .' One of the meanings of the verb *tocar* is 'to assay metals'; (J) follows (S) with 'appeal to it by a word.'

cargarle con la afición: lit. 'to load him with his ruling passion.'

29. *la razón superior:* has the sense of 'opinion' here.

31. Quoted by Addison in the *Spectator*, No. 293.   (J).

33. *Saber abstraer:* lit. 'Know how to withdraw.'
polillas: lit. 'clothes moths.'   Also used of anything which wastes or consumes.

34. *minerva:* lit. 'Minerva,' the goddess of wisdom. Gracián often uses the word in the sense of 'intelligence' or 'wisdom.'

35. *Hacer concepto . . . más:* (A) has 'Peser les choses selon leur juste valeur,' which is very free; (S) is closer with 'Nachdenken, und am meisten über das woran am meisten gelegen.'

36. *también cabe la espera en ella:* lit. 'there is also room for waiting in this matter.'
si bien no se la puede coger al tenor: (A) 'il est impossible de le fixer'; (S) 'obwohl man ihm seinen Gang nicht ablernen kann'; (J) 'although one cannot calculate its path.'   *tenor* has the sense of 'constitution,' 'make-up,' also that of 'literal meaning.'
despejo. A favourite word with Gracián. It has many different meanings and there is no precise English equivalent.

37. *varillas:* lit. 'thrusts with a goad.' (A) has 'Deviner où portent de petits-mots, qu'on nous jette en passant, et savoir en tirer du profit'; (S) renders by 'Stichelreden kennen und anzuwenden verstehen.'

38. *tal vez:* Gracián often uses this adverb in the sense of the modern *tal cual vez* = 'once in a while,' 'occasionally.'

39. *importa conocerla . . . ejercicio.* (J) has 'it is well to know this both for their value in use and for their value in exchange.' This distorts the sense of the original.

40. *algo tiene de estrella:* (S) 'in etwas hängt es von der Gunst der Natur'; (A) renders *estrella* by 'bonne étoile,' which is nearer. The idea is 'lucky star' or, simply, 'luck.'
de la hoja a las hojas: a pun on the two meanings of *hoja*, 'blade of a sword' and 'leaf of a book.'
hay gracia de escritores, y es eterna: (A) 'car il faut rechercher la faveur des écrivains, qui immortalisent les grands exploits'; (S) has 'denn es gibt auch eine Gunst der Schriftsteller, und sie ist unsterblich.' The favour which authors can grant is immortality in their works.

41. *desdorar:* lit. 'to tarnish.'
cordura: lit. 'wisdom, good sense.' Here the idea is one's reputation for possessing wisdom.

42. *natural imperio:* lit. 'command.'   Here the sense is 'power to command.'   (J) renders as 'Born to command,' which is rather free.

secreta: lit. 'secret, hidden.'   The context indicates 'unaccountable' as the most appropriate rendering here.

su respeto: i.e. the respect which they inspire in others.

[*con su*] *amago:* lit. 'hint.'   (A) 'un semblant'; (S) 'eine Miene'; (J) 'a gesture,' is beside the mark here.

43. *sentir:* lit. 'to judge, form an opinion.'

tan imposible al desengaño: lit. 'as impossible for the detection of error,' i.e. 'as useless for the purpose of detecting error.'

fácil al peligro: lit. 'easy for danger,' i.e. 'easy to run into danger.'

lo que es pronto . . . de ella: (A) 'plus son jugement le porte à la censure, plus il se garde de la publier'; (S) 'so bereit er zum Tadel ist so zurück-haltend in der Äusserung desselben'; (J) 'though they have their censure ready they are not ready to publish it,' is weak.

44. *Simpatía con los grandes varones:* the context clearly indicates that reference is made to the feeling of sympathy which great men have for one another.   They intuitively recognize ability in others like them.   (J) 'Sympathy with great minds' must be rejected as it involves a mistrans-lation of *varones* and is generally misleading.

combinar con: lit. 'to unite with.'   Here: 'frequent the society of' is the sense indicated by the context.

prodigio . . . lo ventajoso: (A) 'c'est un instinct secret, que la nature donne à ceux qu'elle veut conduire à l'héroisme'; (S) 'Hierin liegt ein Wunder der Natur, sowohl wegen des Geheimnissvollen darin, als auch wegen des Nützlichen'; (J) ''Tis like a miracle of nature for mystery and for use,' is hardly English.   *oculto* has here the sense of 'secret' = 'unaccountable.'

achaca bebedizos: lit. 'imputes to magic potions.'   cf. (S) 'Zauber-tränken zuschreibt.'

45. *reflexas:* lit. 'reflections.'   (A) has 'réflexion'; (S) 'Schlauheit.' The sense here, to judge by the context, is, rather, 'caution.'

no hay mayor argumento del discurso: (A) 'il n'y a point de meilleure preuve du bon sens, que d'être réflexif'; (S) 'und es giebt keinen sicheren Beweis von Vernunft.'   *argumento* = 'token,' 'proof'; here.

46. *su antipatía:* lit. 'antipathy.'   But the context indicates definite antipathies towards certain individuals.

las previstas prendas: lit. 'the anticipated (disagreeable) qualities.'

es de desdoro de la antipatía: lit. 'is the discredit of antipathy.'   (A) 'il est honteux d'avoir de l'antipathie pour eux' (i.e. great men); (S) 'setzt die Antipathie gegen dieselben uns herab'; (J) 'so dislike to them degrades us.'   The sense is that antipathy towards such men redounds to our dis-credit.

47. *En las grandes capacidades . . . trances. capacidades* (lit. 'capaci-ties') is here best rendered by 'men of great abilities.'

los últimos trances: lit. 'the last stages.' (A) departs from the original with 'Dans les grandes places il y a toujours une grande distance d'un bout à l'autre.' (S) has 'Liegen stets die Extreme sehr weit von einander entfernt, so dass ein langer Weg von einen zum andern ist.' Some kind of paraphrase is necessary in English.

se están en el medio de su cordura: lit. 'are in the middle of their wisdom.' (S) 'halten sich immer im Mittelpunkt ihrer Klugheit'; (J) 'they always keep in the middle of their caution' is not English. 'Wise men take their stand midway,' is the sense of Gracián's here somewhat tortured Spanish.

48. *fondos:* lit. the extent of a man's capacity, his stock of virtues, vices, etc. (J) abandons the original with his title 'Be Thorough' and the phrase 'How much depends upon the person.'

perennidad de concepto: the sense is 'continuity of thought.' (A) departs from the original with 'quand l'entendement est stérile' as does (S) with 'wo keine Quelle von Gedanken fliesst,' although the latter is very near. (J) follows (S) with 'there is no spring of thoughts' (hardly English).

49. *censura:* not, of course, 'blames' in the context, but rather, 'judges,' 'sums up.'

50. ... *ni se roce consigo a solas.* (A) 'que l'on n'ait pas de quoi rougir devant soi-même' is not exact; (S) has 'und mache sich nicht mit sich selbst gemein' which (J) follows with 'or be too familiar with oneself.' All three omit to render *a solas.*

51. *delecto:* lit. 'choice.' cf. (S) 'ohne Wahl ist keine Volkommenheit'; (J) has 'to be choice you must choose,' and this has a Gracianesque flavour. *delecto* = 'discrimination' is, possibly, the best rendering here.

que parece que afectan el errar: (J) 'as if they had tried to go wrong.' This is not quite the idea. One of the meanings of *afectar* is 'to be attached to, or be fond of.' I think this is clearly the sense here.

Gran asunto de la cordura: lit. 'A great concern of wisdom.'

52. *corazón coronado:* lit. 'a crowned spirit.' (A) has 'cœur de roi'; (S) 'vom grossen Herzen'; (J) 'it is the sign of a real man, of a noble heart.' I have adapted (J) here. No literal rendering of the Spanish original is possible in tolerable English.

toda magnanimidad: lit. 'all magnanimity.' A close paraphrase is needed here.

53. *Diligente y inteligente:* lit. 'diligent and intelligent.'
Malogra tal vez ... dictamen. A difficult sentence. (A) has 'Quelquefois le délai fait échouer une entreprise bien concertée'; (S) renders 'und so vereitelt Mangel und Thatkraft bisweilen die Früchte des richtigen Urteils.' (J) has 'remiss action often nullifies prompt judgment.' 'Remiss' here is somewhat ambiguous. The idea is 'procrastination is the thief of time.' I have adopted 'prompt judgment,' although *acertado* = 'prompt' is unusual. The context, however, makes the meaning quite clear and *acertado* = 'accurate' would be inadequate.

54. *Tener bríos a lo cuerdo:* (A) has 'Avoir du sang aux ongles'; (S) 'Haare auf den Zähnen haben'; (J) 'Know how to show your teeth.' All three omit to render *a lo cuerdo*, which is the whole point of the maxim. It is intended to emphasize the contrast between courage and mere rashness.

que valiera más desde luego: (J) completely distorts the meaning here with 'to gain your point at last costs as much trouble as would have gained much more at first.' The sense clearly is '*que valiera más vencer desde luego.*'

la naturaleza acudida: lit. 'attentive Nature.' (J) goes astray with 'wise Nature.' I think 'mother Nature' is the best rendering.

55. ... *con ensanches de sufrimiento:* (A) paraphrases with 'ne s'empresser, ni se passionner jamais c'est la marque d'un cœur qui est toujours au large'; (S) renders 'mit Reichtum an Geduld'; (J) 'dowered with patience' is nearer but does not bring out the idea of '*con ensanches*' = (lit.) 'with dilatations.' I think 'all-embracing patience' is about as close as one can get in tolerable English.

56. *Tener buenos repentes:* lit. 'Have good impulses.' (A) is wrong with 'Trouver de bons expédiens' and it is difficult to justify (S) with 'Geistesgegenwort haben'; (J) misses the mark with 'Have presence of mind.' 'Have good impulses' is weak. The idea is, I think, that one should try to cultivate them. The context does rather suggest 'quick retorts,' but this would be to depart too far from the original.

antiperístasi: lit. the defence put forward by a man charged with a crime that his act was praiseworthy rather than culpable. (J) has 'natures of Antiperistasis,' which is impossible English. I think 'paradoxical' is close enough here.

58. *atemperar:* lit. 'to accommodate.' (J) has 'Adapt yourself to your company' and I have adopted this as the best rendering.

igualmente entendido: lit. 'equally understanding' or 'equally intelligent.' A paraphrase is necessary here to bring out the idea.

59. *Hombre de buen dejo:* (A) goes far from the original with 'L'homme qui se fait désirer et regretter,' as does (S) with 'Das Ende bedenken' and (J) with 'Finish off well.' There seems to be no way in which *Hombre* can be adequately rendered in this context and I suggest 'A happy leave-taking' as the closest approximation to the sense of the Spanish.

60. *y así tiene la mitad andada para los aciertos:* (J) renders 'with a moiety already mastered,' which distorts the original. The idea is that such people are half way along the road to success. *aciertos* = (lit.) successes.

la asistencia al gobernalle: lit. 'presence at the helm.'

o para ejercicio o para consejo: lit. 'either for practice or for counsel.' (J) abandons the original with 'either as pilots or men at the wheel,' but the idea is right.

61. *algún extremo sublime:* (A) 'quelque extrémité sublime' is, surely,

weak; (S) paraphrases with 'der nicht in irgend etwas alle Andern über-
träfe'; (J) 'something pre-eminent,' is weak.

63. *que gana en igualdad:* lit. 'for it gains in equality,' i.e. it helps the one
who has it to win when he and his opponent are equally matched.

fénix: lit. 'Phoenix.' This word is often used in the sense of English
'paragon.'

Álzanse los primeros con el mayorazgo de la fama: mayorazgo = lit.
entailed estate.

pleiteados alimentos: lit. 'portions which are the subject of legal disputes.'
(A) has 'une maigre portion'; (S) 'eingeklagte Alimente'; (J), 'a younger
brother's allowance,' is wrong.

64. *mucho dulce en lisonjas:* lit. 'much sweet in flatteries.'
amargo en chismes: lit. 'bitter in gossip.'
al que aconseja y se queda fuera: lit. 'him who advises and remains outside.'
lición: modern *leccion.* lit. 'lesson.'

65. *Gusto relevante.* (A) 'Le goût fin'; (S) 'Erhabener Geschmack';
(J) 'Elevated taste.'

se heredan con la continuidad: (A) 'et l'on hérite le goût d'autrui à force
de le fréquenter'; (S) and (J) omit.

le tiene en su punto: 'poner en su punto' = 'to rate at its true value.' (J)
goes astray with 'great good luck to associate with the highest taste.'

66. *el rigor de la dirección:* lit. 'the rigour of the aim.'
la puntualidad: lit. 'the method.'

67. *las perfecciones:* lit. 'high gifts.'
el Favonio: lit. Favonius.
se quedan . . . imperceptibilidad: (J) 'remain obscure and unperceived';
'remain unnoticed in their obscurity' is closer.

68. *Dar entendimiento es de más primor que el dar memoria:* lit. 'To
enlighten is of more excellence than to remind.'

cuanto es más: (A) omits; (S) has 'um so viel'; (J) 'the more,' after mis-
rendering the opening sentence as 'It is better to help with intelligence than
with memory.'

advertir: to advise or warn.

que estuvieran en su punto . . . ofrecen: (A) has 'qui seroient excellentes
parce qu'ils n'y pensent pas'; (S) 'die gerade an der Zeit waren, weil solche
sich ihnen nicht darbieten'; (J) 'omit the *à propos* because it does not occur
to them. . . .'

no sea más que dar pie: (A) 'il suffit au premier de frayer le chemin au
second'; (S) 'man gebe nicht mehr als ein Stichwort'; (J) 'give no more
than a hint.' All three depart from the original = 'yield no more than a
foothold.'

cuando toca en utilidad del que despierta: lit. 'when it affects the interests
of the one whose attention you awaken.'

69. *lición:* mod. lección.

70. *vaya a tragos el desengaño:* lit. 'let disappointment go by drops.'

71. *crédito de entendido:* lit. 'the reputation of a prudent person.' The sense is, I think, 'the sign of a prudent person.' (J) renders 'he gets the credit of trustworthiness.'

dependa en su mudanza: lit. 'let him depend in his changing.'

El que ayer fué el blanco . . . su no: lit. 'What was yesterday the white of their "yes" is to-day the black of their "no."'

72. *cuando están afianzados de su dicha . . . seguridad:* (A) 'sous la caution de leur bonne fortune'; (S) 'haben sie nur erst vom Glück Handgeld erhalten'; (J) 'affianced to Fortune.'

73. *un sonriso:* the modern form would be *una sonrisa.*

74. *hurtándoles la cordura en el trato:* lit. 'depriving them of (the chance of learning) wisdom by intercourse with their fellows.'

75. *aún no bien nacido al lucimiento:* lit. 'not yet well born to success.'
atierra: lit. 'destroys,' 'demolishes.' (J) misrenders with 'sharpens.'

78. *bajios:* 'reefs,' 'shoals.' (J) misrenders with 'depths.'

79. *juegan también la pieza del donaire:* lit. 'play also the piece (card) of wit.'
el otro: lit. 'the other man.'

80. *el que tercia:* lit. 'he who joins in [a conversation].'
de qué pie se movió: lit. 'on which foot he moved.'

83. *Será como un echar la capa al toro:* lit. 'It will be like throwing your cloak to the bull . . .'

85. *No ser malilla.* (A) 'Ne se point prodiguer'; (S) 'Nicht die Manille sein'; (J) 'Do not play Manille.' (S) suggests that this is the second-best trump (Manilio) in the game of ombre. (J) favours Littré's view that the reference is to the nine of diamonds which can be 'wild' in the game of manille. *Vide* Appendix.

Rózanse de estas malillas . . . perfecciones. A crux. (A) has 'Ces gens-là perdent toujours, pour avoir voulu trop gagner'; (S) renders 'Diese Manillen nützen die Volkommenheiten jeder Art an sich ab.' (J) has 'These Manilles wear away all kinds of excellence,' which is scarcely English. I think the context makes it clear that the reference is to the versatility of the Jack-of-all-trades which dissipates his energies.

se premian con logros de estimación: lit. 'are rewarded with gains in esteem.'

86. *apodo vulgar:* lit. 'vulgar nickname.' (J) renders 'nickname,' omitting 'vulgar.' The sense of 'vulgar' here is 'common,' i.e. 'widespread,' not 'unseemly.'

echadizos . . . común: lit. 'artfully spread from private envy to general spite.' (J) incorrectly renders *malicia* as 'distrust.'

88. *el trato:* lit. 'social intercourse,' 'dealings with others.' I have

* K

paraphrased rather freely here as there appears to be no neat English equivalent of the original. (J) departs too far from the original with 'Let your behaviour be fine and noble.'

89. *Comprensión de sí:* lit. 'Understanding of oneself.' (J) has 'Know yourself' and I have adopted this as the best rendering in this particular context. Gracián probably had the famous Greek maxim in mind.

tantee la irascible para el empeñarse: a crux. (A) has 'connoître ton activité pour t'engager'; (S) renders 'man untersuche seine Tapferkeit zum Einlassen in Händel'; (J) has 'test the force of your courage in order to apply it.' The Spanish is obscure, but I cannot agree with any of these interpretations. *empeñarse* can have the sense of 'to join battle.' The idea appears to be that one should estimate the extent and justice of one's anger before starting a fight.

90. *acaba presto de dos maneras:* lit. 'ends quickly in two ways.'

92. *trascendental:* 'transcendental' in the sense of 'profound.'

Es un caminar . . . plausible: lit. 'It is a way to security, although not to applause.' (J) renders 'It is the only sure way, though it may not gain so much applause.' This distorts the original badly.

93. *universal:* here used in the sense of 'versatile.'

94. *Incomprensibilidad de caudal:* lit. 'Incomprehensibility of attainments.' *caudal* is frequently used in the sense of 'a man's stock of natural gifts or capabilities.' A paraphrase is necessary here.

96. *que ninguna otra . . . falto:* (A) has 'qu'elle lui suffiroit quand même tout le reste lui manqueroit; (S) renders 'dass die Abwesenheit keines andern den Mann unvollständig macht'; (J) has 'that its absence makes a man imperfect.' All three depart from the original and a neat English rendering is difficult to find.

Nótase más su menos: lit. 'Its least is the more noted,' i.e. the degree in which the quality is lacking will determine the amount of attention which will be given to the deficiency. (J) has 'with other qualities it is merely a matter of more or less,' possibly following the paraphrase of (S) 'nur als ein Mehr oder Minder bemerkt wird.'

97. *obra:* lit. 'manufactures.'

98. *jibias:* 'cuttle-fish.' When pursued, these creatures emit a black fluid which darkens the water around them. (A) abandons the original entirely with 'à ces gens, qui épluchent de si près les paroles, couvre ton cœur d'une haie de défiance et de réserve'; (S) keeps the sense of the Spanish with 'gegen Luchse an Spurgeist, Tintenfische an Verstecktheit'; (J) ignores the lynxes (*linces*) altogether and is satisfied with 'adopt the policy of the cuttle-fish.'

porque: mod. *para que.*

100. *más no parecerlo:* (J) has 'not merely seem to be them.' I think the sense is that one should not put on pious and learned airs.

Pero siempre el desengañado . . . prudencia: (A) has 'Mais la prudence et le
bon esprit ne se repaissent pas de prévention'; (S) 'Und doch war stets die
Aufdeckung des Trugs die Nahrung des denkenden Geistes'; (J) renders
'and yet the discovery of deceit was always thought the true nourishment
of a thoughtful mind.'

The idea is that a wise man does not allow himself to be taken in by
specious views.   He enjoys 'seeing through' things, and seeing things as
they are.   He will accept life as it is rather than as a dream of what we
would like it to be.

101. *con necedad de todos:* lit. 'with the folly of all.'
según votos: lit. 'according to votes.'
No hay defecto sin afecto: lit. 'There is no defect but that there is a liking
for it.'
tienen voto en: lit. 'have a vote in.'

104. *que necesita de advertencia:* 'which requires heed.'
horas contadas: lit. 'counted hours.'

106. *No afectar la fortuna:* (A) has 'Ne point faire parade de sa fortune';
(S) renders 'Nicht mit seinen Glücke prahlen'; (J) has 'Do not parade your
position,' which distorts the original.   The precise meaning of the Spanish
is obscure but I think 'Do not give yourself airs' comes very close to it.

107. *de lo necio:* lit. 'of what is foolish.'

108. *ladear:* the sense here seems to be 'to rub shoulders with,' although
this is not the normal, modern meaning.   (S) has 'Sich gut zu gesellen
verstehen,' and I think he is right; (J) renders the opening phrase as
'The path to greatness is along with others' but does not bring out the
sense of 'quick way,' 'short cut.'
con la comunicación de los extremos . . . .: (A) 'de cette communication des
contraires'; (S) 'durch die Verbindung der Gegensätse'; (J) has 'by
joining extremes.'
porque harán: lit. 'because they will do it.'

109. *galera:* lit. galley.

111. *por el acierto del delecto:* lit. 'by the success (in attainment) of regard.'

112. *Éntrase por el afecto al concepto:* (A) 'C'est par l'affection que l'on
entre dans l'estime'; (S) 'Mittelst des Wohlwollens erlangt man die günstige
Meinung'; (J) 'By gaining their goodwill you gain men's good opinion.'
La formal: 'formal' in the philosophical sense.

114. *hediondeces:* lit. 'stinks.'

115. *donde tercia dependencia:* lit. 'where dependence takes part.'
en la terribilidad de la ocasión: lit. 'in the horribleness of the occasion.'

117. *culpa de cordura:* lit. 'a failing of wisdom.'

118. *que se quedan:* lit. 'that they remain.'

119. *el que quiere hacer casa hace caso:* (A) has 'celui qui veut faire sa

fortune fait cas de tout'; (S) paraphrases with 'und denke dass geschätst sein ein Schats ist'; (J) has, incorrectly, 'know that to be esteemed you must show esteem.' There is here a pun on the words *casa* and *caso* which cannot be rendered in English.

121. *No hacer negocio del no negocio:* lit. 'Do not make business out of what is not business.'
trocar los puntos: lit. 'to change the points.'

124. *absolutamente:* lit. 'absolutely,' 'in an absolute or independent sense.'
sino ser el otro aborrecido: lit. 'but to be the other one detested.'

125. *libro verde:* lit. 'a green book.' *Vide* Appendix, p. 306.
o al derecho o al través: lit. 'either to the right or the reverse.'

126. *Hanse de sellar los afectos:* lit. 'Affections must be covered.'
que si no es casto sea cauto: lit. 'if you cannot be chaste be cautious.'

127. *despejo:* it is difficult to find a precise English rendering of this word. (A) renders it in French by 'le je-ne-sais-quoi'; (S) has 'edle, freie Unbefangenheit'; (J) has 'grace.' Here, I think 'charm' is the nearest equivalent in English. I have slightly re-worded the opening sentence.
añade perfección: lit. 'adds perfection.'
político atajo: lit. 'polite short cut.'

128. *ya que en la posibilidad se violente:* lit. 'since it may overcome repugnance to possibility' (i.e. the possibility of taking action).

129. *más sirve ... compasión:* lit. 'it serves rather as an example of boldness to passion (i.e. hatred) than as a consolation to pity.' A paraphrase is essential here. (J) completely distorts the meaning with 'better be a model of self-reliance opposed to the passion of others than an object of their compassion.'

132. *Usar del reconsejo:* (A) has 'Se r'aviser'; (S) 'Zweimal überlegen'; (J) 'Revise your judgments.' I have adopted (J) as the best approximation.
cordura: lit. 'wisdom.' The context indicates 'discernment' as the best English rendering here.
queda lugar al modo: lit. 'there remains a place for the way (i.e. the manner).'

133. *singulares:* lit. 'singular.' (J) has 'original.' I think the sense is 'singular' in that such people like to be 'singled out' on account of their fads. The context surely makes this clear. 'Notorious' would, if I am correct, be the best rendering.

134. *Doblar los requisitos de la vida:* lit. 'Double the requirements of life.'
No ha de ser única la dependencia: lit. 'Dependence must not be unique.'
término de la permanencia: lit. 'the term of permanency.'
así el arte los de la dependencia: lit. 'so (should) skill those of dependence.'

135. *que añaden lo fiera a lo bestia:* lit. 'who add the wild beast to the animal.'

136. *hojas:* lit. 'leaves.'

sin topar con la sustancia del caso: lit. 'without hitting upon the substance of the matter.'

al centro de la importancia: lit. 'to the centre of the import (of the matter).'

137. *llevándose a sí:* lit. 'carrying himself.'

138. *vado:* lit. 'ford' but the word is used of any expedient adopted to ensure safety. (J) has 'to retire to a harbour and ride at anchor.' This is free but apt and I have adopted it, with the addition of 'safe' (*seguro*) which (J) omits.

caen: lit. 'fall.'

141. *apurando la cordura:* (J) has 'taxing the patience of the wise.' This is apt, but rather free.

va en chapines de entono: lit. 'goes in clogs of arrogance.' (J) is quite incorrect with 'totters along with the aid of stilts.'

143. *la importancia:* lit. 'import,' in the sense of the things which matter most.

144. *Entrar con la ajena para salir con la suya:* lit. 'To enter with (the business or interests of) another in order to emerge with one's own.' (J) renders 'Begin with another's to end with your own,' which is meaningless. A free rendering is necessary here.

porque: mod. *para que.*

aversión: vide Appendix, p. 306.

145. *sacude:* lit. 'jolts.'

adonde le duele a la flaqueza: lit. 'where it hurts weakness.'

146. *arrastra necios por vulgaridad continuada:* lit. 'it drags fools along by their persistent vulgarity.'

cojeando con el tiempo: (J) is very apt with 'limping along on the arm of time,' and I have adopted his rendering.

la otra mitad de la potencia . . . .: *Potencia* = faculty, i.e. here, the faculty of hearing.

El acierto: here, 'Sound judgment.'

148. *el ir sin ella:* lit. 'to go without it.'

razones: lit. 'opinions.'

que le hurtarán todos el trato: lit. 'or all will deprive you of their society.'

vendarán: (J) mistakes this verb for *vender* = 'to sell.' Its literal meaning is 'to bandage.' It is also commonly used in the metaphorical sense of 'to hoodwink.'

149. *testa de hierros:* mod. *testa de ferro* or *testaferro,* 'a scapegoat.'

150. *cosas:* lit. 'things.'

muerden la substancia: lit. 'bite the substance.'

la privación espoleará el deseo: lit. 'the privation (i.e. not being 'in the know') will set spurs to desire.'

151. *tener horas de ella:* lit. 'to have (i.e. "to know") the hours of it.'

el rumbo: lit. 'direction.'

152. *. . . tanto por más cuanto por menos.*   A crux.   (A) omits this altogether; (S) has 'sei es dadurch, dass er über uns, oder dass er unter uns stehe'; (J) has 'the more he does so the less desirable a companion he is'; which preserves the sense, I think, fairly well.   I have adopted his rendering.   A literal translation is impossible.

papel: lit. 'rôle.'

. . . y él el segundo.   The '*él*' should be rendered by 'you,' as the reference is to the formal Spanish '*Vd*' (*Vuestra Merced*), 'your honour.'

o no parece o desaparece: lit. 'it does not show up,' or 'it disappears.'

Fabulla: the reference is to Martial, Book VIII, Ep. 79.

peligrar de mal de lado: lit: 'run into danger by evil at your side,' i.e. by rubbing shoulders with evil.

para hecho: lit. 'for when you are made,' i.e. a 'made man.'

153. *del exceso:* lit. 'of excess,' i.e. of exceeding (surpassing) his achievements.

para igualar al del pasado: lit. 'to equal that of the past,' i.e. to be equal in worth to your predecessor.

el que acabó: lit. 'he who has finished,' i.e. your predecessor.

está en posesión de primero: lit. 'it (i.e. the past) is in possession of the first.'   The sense is 'your predecessor was first in the field.'

añadir prendas: lit. 'to add gifts.'

en el mayor concepto: lit. 'in the greater opinion.'   (A) 'pour lui ôter l'avantage qu'il a d'être plus estimé'; (S) 'um den Andern aus seinem Besitz der höheren Meinung herauszuwerfen.'   (J) 'to oust the other from his hold on public opinion.'

154. *en la espera de la credulidad:* lit. 'in the waiting of credulity.'   (A) 'à la difficulté de croire'; (S) 'die Langsamkeit im Glauben'; (J) 'in slow belief,' is hardly English.   The idea is 'unreadiness to believe.'

155. *es entrar con señorío del afecto:* lit. 'is to enter (i.e. begin) with mastery of the emotions.'

tanteando . . . no más: lit. 'estimating the need of anger up to such a point.'   The tortured construction is pure Graciánese.   Note the reversal of the natural word order 'tanteando la necesidad de enojo . . .'

en una ira: lit. 'in a rage.'

hacer mal a: lit. 'to do harm to.'   (A) goes astray with 'gourmander' (*sic*); (S) has 'bemeisteren'; (J) 'to keep control of.'   I think 'to curb' is the idea.   The analogy is with the methods by which animals are controlled, by the bit, the spur, the whip, etc., and the following word *caballo* clearly suggests 'curb' here.

156. *Amigos de elección:* lit. 'Friends of choice.'

obra: lit. 'acts.'

para la fecundidad de aciertos: lit. 'for the fecundity of successes.'

158. *Hay en esto su arte de discreción:* lit. 'There is in this its art of discretion.'

ente: the 'ens' of the schoolmen = 'being.' 'Quodlibet ens est unum, verum, bonum . . .' a maxim of scholastic philosophy.

los muy salados: (A) 'les meilleurs sont ceux que l'on n'acquiert qu'après avoir longtemps mangé du sel avec eux'; (S) 'die besten sind die von vielen Salz'; (J) 'absolutely the best ones are those well salted.' This, surely, is not an English idiom! One can, however, bring in the idea of 'eating salt with' and so keep fairly closely to the original, cf. (A) and (S).

159. *que quien añade . . . impaciencia:* lit. 'he who increases knowledge increases impatience.'

apele al retiro de sí mismo: lit. 'let him appeal to the inner sanctuary of himself.' (S) 'ziehe sich zurück in sich selbst'; (J) 'retire within himself.' The latter is rather free. I think 'look into his own heart' would be apt here.

161. *defectos dulces:* lit. 'sweet defects.'

se casa y se amanceba: lit. 'marries and illicitly cohabits with.'

162. *apretón de cordeles:* lit. 'a tightening of the cords.' The reference is, probably, to execution by the *garrote.*

gloria: lit. 'heavenly bliss.'

hacer veneno de la felicidad: lit. 'to make poison of happiness.'

sentenciándole . . . suspensión: difficult to render adequately. lit. 'sentencing him to the suspension of so envious a suspense,' a pun on suspension (i.e. hanging) and suspense. (A) has 'en le condamnant au supplice d'attendre en vain que le sujet de ces peines cesse'; (S) 'diesem den Tod durch den Strang, wenn er nicht abwarten will, dass der Neid ihn verzehrt habe'; (J) renders 'the slow death of envy long drawn out.'

163. *la venganza de ensalzado en compasión de caído:* lit. 'revenge upon one in a high position into pity for one who has fallen.'

164. *echar al aire algunas cosas:* lit. 'throw some things into the air.'

166. *cazar:* lit. 'to chase,' 'hunt.'

es el verdadero encandilar: lit. 'is the true way of dazzling them.'

unos para provecho, otros para sombra: lit. 'some for profit, others for (their) shade.'

168. *No dar en:* lit. 'Not to fall into.' (A) 'Ne point donner dans le monstrueux'; (S) 'Nicht zu einem Ungeheuer von Narrheit werden'; (J) 'Do not indulge in the eccentricities of folly.' A literal rendering is difficult because of the context which seems to demand 'have no dealings with.'

la que había de ser . . . imaginado. A crux. (A) 'attendu que ce qui devoit être cause d'une réflexion sérieuse sur ce qui donne matière à la risée publique, fait tomber dans la présomption de croire que l'on est admiré'; (S) 'an die Stelle eines nachdenkenden Bemerkens des fremden Spottes, ist der falsche Dunkel eines eingebildeten Beifalls getreten'; (J) 'instead of paying attention to other people's real derision, men of this kind blind themselves with the unfounded assumption of their imaginary applause.' This is scarcely English!

170. *es asegurar la importancia:* lit. 'is to secure importance.' (A) has

'c'est le moyen de réussir dans les choses d'importance'; (S) 'dadurch
sichert man seine Bedeutsamkeit'; (J) ''Tis a sure means of keeping up
your importance.' I think *importancia* must be paraphrased here in order
to bring out the sense of the original. The idea seems to be 'claim to the
respect of others' but (A) is, I think, just possible.

171. *Si en lo poco se abusa de lo mucho:* (A) 'Si l'on prodigue le beaucoup
pour le peu . . .'; (S) 'Wenn man su geringen Zwecken das Grosse miss-
braucht . . .'; (J) 'If you use up the great for little ends,' is bad.

172. *en un punto de un puntillo:* lit. 'on a point of a punctilio.' (A)
abandons the original with 'en un moment'; (S) has 'in einem Augen-
blick'; (J), 'in a moment,' follows (A). All abandon the original metaphor
which, I think, can be quite well preserved here as 'impaled upon the
point of a punctilio.'

sudor: lit. sweat.

de vidrio: lit. 'of glass.'

173. *Muestran tener la condición más niña que las de los ojos:* difficult to
render well. *niña* = the pupil of the eye; *niño* (adj.) = 'childlike' or,
metaphorically, 'small; petty.' (A) 'Ils se montrent plus tendres à blesser
que les yeux,' is very free; (S) 'Die Beschaffenheit ihres Gemüths ist zarter
als die ihres Augensterns . . .'; (J) 'Their feelings are even more sensitive
than the eye itself.'

desaire: lit. 'annoyance.'

la mitad de: lit. 'half of.' (A) 'tient de la nature du diamant'; (S) 'und
daher ein Amant ein halber Diamant zu nennen'; (J), with 'the Amant is
half adamant,' out-Graciáns Gracián! A free rendering is necessary here.

174. *Para no saber las cosas mal sabidas:* lit. 'In order not to know
things ill tasted.' The pun on the two meanings of 'saber,' 'to know,'
and 'to taste' is untranslatable.

175. *sustancial:* not in the financial sense, here!

176. *Debata en la razón:* (S) 'Man überlege mit der Vernunft'; (J) 'Take
counsel with reason.'

177. *Toda humanidad:* lit. 'Every human quality.'

178. *toca a infelicidad para el remedio:* (A) 'et sonne le toxin (*sic*) aux
approches du mal pour les faire courir au remède'; (S) 'wenn man Unglück
droht, damit man ihm vorbeuge'; (J), 'it always warns them of misfortune
and wards off its effects,' is hardly correct. The idea is, I think, that a
man's heart both forewarns him of disaster and suggests a remedy for it.
The original is obscure.

179. *A tantos pagan pecho . . . se descubre:* a pun on the two meanings
of *pecho* = 'tribute' and 'heart.' (J) 'You must pay ransom to each you tell.'

la ajena tentativa: lit. 'the probing of others.' (S) has 'die
mancherlei Versuche der Andern.' The idea is 'the curiosity of others.'

el tirar varillas: lit. 'throwing darts.'

180. *discurrir:* lit. 'to reason out.'

entrambas partes: lit. 'both sides.'

181. *sangrarse del corazón:* lit. 'to bleed one's heart.' (J) ''tis the lancet of the heart.'

falto: lit. 'deficient.'

182. *su si no:* lit. 'their if not.'

suele vengar: lit. 'is wont to avenge.'

183. *No aprehender fuertemente:* (A) 'Ne se point entêter'; (S) 'Nichts gar zu fest ergreifen'; (J) 'Do not hold your views too firmly.'

cabeças de hierro: lit. 'heads of iron.'

184. *se cose de estos puntos:* lit. 'is embroidered with these points.' (A) 'se coût à petits points'; (S) 'ist aus solchen Dingen zusammengenäht'; (J) 'is woven out of such things.' There is, of course, an untranslatable pun here on two meanings of the word *punto;* viz. 'stitch' and 'sentence.'

185. *Es muy contingente:* lit. 'It is very probable.'

será la primera desempeño de la segunda: lit. 'the first will be a pledge for the second.' (A) 'que la première serve de garant à la seconde, qui ne réussit pas'; (S) 'dann wird er, mag gelingen oder missglücken, der erste seine Ehrenrettung sein'; (J) 'whether it succeed or fail, the first will redeem the second.' I think the sense is that a first shot will *justify* a second, but the Spanish is obscure.

Siempre ha de haber . . . a más: (A) has 'L'on doit toujours avoir son recours à mieux et de beaucoup appeler à davantage'; (S) 'Immer muss man seine Zuflucht zu einer Verbesserung nehmen und sich auf ein Mehreres berufen können'; (J) 'Always have recourse to better means and appeal to more resources.'

186. *autoriçados:* lit. 'authorized.' (A) has 'à la mode'; (S) 'in noch so hohen Ansehen stehen'; (J) goes astray with 'however high placed.'

yerro: there is a pun here on *hierro* = iron, and *yerro* = mistake, error.

Bien pueden estar los vicios realçados, pero no son realces: (A) 'Les vices peuvent bien être exaltés mais non exalter'; (S) 'Die Laster können hoch stehen, sind aber deshalb doch nichts Hohes'; (J) with 'Vices may stand in high place but are low for all that,' departs from the original sense. *realces* should here be rendered by a substantive. I suggest 'adornments.'

187. *por repasión:* i.e. 'through remorse.' (A) has 'par repassion' (par talion); (S) 'durch Vergeltung.'

188. *lo de acá:* lit. 'what is there.'

adelantando las plausibles noticias: (A) 'en y dévelopant des connoissances plausibles'; (S) 'und befordert lobenswerthe Kentnisse'; (J) 'and encourages praiseworthy exertions.' (J) is quite incorrect and (A) and (S) are, I think, wide of the mark. *noticia* can have the sense of English 'news,' especially in the plural, and it can also be the equivalent of English 'knowledge,' 'information,' 'statement.' As in so many cases where Gracián's meaning is ambiguous, we have to rely very much upon the context as a guide to the precise sense in which he uses a word. Here I favour *noticias* = 'statement,' 'observation,' 'remark,' rather than (A) and (S) 'knowledge.' (J) is impossible.

plausibles = 'complimentary' or 'pleasant' is clearly indicated by *Es un político modo . . .'* contrasted with *con el desprecio de lo ausente.* The original is, however, admittedly susceptible of more than one interpretation.

las perfecciones presentes: lit. 'present perfections.'

estas sutilezas del llegar: lit. 'these subtleties of arriving,' i.e. 'subtleties of the *arriviste.*' (S) omits to render *del llegar* and is content with 'alle diese Schliche.'

truecan los sentidos: lit. 'they change the sense(s)' i.e. meaning.

189. *deseo:* lit. 'desire.'

torcedor: anything which causes pain and discomfort, e.g. an instrument of torture, as the thumbscrew, rack, etc. The idea here is that the needs of others can be used to get one's own way.

en la dificultad de la consecución: lit. 'in the difficulty of gaining their object.' (S) renders 'durch Vorstellung der Schwierigkeit des Erlangens . . .'; (J) has 'pointing out the difficulty of satisfaction.' As (J) renders *apetito* by appetite, 'of satisfying it' would, surely, be the obvious rendering in his case. I prefer the more general meaning of *apetito* = desire, which suggests 'fulfilment' for *consecución.*

al paso que crece la repugnancia: lit. 'at the pace at which opposition grows.'

conservar dependencias: lit. 'to preserve dependencies.'

190. *también se dijo 'ventura de fea':* lit. 'it has also been said "the luck of the ugly."'

es arbitrio: lit. 'it is an expedient.'

que nunca se acaba de romper: lit. 'which never finishes breaking.'

191. *con sólo el buen aire de una gorra:* lit. 'with merely the good air of a cap.' (A) has 'par le seul atrait d'une révérence'; (S) 'mit dem schmeichelhaften Hutabziehen'; (J) 'by the grace of their salute.'

desusada: lit. 'obsolete,' 'archaic.' (S) has 'die ungebrauchliche'; (J) follows (S) with 'useless.' I think the context clearly indicates that the sense here is 'overdone,' ancient forms of courtesy being regarded as extravagant. (S) and (J) are wrong here.

193. *al entendido, un buen entendedor:* lit. 'to the understanding person, a person of good understanding.'

194. *pero no tanto que sea desatino . . .:* lit. 'not to such an extent that it should be folly . . .'; (J) 'not so high that you miss your mission at the very beginning of life.'

195. *desfrutar a cada uno:* (A) 'cueïllir ce qu'il y a de bon dans chacun'; (S) paraphrases with 'von Jedem Nütsen zu ziehen verstehen'; (J) 'to know how to make use of every one.'

196. *tienen unos cabida:* lit. 'some have influence.' (S) has 'stehen bei Fürsten and Mächtigen in Ansehen' and (J) follows him with 'some stand high in the favour of . . .'

errar el norte: lit. 'to mistake the course.'

la vecina bocina: lit. 'the neighbouring megaphone.' The reference is to the megaphones which used to be employed in giving orders on board ship. (A) has 'car ce seroit manquer la route que lui marque l'étoile du nord'; (S) 'auf welchen doch der nahe kleine Bär hindeutet'; (J) 'though its neighbour (the pole-star) calls us to it with a voice of thunder.' All three translators have missed the point. A literal rendering would be clumsy, but the idea of the navigator issuing orders should be retained.

197. *que es el sobrehueso de la necedad: sobrehueso* = 'trouble, encumbrance.' (J) has 'the Nemesis.'

198. *remudar:* lit. 'change.'

199. *enlodadas:* lit. 'muddied.' (A) distorts with 'défectueuses'; (S) has 'so mit Koth bespritst an'; (J) 'so besprinkled with dust.'

202. *atenciones:* (A) has 'réflexions'; (S) 'Gedanken'; (J) has 'fruit of thought.'

hazañosos: lit. 'heroic, gallant.' Refers to *hechos,* as *sabios* refers to *dichos.*

204. *basta ofrecerse:* lit. 'it is sufficient that they should present themselves.'

205. *pegando fuego a las maravillas del mundo:* Herostratus set fire to the temple at Ephesus on the night of Alexander's birth, 356 B.C.

207. *Usar del reporte:* (A) 'User de retenue'; (S) 'Sich mässigen'; (J) 'Be moderate.'

Hase de estar . . . acasos: (A) 'Il faut prendre garde à son fait, surtout dans les cas imprévus'; (S) 'Man soll einen Fall wohl überlegen, zumal einen Unfall'; (J), 'One has to consider the chance of a mischance' is incorrect.

209. *por lo introducido:* lit. 'as being accepted.'
(A) 'tout ce que l'exemple et l'usage introduisent a beaucoup de force'; (S) 'Je ne haben viel Gewalt, weil sie eben allgemein eingeführt sind'; (J) 'they are of special power because they are general.'

con descontento de la propia: lit. 'with discontent of their own.'

allende: lit. 'beyond,' 'the other side of.' e.g. *allende el mar* = 'overseas.'

se pudre de: lit. 'is annoyed about.'

210. *jugar de la verdad:* lit. 'play the truth.' (J) has 'to play the card of truth,' and I have followed his rendering here.

Hase de hablar a los presentes en los pasados: lit. 'One must speak to those present (i.e. 'now here') in those of the past.' (J) goes astray with 'Matters of to-day should be treated as though they were long past.' The precise sense of the original is not clear but the context indicates a rendering on the lines I have adopted.

brujulear: lit. 'to divine by conjectures.' (J) has 'for those who understand, a word is sufficient.' The idea is '*verb. sap.*'

211. *ni es de sabios la novedad:* lit. 'nor is surprise of the wise.'

213. *bocadeando:* lit. 'dividing them into small bits.' A paraphrase is

needed here.   (J) has 'some sweet bait brings them into the mouth till they fall from the tongue.'

las redes: lit. 'the nets.'

La detención . . . recato: lit. 'Reserve in the careful man causes the other man, in his caution, to risk his reserve.'   The original is obscure.   (S) has 'Die Zurückhaltung des Aufpassenden macht dass die des Andern die Vorsicht aus der Acht lasst, und so kommt seine Gesinnung an den Tag. . . .'; (J) has 'By reserving your attention the other becomes less attentive,' which distorts the original.

215. *segunda intención:* lit. 'double dealing,' 'duplicity.'   (J) goes wrong with 'second thoughts.'

sea primero: lit. 'should be first.'

las puntas que va echando: lit. 'the suggestions which he is throwing out.'   (A) 'les visées qu'elle prend'; (S) 'die Vorwände, die er . . . aufstellt'; (J) 'the artifices which such a man uses.'

para venir a parar al punto de su pretensión: there is a pun here on the words *punta* and *punto.* It cannot be reproduced in English.   lit. 'to come to a halt at the goal of his pretension.'

216. *en el concepto:* lit. 'in the understanding.'

217. *y pues . . . prevención:* lit. 'and since it happens in reality let it happen in foresight.'

y sirve . . . hizo: lit. 'and the satisfaction from the bad turn which was done to you serves as regret.'

218. *la que nunca obró:* lit. 'which has never done . . .'

leso: lit. 'damaged.'

dañado: lit. 'injured.'

219. *por su casa:* (A) has 'chez eux'; (S) 'für sein eigenes Haus'; (J) 'in their own affairs.'

que temido reflexo: lit. 'than feared (as) cautious.'

220. *exceder:* lit. 'to excel.'   There is a play here on *ceder* and *exceder* which it is difficult to render neatly in English.   (J) is too free with 'To follow the times is to lead them.'   (A) retains the play with 'Savoir céder au tems, c'est excéder.'

entra el desprecio: lit. 'contempt comes in.'

222. *equivalencia:* (A) 'un Janus en équivalent'; (S) 'ein Janus an billigen Urtheil'; (J) 'a Janus for impartiality.'   The latter rendering is incorrect.

Momo: the reference is to Momus, the god of jesting, who blamed the god Vulcan because, in the human form which he had made of clay, no window had been placed in the breast through which whatever was done or thought might be brought to light.

223. *acciones de manía:* lit. 'actions of obsession.'

225. *ir sobre sí:* lit. 'to go over oneself.'

227. *teñir de su color la credulidad:* lit. 'to tinge credulity with their colour.'

228. *opinión:* one of the common meanings of opinion is 'reputation,' i.e. the opinion which others have of one.

229. *con fidelidad:* lit. 'with loyalty.'

231. *está aún muy dentro de su nada:* lit. 'it is still very much within its nothingness.' (A) 'elle est encore bien avant dans le rien'; (S) 'steckt sie noch tief in jenem ihrem Nichts'; (J) 'it is still nothing,' is too free.

232. *manuales:* lit. 'manual.'
parten un cabello: lit. 'share a hair.'
plático: modern *práctico.*

233. *No errarle el golpe al gusto ...:* (A) 'Savoir trouver le goût d'autrui'; (S) 'Den fremden Geschmack nicht verfehlen ...'; (J) is too free with 'Let not the proffered morsel be distasteful.' The literal meaning is 'Do not miss your aim when striking a blow at taste'; (S) is close to the sense but the idea is 'Do not let your judgment of another's taste be mistaken.'

pierden ... agradar: lit. 'they lose the thanks and the gift because they lost the direction of pleasing.' (A) 'on perd et le don et le gré'; (S) 'man verliert alsdann den Dank und das Geschenk'; (J) 'you thereby lose both gift and thanks.'

aporrean el alma: lit. 'they cudgel the soul.'

234. *sin prendas de honra ajena:* lit. 'without pledges of another's honour.'

del provecho en el silencio: lit. 'of advantage in silence.'

del daño en la facilidad: lit. 'of detriment in readiness (i.e. of speech).' The idea of mutual advantage must be brought out. (J) has, too freely, 'Arrange that silence is a mutual advantage, disclosure a danger to both.' cf. (S) 'Man müss so gehen, dass der beideseitige Vortheil im Schweigen, der Schaden in der Mittheilung liege.'

ha de ser el trato de compañía: lit. 'the bargain must be accompanied,' i.e. must be mutual. (J) has 'you must act with a partner.'

para que ... participe: lit. 'in order that the one who is admitted a participant may not be converted into a witness.' (J) 'so that your partner cannot turn king's evidence,' is good, and I have adapted part of this rendering so as to include '*el que se reconoce,*' omitted by (J).

235. *donde no corresponde la villanía:* lit. 'where villainy is not a party to the deal.' (J) is weak with 'unless he is mean.'

237. *Pensará partir peras y partirá piedras:* note the Gracianesque alliteration here. It cannot be carried over literally into English. I have adopted (J) 'You may think you will share pears, but you will only share parings,' with a slight alteration.

238. *echan presto menos:* note word order. The natural one would be 'echan menos presto' or 'presto echan menos.'

239. *reagudo:* lit. 'very acute.'
las sutilezas comúnmente quiebran: lit. 'finenesses usually break.' There

is a play here upon *sutileza* = pointed remark and *sutileza* = fineness, slenderness, e.g. of a foil.

240. *Saber usar de la necedad:* The Scots colloquialism renders the idea exactly.

juega tal vez de esta pieza: lit. 'occasionally plays this piece.'

La sencilla lo es, que no la doble: lit. 'The simple (form) is it (i.e. the card), not the double.' (S) has 'die aufrichtige, nicht die falsche Dummheit ...'; (J) has 'ingenuous folly rather than the pretended.' *doble* is difficult to render literally here.

241. *Da pie ...:* lit. 'It gives a footing.'

Las mayores veras ... burlas: lit. 'The greatest truths have always been born of jests.'

242. *todo pára en parar:* lit. 'everything stops in stopping.'

es defecto de: lit. 'is a defect of,' i.e. arising out of.

244. *Transforman ... ajeno:* cf. (J) 'Some transform favours received into favours bestowed.'

De esta suerte truecan ... activa: lit. 'In this way they change the obligation from passive to active.'

destrocando la necedad ... provecho: (S) '... und solchen Narrenhandel wieder rückgänzig zu machen, indem man ihnen ihre erzeigte Ehre wieder zustellt und dafür seinerseits auch wieder zu dem Seinigen gelangte'; (J) has 'to retaliate on such fools' bargains by paying in their own coin, and so coming by your own again.' This is somewhat free, but a paraphrase is essential. The literal meaning is: 'returning folly, giving them (the fools) back their favour, and each party to the bargain taking his profit.'

248. *No se le lleve el último:* lit. 'Do not let the last thing carry you away.'

252. *el arrimo:* lit. 'the support.' Adriano: the Spanish-Roman emperor, Hadrian. The reference is to a story which relates that an old woman approached Hadrian with a petition and, when repulsed by him, she told him that if, as he alleged, he had no time, he should give up his job. cf. (J), Notes, p. 193.

con tal exceso de ajenos: lit. 'with such an excess of (the affairs of) others.'

253. *aquél ... concepto:* (A) 'avec celui à qui l'on parle'; (S) 'mit dem man zu thun hat ... um ihm eine hohe Meinung einzuflössen.' (A) omits *para el concepto*; (J) has 'if you desire to give him a high opinion of you.'

254. *para el que viene del cielo:* lit. 'for him who comes from heaven.'

257. *zarpa:* lit. 'paw, or claw, of an animal.'

el propio en su afición: lit. 'their own in affection,' i.e. their own pet failing.

258. *alzarse con toda la superintendencia:* (A) 's'élever en prenant toute la surintendance'; (S) 'die ganze Ehre der obern Leitung allein davon zu tragen ...'; (J) misses the mark with 'to carry off the whole glory of success.'

260. *los de la correspondencia:* (A) 'les gens de la correspondance'; (S) 'den entsprechenden Personen'; (J) 'the persons with whom we are connected.'

261. *el foro interno:* lit. 'the interior tribunal,' i.e. of their consciences.

263. *prestarlas:* the modern form. 1653 and 1659 have *prestallas.*

264. *la ajena intención:* lit. 'the purpose of others.'

265. *el Gran Capitán:* Gonzalo de Córdoba (1443–1515).

266. *los insensibles:* (S) 'unempfindlichen Menschen'; (J) 'such men without feeling.'

negóciase . . . soberano: (S) 'So treibt man in der Luft Handel mit der Luft; und der königliche Athem vermag Mut und Kraft einzuflössen'; (J) 'Thus we deal in air and a royal breath can produce courage and power.' *soberano* here = powerful, strong.

268. *caer en la cuenta:* lit. 'to take account of,' i.e. to sum up, (a situation). (A) omits; (S) has 'auf den rechten Weg zu kommen'; (J) 'to get him in the right way,' distorts the original badly. The sense is that there is only one proper way of doing anything.

270. *o quiere ser:* lit. 'or wishes to be.' (A) 'ou veut être'; (S) 'oder will doch sein'; (J) 'or will be so.'

272. *algarabía:* lit. 'gabbling,' 'jargon.'

porque no entiende los términos del buen término: (A) 'parce qu'ils n'entendent rien au savoir-vivre'; (S) 'er versteht die Sprache des guten Vernehmens nicht'; (J) 'the language of good breeding.'

273. *por falto:* lit. 'as lacking,' i.e. in good sense.

por fácil: lit. 'as easy-going.'

274. *un caer en picadura, es suerte:* there is a pun here on the two meanings of *suerte,* 'good luck' and 'a manœuvre in the bullfight.' *picar:* in bullfighting, is to get in a thrust with the goad. (J) has 'to be in vogue is a matter of luck,' which distorts the original.

275. *Corriente, pero no indecente:* lit. 'Easy but not unbecoming.' (J) is very free with 'Join in the game as far as decency permits,' but this is the sense of the original. *Corriente:* I have ventured to use a contemporary expression which, I think, is exact here.

de figura: lit. 'cutting a figure.'

de enfado: lit. 'of vexation,' i.e. 'giving rise to boredom or irritation.'

es ramo de galantería: lit. 'it is a branch of gallantry,' i.e. 'to obey the injunction not to show off is a branch of good manners.'

pasar por donde los más: lit. 'pass where the majority pass.'

un día genial: lit. 'a jovial day,' i.e. 'a holiday.'

que se ganó en toda la seriedad: lit. 'than was won in all seriousness.'

afectar melindres: 'to affect prudish ways.'

276. *los otros:* lit. 'the other (periods).'

277. *Hombre de ostentación:* lit. 'A man of ostentation.'

la ostentativa: (A) 'l'étallage'; (S) 'ausgezeichneten Gaben'; (J) 'ability to display.'   I have adopted (J).

Fué la luz pronto lucimiento de todo lo criado: lit. 'Light was the early display of everything created.'   (J) 'Light was the first thing which caused Creation to shine forth.'   I have slightly adapted (J)'s rendering here.

más cuando la realidad se afianza: lit. 'especially when reality guarantees it.'   (A) 'et particulièrement quand la réalite la cautionne'; (S) 'zumal wenn es sich aufwirklichen Gehalt stützt'; (J) 'especially when combined with real excellence.'

cualquiera a solas fuera violenta: lit. 'any one of them alone would be abortive.'   (A) 'car sans elle toute perfection seroit dans un état violent'; (S) 'denn jedes von beiden allein würde unpassend sein'; (J) 'for one without the other were abortive.'   I have slightly adapted (J) here.

sino por brújula . . . adelantando: lit. 'but rather depicting it (as) through a peep-hole and always moving it further on.'   (A) goes astray with 'seulement par pièces et comme si l'on étoit après à la peindre, pour en découvrir toujours davantage'; (S) has 'von verstohlnen Blicken preiszugeben und dann immer mehr'; (J), 'but to grant stolen glances at it, more and more as time goes on,' distorts the original.   The simile is clearly that of a peep-show.

278. *Huir la nota en todo:* lit. 'Flee notoriety in everything.'

279. *despeñarse:* lit. 'to throw oneself headlong,' i.e. 'to court disaster.'

280. For those who complain of the allegedly unique degeneracy of our own times this Maxim may be a consolation.

andan desmentidas: lit. 'go belied.'

281. *el tibio sí:* lit. 'the tepid yes.'

regüeldos: lit. 'belchings.'

Redujo el juicioso Antígono . . . Cenón: lit. 'The wise Antigonus reduced the whole theatre of his fame to Zeno alone.'

282. *la mucha sustancia:* lit. 'the great substance.'

el que se conserva en el centro de su opinión: lit. 'he who keeps himself in the centre of his reputation.'

283. *exceso de ingenio:* lit. 'excess of genius.'   Here, again, 'excess' has no pejorative sense; 'genius in the highest degree.'

284. *Sea antes avaro que pródigo de sí:* lit. 'Be rather miserly than prodigal with yourself.'

terrero: lit. 'target.'

es tripulado en confusión: (S) 'wird er mit Beschämung fortgeschicht'; (J) 'because he thrusts himself in without shame he is thrust out with it.'

286. *y común:* lit. 'and a general one.'

recibirle: the modern form.   1653 and 1659 have *recebille.*

y las más veces . . . prevenirle: lit. 'and in most cases the astuteness of others will diligently bring this about in order to overcome you.'

287. *porque no acabe de encendérsele la sangre . . . sangriento:* lit. 'because
the blood is hardly fired when it will carry everything out in a bloody way.'
(S) 'denn kaum wird das Blut sich vollends erhisst haben, so wird man
blutig zu Werke gehen'; (J) 'for no sooner is the blood up than it is
spilt.'

288. *Vivir a la ocasión.*   (J) misinterprets here with 'Live for the
moment.'

todo ha de ser al caso: (A) 'mesuré au tems'; (S) 'nach den Umstanden
richten . . .'; (J) 'must be determined by circumstances.'

el norte de la prudencia: lit. 'the direction of prudence.'

290. *que es amor muy de personas:* the meaning is ambiguous.   (A)
has 'il vaut mieux être aimé avec respect qu'avec tendresse.   Tel est
l'amour que demandent les grans-hommes'; (S) renders: 'Man sei eher
im Besitz einer verehrenden als einer hingebenden Liebe: so its sie ganzen
Leuten angemessen'; (J) 'prefer to be loved with respect rather than
with passion, for that is a love suitable for many.'

291. *Saber hacer la tentativa:* lit. 'Know how to make examination.'
detención: lit. 'delay.'
el ajeno: i.e. *el ajeno juicio.*

292. *Venza el natural:* lit. 'Let natural endowment overcome . . .'
Un caudal con ensanche: lit. 'A stock of gifts with (a capacity for) enlarge-
ment.'   (A) 'Un homme qui a de quoi fournir'; (S) 'Ein umfassender
Geist'; (J) 'An extensive capacity.'   The whole sentence *Un caudal . . .
empleos* defies literal translation and a paraphrase is necessary.   The idea
is that ability develops and reveals itself more and more with every fresh
responsibility undertaken.

293. *La compostura:* 'Composure.'   (J) has 'A composed bearing.'
The context clearly indicates 'deportment.'   *compostura* can have the sense
of 'the way in which something is put together or made up,' in this case, a
man's whole bearing.

habla por sentencias, obra con aciertos: (S) 'Ihre Reden sind Sentenzen,
ihr Wirken gelingende Thaten'; (J) has 'with men of this kind sentences are
orations and acts are deeds,' which does not appear to mean very much!
Sentencia has various meanings, among which are 'aphorism' and 'decision
of a judge.'   Gracián is, I think, punning on all the possible meanings,
including the simple 'sentence.'   The idea is that their words reveal sound
judgment and good sense.   *aciertos:* lit. 'successful hits.'

294. This Maxim anticipates the modern psychological doctrine of
'rationalization.'

y abunda de razones en su aprehensión: (A) 'et abonde en raisons dans tout
ce que son appréhension lui répresente'; (S) 'und glaubt einen Überfluss
an Gründen für dieselben zu haben'; (J) 'and imagines he has abundant
grounds for them.'   The literal sense is 'and abounds in reasons for
holding them.'

y así el recelo . . . ajeno: (A) 'et par là son doute corrigera l'entêtement des autres'; (S) 'dann wird das Misstrauen gegen sich selbst sein Urtheil über das Benehmen des Gegners berichtigen'; (J) 'for his decision of his opponent's view may cast doubt on his own.' (J) completely distorts the original.

295. *las hormiguillas del honor:* lit. 'the little ants of honour.'

298. *gusto relevantemente jocundo:* (J) abandons the original with 'a pleasant and refined taste.' (S) has 'ein zugleich erhabener und angenehmer Geschmack.' The precise sense in which Gracián uses *jocundo* = 'jovial,' 'jolly,' 'cheerful,' is not very clear.

gusto is, I think, used here in its sense of 'inclination' or 'disposition' rather than 'taste.'

Entendimiento del bueno: lit. 'The understanding of the good man.'

ofréceseles mucho y bien: lit. 'there presents itself to them a great deal and (that) good.'

299. *es grande la baja de la segunda vez:* lit. 'the lowering of the second time is great.'

300. *Tres eses hacen dichoso:* (A) 'Trois S le font heureux, la Santé, la Sagesse, la Sainteté'; (S) 'Drei Dinge, welche im Spanischen mit einem S anfangen, machen glücklich: Heiligkeit, Gesundheit und Weisheit.' This is a, perhaps unavoidably, clumsy rendering. (J) has 'Three HHH's make a man happy, Health, Holiness, and a Headpiece.' The rendering 'Saintly, Sound, and Sensible' seems an obvious solution.

APPENDIX

The following is a brief summary of the more important comments which A. Morel-Fatio makes upon the text of the *Oráculo* and upon a number of passages in Schopenhauer's rendering. The Maxims concerned are indicated by their numbers. (M-F = Morel-Fatio.)

5. *entretenerla, no satisfacerla.* The 'la' here, says M-F, refers to 'dependencia.'

15. *valientes.* Gracián uses this word in the sense of 'bravoes' or 'champions.' (J) 'champions of intellect.' (Cf. M-F.)

21. *obre.* Both 1653 and 1659 have 'obre.' (A), (S), and (J) render as though the Spanish text had 'abra' (present subjunctive of 'abrir,' 'to open'). The context, 'a las puertas de la Fortuna,' certainly suggests 'abra' and the translators may have regarded 'obre' as a misprint. This, however, presumes *two* typographical errors, and, in view of the fact that 'obre,' in the sense of 'sets to work,' is quite possible here, the assumption is scarcely justifiable. (Cf. M-F.)

23. *sino.* M-F cites the *Criticón*, iii, 9: 'No hallarás sí sin no, ni cosa sin un si no,' to support his rendering: 'Évitez les taches: il n'y a pas de perfection où l'on ne trouve quelque chose à reprendre,' and approves (A) 'à toute perfection il y a un si et un mais.'

48. *No hay en éstos donde parar, o todo pára.* (S) has 'an solchen ist gar nichts, wobei man lange weilen konnte, obwohl sie lanweilig genug sind.' As M-F rightly observes: 'il n'y a rien de tel dans le texte'!

50. *ni se roce consigo a solas.* 1653 and 1659 both have 'se rose.' M-F suggests that this may be a typographical error for 'se roze' (mod. 'se roce'). The context indicates that he is correct in his assumption.

305

59. *afortunados.* (S) completely reverses the sense with 'Unglückskinder.' (Cf. M-F.)

80. 1659 has *Sea la reflexa contraste de lo farto y de lo falso.* M-F rightly regards 'farto' as a typographical error for 'falto.' In the 1653 edition the consonant before the 't' has been dropped and 1659 wrongly inserts 'r.'

85. M-F cites Lorenzo Franciosini's *Vocabolario italiano e spagnuolo,* 'Servir de malilla o como malilla: vale servire a far ogni cosa.' 'Malilla' is the diminutive of 'mala,' 'a bag.' Cf. English 'small hold-all.' The Spanish Academy's Dictionary gives 'comodín' (English, 'something useful for all purposes') as one of the meanings of 'malilla.' (*Vide supra,* Notes to 85, *No ser malilla.*)

104. *residencia.* M-F points out that this word is used here in a technical, legal sense. (English, 'court,' 'tribunal.')

120. *cabezas.* The sense here, says M-F, is 'the *élite,*' not 'the majority.'

122. M-F suggests 'entremetimiento' in place of 'entretenimiento' (1653 and 1659).

125. *libro verde.* M-F says that the reference is to the 'libro verde' of Aragon, a 'black' (*lit.* 'green') list of 'new Christians' drawn up at the close of the fifteenth century.

126. *y los necios mienten las por hacer* (1653 and 1659). M-F suggests that we should read 'mientan' = 'announce' or 'declare.' (S) has 'lügen.' He did not spot the fairly obvious misprint. (J) has the right idea with 'but fools boast of them' (*i.e.* their follies).

144. *aversión.* M-F suggests this reading instead of 'versión' (1653 and 1659). The latter he regards as a misprint.

145. M-F suggests 'entremetimiento' in place of 'entretenimiento' (1653 and 1659).

149. *testa de hierros.* M-F points out that there is here a pun on 'hierro,' 'iron,' and 'yerro,' 'mistake.' The usual form is 'testaferro' ('scapegoat').

172. *hiela.* Both 1653 and 1659 have 'y el a,' an obvious misprint. (Cf. M-F.)

180. . . . *si es discreto, tampoco.* M-F says that the sense is 'si (el enemigo) es discreto tampoco' not, as (S) has it, 'ist er (*i.e.* 'il necio') hingegen ein wenig klug.'

194. *pero no tanto que sea desatino.* M-F maintains that there should be a full stop after 'desatino' and that 'Al comenzar' opens a new sentence. 1653 and 1659 have no full stop.

241. *A lo mejor se han de dejar, y lo más seguro es no levantarlas.* M-F says: 'Le sens est, il faut cesser les plaisanteries au meilleur moment, c'est-à-dire quand elles n'ont pas encore causé d'offenses, et le plus sûr est encore de n'en point risquer.'

242. *Estos acaban las cosas, aquellos acaban con ellas.* M-F says the sense is: 'Les premiers finissent les affaires, les seconds finissent en même temps que les affaires.'

279. *No hay cuidado más logrado que en espías.* M-F prefers (A) 'Il n'y a point de peine mieux employé que celle d'épier' to (S) 'Keine Sorgfalt ist besser angewandt, als die gegen Spione.'

280. *a uso ya de todo el mundo.* M-F points out that this is a reference to a proverb: 'A uso (or 'a fuer') de Aragón, a buen servicio, mal galardón.' The 'uso,' says Gracián, is now world wide.

281. *porque regüeldos de aristas no alientan.* M-F points out that Courbeville reads 'regojos' for 'regüeldos' and 'alimentan' for 'alientan.' Both 1653 and 1659 have 'regüeldos' and 'alientan.' (S) omits the phrase altogether. M-F attributes Jacobs's bowdlerizing to English prudery!